GOVERNMENT PROCEDURES AND OPERATIONS

FEDERAL FUNDS

A SELECTION OF PROGRAMS

GOVERNMENT PROCEDURES AND OPERATIONS

Additional books in this series can be found on Nova's website under the Series tab.

Additional E-books in this series can be found on Nova's website under the E-book tab.

GRANTS AND FUNDING

Additional books in this series can be found on Nova's website under the Series tab.

Additional E-books in this series can be found on Nova's website under the E-book tab.

GOVERNMENT PROCEDURES AND OPERATIONS

FEDERAL FUNDS

A SELECTION OF PROGRAMS

KIERAN SACCOCCIO
EDITOR

nova publishers
New York

For permission to use material from this book please contact us:
Telephone 631-231-7269; Fax 631-231-8175
Web Site: http://www.novapublishers.com

Additional color graphics may be available in the e-book version of this book.

Library of Congress Cataloging-in-Publication Data

ISBN: 978-1-62618-005-5

Published by Nova Science Publishers, Inc. † New York

CONTENTS

PREFACE

This book provides an overview of select programs using federal funds with a focus on: the Global Security Contingency Fund (GSCF); the history, administration and common usage of the Judgment Fund; the Crime Victims Fund; the Housing Trust Fund; background and options for reform for the Universal Service Fund; the Reclamation Fund; an overview, funding history and issues of the Land and Water Conservation Fund; the Drinking Water State Revolving Fund (DWSRF); and the International Species Conservation Fund.

Chapter 1 - The new Global Security Contingency Fund (GSCF), established by Congress in December 2011, responds to long-standing congressional concerns that the U.S. government needs to address multiple deficiencies that have undermined interagency efforts abroad, in particular efforts to meet emergent challenges.

Created as a four-year pilot project by the FY2012 National Defense Authorization Act (P.L. 112-81), Section 1207, the GSCF is jointly administered and funded by the Department of State and the Department of Defense (DOD).

The GSCF provides resources for training and other support to enable foreign military and security forces to conduct security and counterterrorism operations and participate in coalition operations, as well as for justice sector, rule of law, and stabilization programs. The GSCF is placed under the State Department budget. Although decisions are to be jointly made by the Secretaries of State and Defense, the mandated mechanism puts the Secretary of State in the lead. (The legislation also includes three one-year transitional authorities for counterterrorism and peacekeeping assistance to Africa and Yemen, for which the Secretary of Defense has the lead.)

The GSCF is seen as an important step in improving U.S. efforts to deal with crises and emergent threats and to take advantage of unexpected opportunities. It incorporates features of previous legislation and reflects recommendations to improve current national security structures and practices. Many hope that it will provide a model for interagency cooperation on security assistance that will overcome the disadvantages of the current system of agency-centric budgets and efforts.

The FY2012 omnibus appropriations act (P.L. 112-74) does not appropriate new monies to the fund for regular budget programs, but permits DOD and the State Department to transfer up to $250 million to the GSCF from other accounts, with a limit of $200 million from DOD and $50 million from State from specified accounts. (P.L. 112-74 specifies that these transfer authorities are in addition to any other transfer authorities available to these departments.) The FY2012 NDAA authorizes a higher limit for FY2012 of $350 million. (This authorized amount includes both GSCF funding and up to $150 million in funding for the one-year transitional authorities.) For FY2013 and future years, the FY2012 NDAA sets a limit of $300 million. The FY2012 NDAA also provides that the State Department contribution shall not be less than 20% of the total amount required for a specific activity, and the DOD contribution not more than 80%.

In its February 2012 FY2013 budget submission, the State Department requested a $25 million GSCF appropriation, and $50 million in transfer authority. DOD did not request an appropriation or any new transfer authority.

Issues that Congress may choose to consider include the State Department's ability and capacity to lead GSCF activities; possible funding and flexibility drawbacks for DOD; the desirability of providing DOD with authority to train non-military security forces, including law enforcement; and the potential effectiveness of GSCF programs in the absence of a strategy for security assistance. In the context of FY2013 appropriations action, Congress may consider whether to provide a specific GSCF appropriation. The Senate version of the FY2013 Department of State, Foreign Operations and Related Appropriations Act (S. 3241) would appropriate $25 million to the GSCF.

Chapter 2 - The Judgment Fund is a permanent, indefinite appropriation that was created by Congress in 1956 to pay judgments entered against the United States. Generally, the United States cannot be sued unless it has waived its sovereign immunity. Originally, such waivers were rare, so individual claims were assigned to congressional committees, which in turn appropriated funds to satisfy the judgments. Prior to the creation of the Judgment Fund, the number of claims grew rapidly, taking up an increasing amount of Congress's time and resources. Eventually, the Judgment Fund was created to reduce Congress's workload, so that individual appropriations were not needed for each award entered.

The Fund's administration has changed substantially since its inception, with varying degrees of control and oversight by Congress, the Government Accountability Office, and the Treasury Department. Originally, the Fund was limited to claims of less than $100,000, entered by the Court of Federal Claims or a U.S. District Court. As payments grew in size, Congress transferred authority to the Justice Department to make payments on behalf of the United States, as certified by the Attorney General.

Today, the Fund is administered by the Financial Management Service in the Treasury Department and is only accessible when certain closely circumscribed statutory requirements are met. Most importantly, an agency may not access the Fund when there is another appropriation that may be applied or when the plaintiff prevailed through an administrative remedy. In addition, the fund can only be used for monetary awards that are final, meaning the award cannot be changed or overturned. The awards must result from claims that were or could have been litigated in court.

This report sets out specific instances in which the Fund can be accessed and illustrates the procedural mechanisms for obtaining payment under certain statutory causes of action. Although primarily used for the payment of principal awards, attorneys' fees and interest on awards may also be paid from the Fund. At the court's discretion, certain costs enumerated in 28 U.S.C. § 1920 may be awarded to the prevailing party. In addition, certain statutes, such as the Federal Tort Claims Act, provide that attorneys' fees may be recovered by the prevailing party. In addition, interest that accrues after the judgment may also be payable from the Fund. This report provides examples of how the payments from the Fund may be made under the Equal Access to Justice Act, Contract Disputes Act, Notification and Federal Employee Antidiscrimination Act (No FEAR Act), and through tribe-specific judgment funds.

In addition, this report will briefly highlight several recently proposed changes to the Judgment Fund's administration. The Judgment Fund Transparency Act of 2011 (H.R. 1446) would require the Secretary of the Treasury to post the claimant, agency, fact summary, and payment amount for each claim paid out of the Fund. The Government Transparency and Recordkeeping Act of 2012 (S. 3415) would require the Secretary to publicly report all payments from the Fund under the Equal Access to Justice Act since 2003 and all future claims. Amendments to the No FEAR Act that were proposed in H.R. 6780 (110th Congress) and H.R. 67 (111th Congress) would have impacted reimbursement of the Fund for payments under the No FEAR Act.

Chapter 3 - In 1984, the Crime Victims Fund (CVF) was established by the Victims of Crime Act (VOCA, P.L. 98-473) to provide funding for state victim compensation and assistance programs. Since 1984, VOCA has been amended several times to support additional victim-related activities. These amendments established within the CVF (1) discretionary grants for private organizations, (2) the Federal Victim Notification System, (3) funding for victim assistance staff within the Federal Bureau of Investigation and Executive Office of U.S. Attorneys, (4) funding for the Children's Justice Act Program, and (5) assistance and compensation for victims of terrorism.

In 1988, the Office for Victims of Crime (OVC) was formally established within the Department of Justice (DOJ) to administer the CVF. As authorized by VOCA, the OVC awards CVF money through grants to states, local units of government, individuals, and other entities. The OVC also distributes CVF money to specially designated programs, such as the Children's Justice Act Program and the Federal Victim Notification System.

Deposits to the CVF come from criminal fines, forfeited appearance bonds, penalties and special assessments collected by the U.S. Attorneys' Offices, federal courts, and Federal Bureau of Prisons. Since 2002, Congress has allowed gifts, bequests, and donations from private entities to be deposited into the CVF.

When the CVF was created in 1984, Congress placed a cap on how much money could be deposited into the CVF each year. Congress eliminated the cap for deposits in 1993. In FY2000, Congress established a cap on the amount that would be available for distribution in a fiscal year to ensure the stability of funds for crime victims programs and activities. Since 2000, Congress has established the yearly CVF cap as a part of DOJ's annual appropriation. For the last several years, Congress has set the CVF distribution cap at $705 million.

In considering the CVF allocation and future caps, there are several issues on which policymakers may deliberate. Congress may consider whether to adjust the manner in which the CVF is allocated, amend VOCA to accommodate additional victim activities or groups, adjust the cap and allow use of the CVF for grant programs other than those explicitly authorized by VOCA, or make other adjustments to the CVF cap—such as eliminate the cap altogether.

Chapter 4 - On July 30, 2008, President Bush signed into law the Housing and Economic Recovery Act of 2008 (P.L. 110-289), which included the establishment of a national Housing Trust Fund. In general, affordable housing trust funds provide dedicated, permanent sources of funding for affordable housing that do not require annual appropriations. Several states and many localities across the United States already have their own affordable housing trust funds, and for years affordable housing advocates had worked to get such a fund created on a national level. Opponents of a national affordable housing trust fund argued that it would be duplicative of other affordable housing programs.

The Housing Trust Fund created by P.L. 110-289 would provide formula-based grants to states to use for affordable housing activities. By statute, most of the funding would have to be used for rental housing; states could use up to 10% of their grants for homeownership activities. Furthermore, all of the funds would have to benefit very low- or extremely low-income households, with at least 75% of the funding for rental housing being used exclusively for the benefit of extremely low-income households.

P.L. 110-289 directed Fannie Mae and Freddie Mac to annually contribute a percentage of the dollar volume of mortgages that they purchased to the Housing Trust Fund as the fund's dedicated funding source. However, the law also gave the director of the Federal Housing Finance Agency (FHFA), Fannie and Freddie's regulator, the authority to suspend those contributions if he determined that they were contributing to financial trouble at the agencies. On September 7, 2008, Fannie and Freddie were placed in conservatorship, and in November 2008, the director of FHFA suspended their contributions to the Housing Trust Fund. The Fund had not yet received any funding at the time the contributions were suspended.

It is unclear whether contributions from Fannie Mae and Freddie Mac to the Housing Trust Fund will ever be reinstated. Advocates have begun searching for a new source of funds for the program. Several pieces of legislation have been introduced in the 112th Congress that include funding for the Housing Trust Fund, and similar legislation had been introduced in previous Congresses. However, no funding has been provided to the program as of the date of this report. Legislation has also been introduced in the 112th Congress that would eliminate the Housing Trust Fund entirely.

Chapter 5 - The concept that all Americans should be able to afford access to the telecommunications network, commonly called the "universal service concept" can trace its origins back to the 1934 Communications Act. Since then, the preservation and advancement of universal service has been a basic tenet of federal communications policy, and Congress has historically played an active role in helping to preserve and advance universal service goals. The passage of the Telecommunications Act of 1996 (P.L. 104-104) not only codified the universal service concept, but also led to the establishment, in 1997, of a federal Universal Service Fund (USF or Fund) to meet the universal service objectives and principles contained in the 1996 act. According to Fund administrators, from 1998 through end of year 2010, $73.7 billion was distributed, or committed, by the USF, with all 50 states, the District of Columbia, and all territories receiving some benefit.

The Federal Communications Commission (FCC) is required to ensure that there be "specific, predictable and sufficient ... mechanisms to preserve and advance universal service." However, changes in telecommunications technology and the marketplace, while often leading to positive benefits for consumers and providers, have had a negative impact on the health and viability of the USF, as presently designed. These changes have led to a growing imbalance between the entities and revenue stream contributing to the fund and the growth in the entities and programs eligible to receive funding. The desire to expand access to broadband and address what some perceive as a "digital divide" has also placed focus on what role, if any, the USF should take to address this issue. The FCC's national broadband plan, *Connecting America: The National Broadband Plan*, calls for a major restructuring of the USF to enable it to take a major role in achieving the goal of nationwide broadband access and adoption. The FCC has initiated a series of proceedings to achieve this goal.

There is a growing consensus among policy makers, including some in Congress, that significant action is needed not only to ensure the viability and stability of the USF, but also to address the numerous issues surrounding its appropriate role in a changing marketplace. How this concept should be defined, how these policies should be funded, who should receive the funding, and how to ensure proper management and oversight of the Fund are among the issues framing the debate.

The current policy debate has focused on five concerns: the scope of the program; who should contribute and what methodology should be used to fund the program; eligibility criteria for benefits; concerns over possible program fraud, waste, and abuse; and the impact of the Antideficiency Act (ADA) on the USF.

It is anticipated that Universal Service Fund reform will continue to be a topic of congressional interest. The House Energy and Commerce Committee and the Senate Commerce, Science, and Transportation Committee have included USF reform on their agendas of issues for consideration and oversight. Three stand-alone measures (H.R. 2163, H.R. 3118, S. 297) relating to USF have been introduced to date.

Chapter 6 - The Reclamation Fund was established in 1902 to fund the development of irrigation projects on arid and semiarid lands of the 17 western states. It originated as a revolving fund for construction projects and was supported by the proceeds of the sale of land and water in the western United States. Over time, it was amended to receive proceeds from a number of other sources. It is currently derived from repayments and revenues associated with federal water resources development as well as the sales, rentals, and leases (including natural resource leasing) of federal land in the western United States. Portions of the fund's balance are appropriated annually by Congress for multiple purposes, including some of the operational expenditures of the Bureau of Reclamation (Reclamation) and the Power Marketing Administrations. Through FY2011, collections deposited into the Reclamation Fund totaled more than $40 billion, while total appropriations from the fund totaled approximately $30 billion.

The Reclamation Fund did not finance all Reclamation investments in the western United States. As a result of limited funding availability, a number of large dams and other Reclamation investments were financed by the General Fund of the U.S. Treasury. Notwithstanding advances to the Reclamation Fund by Congress in 1910 and 1931, deposits into and appropriations out of the fund have been roughly equal over time. From the 1940s until the 1990s, the fund maintained a small, relatively stable balance. Beginning in the mid-1990s, balances in the fund began to increase significantly as receipts from mineral leasing and power sales increased, while appropriations from the fund largely remained static. By the end of FY2011, the fund had a balance of more than $9.6 billion, and it is expected to continue to grow.

Receipts deposited into the Reclamation Fund are made available to Reclamation by Congress through annual discretionary appropriations bills, which are subject to congressional budgetary allocations. Some have proposed that Congress appropriate some portion of the surplus balance in the Reclamation Fund to reclamation activities in western states, including new water storage projects or the rehabilitation of existing projects. These interests argue that the Reclamation Fund was set up to benefit western states and should now be used to increase investments in these areas.

As the balance of the Reclamation Fund continues to increase, Congress may reevaluate the Reclamation Fund's status, including its financing of new or ongoing activities. The Omnibus Lands Act of 2009 (P.L. 111-11) included provisions that will transfer $120 million per year from the fund from FY2020 through FY2034, without further appropriation, to a separate fund that provides for Indian Water Settlement construction projects. In the 112th Congress, a bill before the Senate (S. 3385) proposes to transfer another $80 million per year that would otherwise go to the Reclamation Fund from FY2013 through FY2029 for the construction of rural water projects. Major changes to the fund's mechanics may have scoring implications in the annual budgetary context and under congressional pay-as-you-go rules.

Chapter 7 - The Land and Water Conservation Fund (LWCF) Act of 1965 was enacted to help preserve, develop, and assure access to outdoor recreation facilities to strengthen the health of U.S. citizens. The law created the Land and Water Conservation Fund in the U.S. Treasury as a funding source to implement its outdoor recreation goals.

The LWCF has been the principal source of monies for land acquisition for outdoor recreation by the four federal agencies—the National Park Service, Bureau of Land Management, Fish and Wildlife Service, and Forest Service. In the past, Congress typically has identified which areas are to be acquired with the funds it provides. The LWCF also funds a matching grant program to assist states in recreational planning, acquiring recreational lands and waters, and developing outdoor recreational facilities. A portion of the appropriation is divided equally among the states, with the remainder apportioned based on need, as determined by the Secretary of the Interior. The states award their grant money through a competitive selection process based on statewide recreation plans and establish their own priorities and criteria. Finally, beginning in FY1998, LWCF has been used to fund other federal programs with related purposes.

The LWCF is authorized at $900 million annually. While the fund accrues revenues and collections from multiple sources, nearly all of the revenues are derived from oil and gas leasing in the Outer Continental Shelf. Congress determines the level of appropriations each year, and yearly appropriations have fluctuated widely since the origin of the program. Of the total revenues that have accrued throughout the history of the program ($33.5 billion), less than half have been appropriated ($15.8 billion). FY2001 marked the highest funding ever, with appropriations exceeding the authorized level by reaching nearly $1 billion. For FY2011, the most recent fiscal year, the appropriation was $300.5 million.

The $15.8 billion appropriated throughout the history of the program has been unevenly allocated among federal land acquisition (62%), the state grant program (26%), and other programs (12%). Similarly, federal land acquisition funds have been allocated unevenly among the four federal agencies. More recent legislation (P.L. 109-432) provided that a portion of revenues from certain OCS leasing are provided without further appropriation to the state grant program. These funds are to supplement any funds appropriated by Congress.

There is a difference of opinion as to the appropriate level of funds for LWCF and how those funds should be used. Current congressional issues include deciding the amount to appropriate for land acquisition and identifying which lands should be acquired; deciding the level of funding for the state grant program and how funds should be allocated among the states; and determining which, if any, other programs to fund from the LWCF. The primary context for debating these issues is Interior appropriations legislation. Other issues of current debate include whether the LWCF should be permanently appropriated at the authorized level of $900 million, and whether revenues from additional activities should be directed to the LWCF.

Chapter 8 - The Safe Drinking Water Act (SDWA) Amendments of 1996 authorized a drinking water state revolving loan fund (DWSRF) program to help public water systems finance infrastructure projects needed to comply with federal drinking water regulations and to meet the act's health objectives. Under the program, states receive capitalization grants to make loans to public water systems (privately and publicly owned) for drinking water projects and certain other SDWA activities. Since FY1997, Congress has provided more than $16 billion for this program, including $2 billion in the supplemental funding the American Recovery and Reinvestment Act of 2009 (ARRA; P.L. 111-5). Through June 2010, the DWSRF program had provided a total of $14.6 billion in assistance and supported 8,519 projects; with the 20% state match, bond proceeds, and other funds, the program had provided a total of $20.027 billion in assistance.

The Environmental Protection Agency's (EPA's) latest (2007) survey of capital improvement needs for public water systems indicated that water systems need to invest $334.8 billion on infrastructure improvements over 20 years to ensure the provision of safe water. EPA reports that this amount is similar to the 2003 needs estimate of $276.8 billion ($331.4 billion when adjusted to 2007 dollars). The latest survey reflects continued improvement in the reporting of needs for infrastructure rehabilitation and replacement, and also reporting funding needs related to compliance with SDWA regulations and security-related needs.

Key program issues include the gap between estimated needs and funding; the growing cost of complying with SDWA standards, particularly for small communities; the ability of small or economically disadvantaged communities to afford DWSRF financing; and the broader need for cities to maintain, upgrade, and expand infrastructure unrelated to SDWA compliance.

ARRA provided $2 billion for the DWSRF program for drinking water infrastructure projects, and $4 billion for a similar Clean Water SRF to fund municipal wastewater infrastructure projects in the form of capitalization grant loans. Under the DWSRF program, the supplemental funding was also allocated as capitalization grants to the states, which states use to provide financial assistance (subsidized loans and grants) to public water systems for infrastructure projects. The ARRA supplemental funding, and subsequent appropriations, have come with new requirements (such as a 20% reserve for "green" projects and the application of Davis-Bacon prevailing wage requirements to projects receiving any DWSRF funding). States have expressed concern that the added requirements have reduced their ability to determine project priorities, increased project costs, and placed new strains on the state/federal partnership.

In the 112th Congress, congressional action has focused on appropriations. For FY2012, the President requested $999.0 million for the DWSRF program, and Congress provided $919.4 million in P.L. 112-74 (before applying an across-the-board rescission of 0.16%). In this act, Congress made the green infrastructure reserve discretionary, and expanded the application of Davis-Bacon requirements to the DWSRF program to include FY2012 and all future years. The Administration has requested $850 million for the program for FY2013. Other approaches to financing water infrastructure also have been proposed. For example, H.R. 402 would establish a National Infrastructure Development Bank, and H.R. 1802 and S. 939 would remove the volume cap on private activity bonds for drinking water and wastewater facilities; the Senate Finance Committee's Surface Transportation Reauthorization bill includes similar provisions.

Chapter 9 - International species conservation is addressed by several funds, including those under the Multinational Species Conservation Fund (MSCF) and the Neotropical Migratory Bird Conservation Fund (NMBCF). This report provides a brief overview of MSCF and NMBCF and their funding and legislative status.

In: Federal Funds: A Selection of Programs
Editor: Kieran Saccoccio
ISBN 978-1-62618-005-5

Chapter 1

GLOBAL SECURITY CONTINGENCY FUND (GSCF): SUMMARY AND ISSUE OVERVIEW*

Nina M. Serafino

SUMMARY

The new Global Security Contingency Fund (GSCF), established by Congress in December 2011, responds to long-standing congressional concerns that the U.S. government needs to address multiple deficiencies that have undermined interagency efforts abroad, in particular efforts to meet emergent challenges.

Created as a four-year pilot project by the FY2012 National Defense Authorization Act (P.L. 112-81), Section 1207, the GSCF is jointly administered and funded by the Department of State and the Department of Defense (DOD).

The GSCF provides resources for training and other support to enable foreign military and security forces to conduct security and counterterrorism operations and participate in coalition operations, as well as for justice sector, rule of law, and stabilization programs. The GSCF is placed under the State Department budget. Although decisions are to be jointly made by the

* This is an edited, reformatted and augmented version of the Congressional Research Service Publication, CRS Report for Congress R42641, dated August 1, 2012.

Secretaries of State and Defense, the mandated mechanism puts the Secretary of State in the lead. (The legislation also includes three one-year transitional authorities for counterterrorism and peacekeeping assistance to Africa and Yemen, for which the Secretary of Defense has the lead.)

The GSCF is seen as an important step in improving U.S. efforts to deal with crises and emergent threats and to take advantage of unexpected opportunities. It incorporates features of previous legislation and reflects recommendations to improve current national security structures and practices. Many hope that it will provide a model for interagency cooperation on security assistance that will overcome the disadvantages of the current system of agency-centric budgets and efforts.

The FY2012 omnibus appropriations act (P.L. 112-74) does not appropriate new monies to the fund for regular budget programs, but permits DOD and the State Department to transfer up to $250 million to the GSCF from other accounts, with a limit of $200 million from DOD and $50 million from State from specified accounts. (P.L. 112-74 specifies that these transfer authorities are in addition to any other transfer authorities available to these departments.) The FY2012 NDAA authorizes a higher limit for FY2012 of $350 million. (This authorized amount includes both GSCF funding and up to $150 million in funding for the one-year transitional authorities.) For FY2013 and future years, the FY2012 NDAA sets a limit of $300 million. The FY2012 NDAA also provides that the State Department contribution shall not be less than 20% of the total amount required for a specific activity, and the DOD contribution not more than 80%.

In its February 2012 FY2013 budget submission, the State Department requested a $25 million GSCF appropriation, and $50 million in transfer authority. DOD did not request an appropriation or any new transfer authority.

Issues that Congress may choose to consider include the State Department's ability and capacity to lead GSCF activities; possible funding and flexibility drawbacks for DOD; the desirability of providing DOD with authority to train non-military security forces, including law enforcement; and the potential effectiveness of GSCF programs in the absence of a strategy for security assistance. In the context of FY2013 appropriations action, Congress may consider whether to provide a specific GSCF appropriation. The Senate version of the FY2013 Department of State, Foreign Operations and Related Appropriations Act (S. 3241) would appropriate $25 million to the GSCF.

INTRODUCTION

At the Obama Administration's request, in December 2011 Congress enacted into law a new, joint State Department and Department of Defense (DOD) Global Security Contingency Fund (GSCF) to assist countries with emergent security-related needs. The Administration proposed the GSCF with its FY2012 budget submission as a "pilot project" for State and the DOD to jointly fund and plan security efforts.[1] These efforts include programs to provide training and support for foreign governments' security and counterterrorism operations, as well as justice sector, rule of law, and stabilization programs.

As proposed, the GSCF's stated purpose was to enable the United States to better "address rapidly changing, transnational, asymmetric threats, and emergent opportunities."[2] "Pooled" DOD and State Department funds would be used to develop interagency responses to build the security capacity of foreign states, prevent conflict, and stabilize countries in conflict or emerging from conflict.

Demonstrating its interest in the experiment, Congress provided GSCF authority as Section 1207[3] of the FY2012 National Defense Authorization Act (P.L. 112-81) for four fiscal years rather than the three years requested.[4] As enacted, Section 1207 also contains two transitional authorities for counterterrorism operations and peacekeeping support in Africa and one for counterterrorism assistance in Yemen. All three transitional authorities expire at the end of FY2012.

Many see the GSCF as an innovative first step in addressing the problems inherent in the current agency-based budgeting and program development systems that impede rapid U.S. responses to events abroad. Although some view the GSCF primarily as a means to provide DOD funds for activities usually conducted by the State Department, with its relatively smaller budget, others look to the GSCF as a possible means to foster more timely, coherent, and effective U.S. government responses to emerging threats and opportunities and to provide an impetus for improving interagency coordination in security and stabilization missions.

This report provides basic information on the GSCF legislation. It starts with a brief discussion of the origins of the legislation, then summarizes the legislation's provisions. It concludes with a short analysis of salient issues.

ORIGINS

The GSCF concept has its origins in long-standing perceptions that multiple deficiencies in current national security structures and practices have undermined U.S. efforts to respond rapidly and effectively to emergent situations abroad. Analysts have identified the U.S. government's current agency-centric national security system as a key impediment to rational budgeting and planning for national security efforts that require contributions from multiple agencies. Analysts have long proposed changes to address deficiencies along the following lines:[5]

- *Provide the State Department with a flexible funding account to respond to emerging needs and crises*. For many years, the George W. Bush Administration repeatedly sought a State Department emergency response fund that would facilitate immediate responses to crises and emerging threats. Congress denied such requests several times, but in 2005 it authorized DOD to transfer up to $100 million of its own funds to the State Department for such purposes.[6] "Section 1207" authority expired at the end of FY2010; in FY2011, Congress established a U.S. Agency for International Development (USAID) account, the Complex Crises Fund, for the same purposes, with a $50 million appropriation in FY2011 and $40 million in FY2012 ($30 million of which is for Overseas Contingency Operations). It has not made a similar account available to the State Department.
- *Develop mechanisms to promote greater interagency cooperation in planning security and stabilization programs*. Analysts point to many problems inherent in programming by individual agencies. Because agencies usually do not consult or coordinate with others when planning programs, there can be unnecessary duplication and overlap. Also, because agencies conduct programs targeted at the issues that fall under their purview, there are often serious gaps. Of particular concern are the "governance gaps" (i.e., the formulation of security assistance programs to train and equip military forces without components to improve the ability of government institutions to manage those forces). The goal of greater interagency cooperation is to develop coherent security and stabilization programs that address all elements of a problem.

- *Clarify and rationalize security roles and missions.* The appropriate division of labor between the State Department and DOD, especially for security assistance, is a matter of debate. Since military assistance first became a significant component of U.S. foreign policy after World War II, oversight of those programs has always been vested in a civilian, usually the Secretary of State. In 1961, Congress made the Secretary of State responsible, by law, for "the continuous supervision and general direction" of that assistance.[7] Beginning in the 1980s, however, Congress has called on DOD to contribute its manpower and funding to an increasingly broad range of national security efforts under new DOD authorities. After the terrorist attacks on the United States of September 11, 2001 (9/11), DOD has requested and Congress has approved multiple new DOD authorities. Some fill gaps when civilian funding and personnel are not available Others, DOD argues, provide a means to address critical needs in an effort to protect U.S. troops and minimize U.S. military operations. The goal is to reach agreement on an appropriate model for post-9/11 civil-military activities and missions, either by strengthening the State Department's ability to lead and conduct security assistance programs on its own or by creating new modes of sharing responsibility.
- *Create a "unified" budget system for national security missions along functional rather than agency lines.* For over a decade, analysts have urged the U.S. government to consolidate budgets for national security activities. In particular, they have recommended that the White House present Congress annually with either a unified national security budget or a series of unified budgets for a specific multi-agency national security activity, such as counterterrorism or security assistance. The goal is to rationalize government-wide resource allocation and promote due consideration of the tradeoffs involved in allocating those resources. Unified budgets are also recommended as a means to provide greater transparency and accountability in U.S. government spending, and facilitate congressional oversight of national security programs.

The Obama Administration presented the GSCF as a means of identifying potential difficulties in combining State Department and DOD funds and testing the possibilities for combining agency expertise and efforts to conduct security activities. If successful, the GSCF may provide impetus to these changes and set a precedent for broader interagency funding and efforts.

BASIC PROVISIONS

Uses and Approval Processes

Assistance may be provided under the three-year GSCF authority for three purposes, as detailed below. Assistance "may include the provision of equipment, supplies, and training." (GSCF funds would be available to either the Secretary of State or the Secretary of Defense for such assistance.) The GSCF planning and approval processes are managed in the Department of State by the Bureau of Political-Military Affairs and in the Defense Department by the Partnership Strategy and Stability Operations office under the Under Secretary of Defense for Policy.

The first two GSCF purposes and uses—security and counterterrorism training, and coalition support—are similar to those of the Global Train and Equip authority provided by Section 1206 of the FY2006 NDAA, P.L. 109-163, as amended. There are, however, four differences.[8] For Section 1206 programs, the Secretary of Defense is in the lead. In addition, Section 1206 may only be used to assist military forces and maritime security forces, not the full range of security forces permitted by Section 1207. Further, GSCF counterterrorism assistance may be provided to the foreign government agencies responsible for the military and specified security forces receiving assistance. Section 1206 has no such provision. Finally, GSCF authority is provided notwithstanding any other provision of law with two exceptions (see below), while Section 1206 has no notwithstanding provision.

Security and Counterterrorism Training

Section 1207 (b)(1)(A) authorizes the use of the GSCF "to enhance the capabilities of military forces and other security forces responsible for conducting border and maritime security, internal security, and counterterrorism operations, as well as the government agencies responsible for such forces." Recipient countries would be designated by the Secretary of State with the concurrence (i.e., approval) of the Secretary of Defense. Programs to provide this support would be jointly formulated by the Secretary of State and the Secretary of Defense, and approved by the Secretary of State, with the concurrence of the Secretary of Defense before implementation.

Coalition Support

Section 1207 (b)(1)(B) permits GSCF assistance to national military forces and other specified security forces to enable them to "participate in or support military, stability, or peace support operations consistent with United States foreign policy and national security interests." Just as with security and counterterrorism training assistance, recipient countries would be designated by the Secretary of State with the concurrence of the Secretary of Defense. These programs are also jointly formulated by the Secretary of State and the Secretary of Defense, and approved by the Secretary of State, with the concurrence of the Secretary of Defense, before implementation.

Justice Sector, Rule of Law, and Stabilization Assistance

Section 1207(b)(2) authorizes using the GSCF to assist the justice sector (including law enforcement and prisons), and to conduct rule of law programs and stabilization efforts "where the Secretary of State, in consultation with the Secretary of Defense, determines that conflict or instability in a region challenges the existing capability of civilian providers to deliver such assistance." The Secretary of State also designates recipients of this type of assistance and implements activities with the concurrence of the Secretary of Defense. However, unlike the preceding types of assistance where the Secretaries of State and Defense would jointly formulate programs, the Secretary of State formulates these programs in consultation with the Secretary of Defense. State and DOD staff will determine an appropriate consultation mechanism.

Transitional Authorities for Horn of Africa Counterterrorism and Peacekeeping and Yemen Counterterrorism

In addition to the GSCF authority requested by the Administration, Section 1207(n) establishes three new transitional authorities that would permit the Secretary of Defense, with the concurrence of the Secretary of State, to assist counterterrorism and peacekeeping efforts in Africa and Yemen during FY2012. Assistance may include the provision of equipment, supplies, and training, as well as assistance for minor military construction, for the following purposes:

- "To enhance the capacity of the national military forces, security agencies serving a similar defense function, and border security forces of Djibouti, Ethiopia, and Kenya to conduct counterterrorism operations against al-Qaeda, al-Qaeda affiliates, and al Shabaab."

- "To enhance the capacity of national military forces participating in the African Union Mission in Somalia to conduct the counterterrorism operations described" above.
- "To enhance the ability of the Yemen Ministry of Interior Counter Terrorism Forces to conduct counter-terrorism operations against al-Qaeda in the Arabian Peninsula and its affiliates."

Funding Provisions and Expiration

The FY2012 NDAA establishes a GSCF account "on the books of the Treasury of the United States"; the FY2012 omnibus appropriations act (P.L. 112-74)[9] specifies that it has been placed under the State Department. The NDAA provides that the contribution of the Secretary of State to an activity shall not be less than 20% of the total amount required for that activity, and the contribution of the Secretary of Defense shall not be more than 80%.

Funding Snapshot

The FY2012 appropriations act provides no new money for the fund, but permits DOD and the State Department to transfer up to $250 million from other, specified accounts during FY2012.

The limits that may be transferred are $200 million from DOD and $50 million from State from the specified accounts. (The FY2012 appropriations act also states that these transfer authorities are in addition to any other transfer authorities available to these departments.)

Under the FY2012 NDAA, monies may be transferred from the GSCF to the "agency or account determined to be the most appropriate to facilitate" assistance. (No official is specified as responsible for the determination.) As noted above, the main GSCF authority expires on September 30, 2015, but amounts appropriated or transferred before that date for programs already in progress would remain available until the programs are completed.

FY2012 authorization and appropriations amounts for the GSCF differ. The FY2012 NDAA authorized a limit of $350 million for FY2012 (i.e., $100 million more than the new transfer authority provided in the appropriations acts). The FY2012 appropriations transfer authorities are solely for the GSCF. The FY2012 NDAA authorized amount, however, covers funding for both the

GSCF and for the three transitional authorities. The FY2012 NDAA permits up to $150 million for the transitional authorities. Thus, if State and DOD choose to fund the transitional authorities up to the full amount, the FY2012 NDAA authorized amount available for GSCF programs would be $200 million, or $50 million less than the amount provided by the new transfer authorities provided by the appropriations act.

For FY2013-FY2015, the FY2012 NDAA stipulates that the authorized amount may not exceed $300 million.[10]

Funding Provisions by Agency

DOD FY2012 Funding Provisions

Section 8089 of the P.L. 112-74 omnibus appropriations act provides that DOD may transfer up to $200 million in DOD funds to the GSCF. The FY2012 NDAA does not authorize new funds to effect that transfer, but provides that DOD may transfer up to $200 million per fiscal year[11] from its defense-wide operation and maintenance account to the GSCF. Section 8089 provisions are subject to the FY2012 NDAA cap on total funding and limit of no more than 80% on the DOD contribution.

Table 1. GSCF Funding Limits
($ Millions)

Fiscal Year	Appropriations Request		NDAA Authorization			Appropriations Authority to Transfer Funds to GSCF from Specified Accounts			Appropriations Specifically for GSCF	
	DOD	State	DOD	State	Combined	DOD	State	Combined	DOD	State
FY2012	0[a]	50[a]	200	NA	350	200	50	250	0	0
FY2013	0	25[b]	200	NA	300	NYD	NYD	NYD	NYD	NYD
FY2014-FY2015	NYD	NA	200	NA	300	NYD	NYD	NYD	NYD	NYD

Note: NA = Not Applicable; NYD = Not Yet Determined.

a. The Administration also requested a total transfer authority of $500 million, without further specification.

b. The Administration also requested a $50 million transfer authority.

State Department FY2012 Funding Provisions

The State Department requested a $50 million appropriation as its contribution to the GSCF in FY2012. Just as with DOD, however, the P.L. 112-74 appropriations act provides no new monies for the State Department contribution to the fund. Instead, Section 8004 of this act permits the State Department to transfer to the GSCF up to $50 million from funds appropriated to three accounts in the State Department Overseas Contingency Operations section of the act, that is, Foreign Military Financing (FMF), International Narcotics Control and Law Enforcement (INCLE), and the Pakistan Counterinsurgency Capability Fund (PCCF).[12] Section 8004 provisions are subject to the FY2012 NDAA cap on total funding and limit of no less than 20% on the State Department contribution.

Funding for FY2012 Transitional Authorities

Of the authorized $350 million, the FY2012 NDAA states that up to $150 million may be dedicated to two specified purposes.

- Up to $75 million may be used to improve counterterrorism operations in Africa. This assistance may be used to enhance “the capacity of the national military forces, security agencies serving a similar defense function, and border security forces of Djibouti, Ethiopia, and Kenya to conduct counterterrorism operations against al- Qaeda, al-Qaeda affiliates, and al Shabaab” and the capacity “of national military forces participating in the African Union Mission in Somalia to conduct counterterrorism operations” against those same forces.
- Up to $75 million may be used to enhance the ability of the Yemen Ministry of Interior Counterterrorism Forces to conduct counterterrorism operations against al- Qaeda in the Arabian Peninsula and its affiliates.[13]

FY2013 Funding Request and Congressional Action

In its FY2013 budget submission, the State Department requests a $25 million GSCF appropriation and a $50 million transfer authority. DOD does not request an appropriation or any new transfer authority. The Senate version of the FY2013 Department of State, Foreign Operations and Related Appropriations Act (S. 3241) would appropriate $25 million to the GSCF, but does not provide specific transfer authority. The House version of the bill (H.R. 5857) has no GSCF provisions.

LIMITATIONS, CONDITIONS, AND EXEMPTIONS

Congress provides GSCF authority notwithstanding any other provision of law, with two exceptions. These are the Foreign Assistance Act (FAA) of 1961, as amended (P.L. 85-195), Section 620A prohibition on assistance to governments supporting international terrorism, and the FAA Section 620J prohibition on assistance to foreign security forces for which the Secretary of State has determined there is credible evidence of gross violations of human rights (the "Leahy Amendment"). The legislation makes clear that the four-year GSCF authorization is not intended to replace other legislation.[14] GSCF programs are required to include elements to promote the observance of and respect for human rights and fundamental freedoms, as well as respect for legitimate civilian authority.

The notwithstanding provision does not extend to the transitional authorities. Two limitations apply to the transitional authorities. Funding cannot be used "to provide any type of assistance that is otherwise prohibited by any provision of law." It also cannot be used to provide a country with assistance that it is otherwise prohibited from receiving by any other provision of law.

CONGRESSIONAL OVERSIGHT

GSCF reporting requirements are extensive, but not unusual. The authorizing legislation requires the Secretary of State, with the concurrence of the Secretary of Defense, to notify specified congressional committees at three points. The committees to be notified are the House and Senate Appropriations Committees and Armed Services Committees, the House Committee on Foreign Affairs, and the Senate Committee on Foreign Relations.

- The first notification requirement mandates that the Secretary of State, with the concurrence of the Secretary of Defense, notify Congress 15 days after the date on which all necessary guidance has been issued and the processes for implementing programs "are established and fully operational." A similar notification is required for the transitional authorities.

- The Secretary of State, with the concurrence of the Secretary of Defense, must also notify the specified committees not less than 15 days before initiating an activity. No funds may be transferred into the fund until 15 days after Congress is notified. The notification regarding the initiation of program activities is to include a detailed justification for the program, its budget, execution, plan and timeline, a list of other security-related assistance or justice sector and stabilization assistance being provided to that country that is related to or supported by that activity, and any other appropriate information. The transitional authorities carry similar reporting requirements.
- A third requirement is for an annual report on programs, activities, and funding, jointly submitted by the Secretary of State and the Secretary of Defense. The first report is to be provided no later than October 30, 2012. Subsequent reports are to be provided annually thereafter.

The appropriations legislation requires the State Department to notify the appropriations committees 15 days prior to making any transfers from the INCLE, FMF, and PCCF accounts to the GSCF in accordance with regular notification procedures, including a detailed justification, implementation plan, and timeline for each proposed project. It is not, however, subject to prior consultation with the appropriations committees. It requires DOD to notify the congressional defense committees in writing 30 days prior to making transfers to the GSCF with the source of funds and a detailed justification, execution plan, and timeline for each proposed project.

Current Status of GSCF Assistance and Organization

As of the date of this report, no GSCF assistance has been provided.[15] The departments are developing an interagency consensus on national priorities for security sector assistance, as well as a FY2012 assistance plan. DOD and State staff have examined various proposals, but none has yet been deemed by both departments of sufficient priority to merit funding.

The House Armed Services Committee, in its report on the National Defense Authorization Act for FY2013 (H.R. 4310), has expressed concern with the GSCF decision-making process. It stated its expectation that the departments "begin exercising the authority in a timely manner."[16]

ISSUES FOR CONGRESS IN BRIEF

For some policymakers and analysts, the GSCF proposal is a positive, long-awaited first step toward the development of integrated, interagency funding streams for agencies that carry out related programs. For others, the GSCF proposal and specific provisions of the bill raise a number of issues, some of which are summarized below.[17]

The State Department's Ability and Capacity to Lead the GSCF

The GSCF puts the State Department, in the person of the Secretary of State, in the lead for all but the transitional authorities for the Horn of Africa and Yemen. Some who have viewed Congress's approval of many new DOD security assistance authorities since 9/11 as a gradual erosion of the traditional State Department lead on security assistance[18] may see the GSCF as a welcome reversal of that trend.

Nevertheless, some may wonder about the extent to which the Secretary of State may actually exercise control if DOD provides most GSCF funding. This may be especially true as the Secretary of Defense will be providing funds through an authority that permits the transfer of funds from one activity to another but stipulates that the funds may only be transferred to a higher priority activity. Activities that may be high priority for State are not necessarily high priority for DOD.

Advocates of greater State Department control would prefer that Congress dispense with the GSCF "pooled" fund and appropriate substantially more security assistance and related DOD funding (particularly "Section 1206" building partnership capacity funding[19]) directly to the international affairs budget, just as FMF, INCLE, and PCCF are currently appropriated. Some fear that the decision to pool DOD and State Department funds rather than to appropriate funds directly to the State Department budget will perpetuate the State Department's lack of capacity to handle security assistance rather than resolve it.[20] On the other hand, others are concerned that including all GSCF funding in the international affairs budget would leave GSCF activities vulnerable to possible cuts by Congress or by the State Department itself as part of overall State Department budget reductions.

Many analysts are concerned that the State Department lacks the capacity to plan and direct an increased number of security assistance and related governance and rule of laws programs[21] without increasing the size of its staff. Some also view the State Department as lacking the institutional interest and will necessary to plan and oversee[22] a large security assistance portfolio. But others may point to the State Department's creation of new programs under the Security Assistance peacekeeping account (PKO) as evidence of State's interest in this program area.

Possible Drawbacks for DOD

For DOD, the GSCF may be perceived as entailing disadvantages as well. While some perceive the GSCF's ability to tap DOD funds for State Department programs of mutual interest as beneficial, others see this effort as a problematic and unwarranted diversion of DOD funds, particularly in an increasingly constrained budget environment. In addition, some analysts believe that DOD at times needs to ensure the integrity of its own missions by the use of security and stabilization assistance. Because GSCF purposes overlap those of DOD's "Section 1206" train and equip authority, where the Secretary of Defense is in the lead, some analysts view a successful GSCF effort as someday leading to the elimination of Section 1206 and similar authorities. For some analysts, such a move would mean sacrificing some of the control and flexibility of programs provided through a DOD authority.

DOD Authority to Train Foreign Security Forces

The GSCF proposals also raise the continuing concern about DOD's role in training security forces with law enforcement functions. The GSCF legislation provides DOD with authority to train and otherwise assist a wider range of foreign security forces than previously permitted. Since FY2006, in conjunction with DOD requests for an expansion of Section 1206 authority, Congress has repeatedly rejected providing DOD with authority to train and assist police and other non-military forces, except for foreign maritime security forces. (Congress has, however, specifically provided DOD with authority to train police in Afghanistan and Iraq.) The GSCF provides authority for assistance to "security forces responsible for conducting border and maritime security, internal security, and counterterrorism operations, as well as the government agencies responsible for such forces," without any limitation on the agency that could provide such assistance. Opponents of this extension have argued that training security forces that perform law enforcement functions is a civilian, not a DOD, function because military skills and culture are distinct from those of civilian law enforcement. Proponents see sufficient overlap, particularly for security forces that operate in lawless border areas and those that exercise counterterrorism functions, to validate this expansion. Some analysts state that the GSCF joint State-DOD program development provisions reduce the risks of the "militarization" of law enforcement efforts.

Strategic Framework

Some analysts express concern that the Administration has requested a new security assistance funding mechanism without first establishing a strategic framework that would set priorities and clarify department and agency roles in security assistance. Early on, the Obama Administration undertook a National Security Council-led review of security assistance to establish such a framework, but that effort has not yet concluded. Some analysts state that it stalled over the issue of an appropriate division of responsibilities between DOD and the State Department.

Some now look to the GSCF process as the crucible for competing conccpts of rcsponsibilitics— whcthcr to rcinvigoratc thc traditional Statc Department lead on all security assistance, placing all security assistance resources under the State Department budget, or to develop a new paradigm of shared responsibilities—and new arrangements. Given the Administration's characterization of the GSCF as an experiment intended to identify issues in interagency collaboration, the GSCF may contribute to the goals of the review. Or, if DOD and the State Department are unable to agree decisively upon a division of labor, Congress may opt to consider further legislation.

LOOKING AHEAD: FY2013 FUNDING AND BEYOND

Even though the GSCF has been authorized for four years, through FY2015, Congress may monitor its use closely and consider in-course changes. For instance, one necessary change may be in the source of GSCF funding. For FY2012, Congress, in its appropriations action, provided for the GSCF to be funded through transfers from specified State Department and DOD accounts, not through new appropriations. The FY2012 NDAA transfer authority for funds from specified DOD accounts to the GSCF extends through FY2015, but there is no corresponding State Department long-term transfer authority. (The House-passed FY2013 Foreign Relations Authorization Act, H.R. 6018, has no GSCF provision.) Without a new State Department transfer authority, FY2012-FY2015 GSCF activities will depend on either a sizable FY2012 State Department transfer from specified accounts as permitted by the FY2012 omnibus appropriations act or on future annual appropriations. As mentioned above, the Senate version of the FY2013 Department of State, Foreign Operations and Related Appropriations Act (S. 3241) would appropriate $25 million to the GSCF, as requested by the Administration, but there is no corresponding provision in the House version of the bill (H.R. 5857).

End Notes

[1] Its origin was a broader mechanism proposed by former Secretary of Defense Robert M. Gates to Secretary of State Hillary Clinton in 2009 to create a joint State-DOD "pool" of funds to build the security capacity of foreign states, prevent conflict, and stabilize countries in conflict or emerging from conflict. In public *fora*, Gates advocated the pooled fund concept as a means to "incentivize collaboration between different agencies of our government." Office of the Assistant Secretary of Defense (Public Affairs) Speechwriters Office, "Remarks as Delivered by Secretary of Defense Robert M. Gates, The Nixon Center's Distinguished Service Award, The Nixon Center, Washington, D.C.," press release, February 24, 2010, http://www.usglc.org/USCLCdocs/Secretary%10of%20Defense%20Gates%20-%20Nixon%20Center.pdf.

[2] State Department FY2012 Congressional Budget Justification (CBJ), February 2011, p. 161.

[3] This Section 1207 is not the same as the controversial Section 1207 Security and Stabilization Assistance provision of the National Defense Authorization Act of FY2006 (P.L. 109-163),

as amended, that authorized the Secretary of Defense to transfer up to $100 million per fiscal year in defense articles, services, training or other support for reconstruction, stabilization, and security activities abroad. That authority expired in FY2010.

[4] The final legislation retains the basic concept and fundamental elements of the Administration's request, but incorporates compromises regarding differing uses, restrictions, and funding amounts among the Administration, House, and Senate versions of the bill. The House version was contained in Section 1204 of H.R. 1540, the FY2012 National Defense Authorization Act (NDAA), as passed by the House May 26, 2011. The identical measure was incorporated as Section 924 in H.R. 2583, the Foreign Relations Authorization Act for FY2012, as passed by the House Foreign Affairs Committee on July 21, 2011. The Senate Armed Service Committee (SASC) incorporated its proposal as Section 1207 of S. 1253, the version of the FY2012 NDAA that SASC reported to the Senate on June 22, 2011 (S.Rept. 112-26). Earlier, SASC had incorporated the Administration's proposal, submitted to Congress on May 6, in its courtesy version of the FY2012 NDAA, S. 981, Section 1214, introduced May 12, 2011.

[5] These proposals are contained in a variety of reports by government agencies as well as non-governmental defense and foreign affairs research organization. See, for example, U.S. Department of State and United States Agency for International Development, *The Quadrennial Diplomacy and Development Review* (QDDR), Washington, D.C., December 2010, p. 203; Gordon Adams and Rebecca Williams, *A New Way Forward: Rebalancing Security Assistance Programs and Authorities*, Henry L. Stimson Center, Washington, DC, March 2011, p. 34; Project on National Security Reform, *Turning Ideas Into* Action, September 2009, p. 219; RAND and the American Academy of Diplomacy, *Integrating Instruments of Power and Influence: Lessons Learned and Best Practices, Report of a Panel of Senior Practitioners*, 2008, pp. 22-23; Center for Strategic and International Studies, *Integrating 21st Century Development and Security Assistance*, 2007, p. 38. For a CRS overview of the unified budget issue, see CRS Report R42133, *Building Civilian Interagency Capacity for Missions Abroad: Key Proposals and Issues for Congress*, by Nina M. Serafino, Catherine Dale, and Pat Towell, pp. 52-56, hereafter referred to as CRS Report R42133.

[6] Section 1207 of the FY2006 NDAA, P.L. 109-163, as amended. See CRS Report RS22871, *Department of Defense "Section 1207" Security and Stabilization Assistance: Background and Congressional Concerns*, FY2006-FY2010, by Nina M. Serafino.

[7] The Foreign Assistance Act, as amended, Section 622(c) (P.L. 85-195, 22 U.S.C. 2382), provides that the Secretary of State, under the direction of the President, "shall be responsible for the continuous supervision and general direction of economic assistance, military assistance, and military education and training programs ... to the end that such programs are effectively integrated both at home and abroad and the foreign policy of the United States is best served thereby." Section 623 establishes the role of the Secretary of Defense regarding security assistance provided under the FAA, giving him primary responsibility for (1) the determination of military end-item requirements; (2) the procurement of military equipment in a manner which permits its integration with service programs; (3) the supervision of end-item use by the recipient countries; (4) the supervision of the training of foreign military and related civilian personnel; (5) the movement and delivery of military end-items; and (6) within the Department of Defense, the performance of any other functions with respect to the furnishing of military assistance, education and training...." The Secretary of Defense is also charged with responsibility for determining "priorities in the procurement, delivery, and allocation of military equipment...."The term military assistance has gradually replaced by the more generic term "security assistance." There are no standard U.S. government definitions for either military assistance or security assistance.

[8] See CRS Report RS22855, *Security Assistance Reform: "Section 1206" Background and Issues for Congress*, by Nina M. Serafino.

[9] Consolidated Appropriations Act, P.L. 112-74, signed into law December 23, 2011.

[10] The authorization act (FY2012 NDAA, P.L. 112-81) also provides the Secretary of State with the authority (under section 635(d) of the Foreign Assistance Act of 1961, as amended) to accept contributions in the form of "money, funds, property, and services." Any amounts in the fund would be available until expended. GSCF monies could be used for necessary administrative expenses.

[11] This transfer authority is provided "in accordance with established procedures for reprogramming under section 1001 of this Act (P.L. 112-81) and successor provisions of law." Section 1001 places a number of restrictions on reprogramings, which can total no more than $4 billion and must be made from a lower to a higher priority program. Section 1001 also provides that the amount transferred is consider to increase the amount authorized for the account to which it is transferred. Transfer authority is also provided by Division A of the Consolidated Appropriations Act, P.L. 112-74, Department of Defense Appropriations Act, 2012, Section 8089.

[12] Division I, Department of State, Foreign Operations, and Related Programs Appropriations Act, 2012, Title VIII, Overseas Contingency Operations, Section 8004.

[13] For more information on counterterrorism efforts in Africa and U.S. support for those efforts, see CRS Report R41473, *Countering Terrorism in East Africa: The U.S. Response*, by Lauren Ploch Blanchard. For more information on Yemen and U.S. assistance to Yemen, see CRS Report RL34170, *Yemen: Background and U.S. Relations*, by Jeremy M. Sharp.

[14] Section 1207(e) states that the "authority to provide assistance under this section is in addition to any other authority to provide assistance to foreign nations."

[15] On June 15, 2012, however, DOD notified the Congress of plans for assistance to Yemen under the transitional authority of Section 1207(n)(1)(C).

[16] U.S. Congress, House Committee on Armed Services, *National Defense Authorization Act for Fiscal Year 2013*, Report on H.R. 4310 together with Additional and Dissenting Views, 112th Cong., 2nd sess., May 11, 2012, H.Rept. 112-479 (Washington: GPO, 2012), p. 257.

[17] For more background on security assistance and a fuller exploration of associated issues, see CRS Report RS22855, *Security Assistance Reform: "Section 1206" Background and Issues for Congress*, by Nina M. Serafino, and CRS Report R41817, *Building the Capacity of Partner States Through Security Force Assistance*, by Thomas K. Livingston.

[18] See footnote 7.

[19] First authorized by Section 1206 (Authority to Build Partnership Capacity of Foreign Military Forces) of the FY2006 NDAA, P.L. 109-163, and subsequently extended and amended.

[20] Gordon Adams and Rebecca Williams, *A New Way Forward: Rebalancing Security Assistance Programs and Authorities*, The Henry L. Stimson Center, Washington, DC, March 2011, pp. 25,30.

[21] For more on this topic, see CRS Report R42155, pp. 57-60.

[22] As with other security assistance programs under both State Department and DOD leads, it is anticipated that GSCF programs will be implemented and managed by the Defense Security Cooperation Agency, a DOD agency jointly funded by State and DOD.

In: Federal Funds: A Selection of Programs ISBN 978-1-62618-005-5
Editor: Kieran Saccoccio

Chapter 2

THE JUDGMENT FUND: HISTORY, ADMINISTRATION, AND COMMON USAGE*

Vivian S. Chu and Brian T. Yeh

SUMMARY

The Judgment Fund is a permanent, indefinite appropriation that was created by Congress in 1956 to pay judgments entered against the United States. Generally, the United States cannot be sued unless it has waived its sovereign immunity. Originally, such waivers were rare, so individual claims were assigned to congressional committees, which in turn appropriated funds to satisfy the judgments. Prior to the creation of the Judgment Fund, the number of claims grew rapidly, taking up an increasing amount of Congress's time and resources. Eventually, the Judgment Fund was created to reduce Congress's workload, so that individual appropriations were not needed for each award entered.

The Fund's administration has changed substantially since its inception, with varying degrees of control and oversight by Congress, the Government Accountability Office, and the Treasury Department. Originally, the Fund was limited to claims of less than $100,000, entered by the Court of Federal Claims or a U.S. District Court. As payments grew in size, Congress transferred

* This is an edited, reformatted and augmented version of the Congressional Research Service Publication, CRS Report for Congress R42835, dated November 26, 2012.

authority to the Justice Department to make payments on behalf of the United States, as certified by the Attorney General.

Today, the Fund is administered by the Financial Management Service in the Treasury Department and is only accessible when certain closely circumscribed statutory requirements are met. Most importantly, an agency may not access the Fund when there is another appropriation that may be applied or when the plaintiff prevailed through an administrative remedy. In addition, the fund can only be used for monetary awards that are final, meaning the award cannot be changed or overturned. The awards must result from claims that were or could have been litigated in court.

This report sets out specific instances in which the Fund can be accessed and illustrates the procedural mechanisms for obtaining payment under certain statutory causes of action. Although primarily used for the payment of principal awards, attorneys' fees and interest on awards may also be paid from the Fund. At the court's discretion, certain costs enumerated in 28 U.S.C. § 1920 may be awarded to the prevailing party. In addition, certain statutes, such as the Federal Tort Claims Act, provide that attorneys' fees may be recovered by the prevailing party. In addition, interest that accrues after the judgment may also be payable from the Fund. This report provides examples of how the payments from the Fund may be made under the Equal Access to Justice Act, Contract Disputes Act, Notification and Federal Employee Antidiscrimination Act (No FEAR Act), and through tribe-specific judgment funds.

In addition, this report will briefly highlight several recently proposed changes to the Judgment Fund's administration. The Judgment Fund Transparency Act of 2011 (H.R. 1446) would require the Secretary of the Treasury to post the claimant, agency, fact summary, and payment amount for each claim paid out of the Fund. The Government Transparency and Recordkeeping Act of 2012 (S. 3415) would require the Secretary to publicly report all payments from the Fund under the Equal Access to Justice Act since 2003 and all future claims. Amendments to the No FEAR Act that were proposed in H.R. 6780 (110th Congress) and H.R. 67 (111th Congress) would have impacted reimbursement of the Fund for payments under the No FEAR Act.

INTRODUCTION

The Judgment Fund (or Fund) is a permanent appropriation enacted by Congress in 1956. The Fund is an unlimited amount of money set aside to pay judgments against the United States. It is only accessible when the United States has waived its sovereign immunity and certain statutory conditions are met. The Fund has evolved in administration and function over the last half century and has been subject to limiting principles. Most importantly, the Judgment Fund cannot be used in place of a specific appropriation. The Fund remains a source of continued controversy and discussion, especially in the current fiscal environment. During the budget uncertainties in the 1990s, federal agencies became increasingly concerned about the Judgment Fund's solvency, as statutory and constitutional constraints precluded the agencies from obligating funds where appropriated money is not available.[1]

This report reviews the history of the Judgment Fund, which has been administered through different agencies and with variable levels of congressional oversight since its inception. This report also outlines specific instances in which the Fund may be accessed, and when costs other than the principal award may be paid. Finally, this report provides examples of how and when the Judgment Fund may be accessed, as well as instances of when tribal judgment funds are implicated.

HISTORY AND OVERVIEW OF THE JUDGMENT FUND

Basic Framework for Litigating against the United States

The U.S. government has sovereign immunity, meaning it cannot be sued unless it has waived immunity or consented to suit.[2] Article III, Section 2 of the U.S. Constitution immunizes federal officials from lawsuit, disallows suits against the federal government by the states, and has been interpreted to prohibit suits against the federal government generally.[3] Under limited circumstances, the United States has waived sovereign immunity; it has done so in a constitutional provision, by express statutory authority, or through a contract.[4] Therefore, the United States can be sued pursuant to certain statutes, most commonly the Federal Tort Claims Act.[5] The Tucker Act,[6] the Military Personnel and Civilian Employees Claims Act,[7] and the Federal Employees Compensation Act[8] are other examples of sovereign immunity waivers passed in the last century.[9] These statutes often contain substantial limiting principles and have been narrowly construed by courts.[10]

Congress must make provisions to pay judgments when suits against the United States are successful. Appropriated funds may not be used to satisfy claims unless there is specific statutory authority that allows the claim to go forward and provides a source of funds to pay any award.[11] In the wake of several legislative enactments waiving the United States' sovereign immunity, Congress enacted the Judgment Fund in an effort to reduce the need to allocate specific appropriations for payment of claims.[12]

Awards Prior to the Creation of the Judgment Fund

While waiver of sovereign immunity was less common in the early Republic than it is today, determining and settling claims against the United States occupied a substantial amount of Congress's time since its first session.[13] As early as the Continental Congress, the legislature established committees to audit and settle claims against the United States. The structure and staffing of these committees left most of them with an overwhelming workload, as claims from the War for Independence multiplied and dragged on.[14]

Therefore, one of Congress's first priorities after the ratification of the Constitution was establishing an executive branch agency that could manage payments of claims against the United States. In its first session, Congress established the Treasury Department in the Treasury Bill of 1789, with an extremely detailed enabling statute that left Congress with substantial control over monetary policy but little ministerial responsibility.[15] Among other things, the act authorized the Treasury Department to settle all claims and accounts, delegating to the Auditor the duty to examine claims and to the Comptroller the duty to approve or disapprove of the Auditor's finding.[16] In the event a claim was disputed by the government, the Treasury Department disallowed the claim and accepted the government's facts.[17] If the claim was denied by the Treasury Department, the claimant could petition Congress directly. Congress, in turn, made specific appropriations for each claim validated by the Department or through the petition process. This resulted in many claims waiting in limbo, where the Auditor and Comptroller had agreed to pay the claim, but where Congress had yet to make an appropriation to satisfy the judgment.[18]

By 1855, Congress was still dedicating a large portion of its resources to passing appropriations to satisfy claims against the United States, and hearing petitions from claims that were denied by the Treasury Department.[19] In order to reduce its workload, Congress established the Court of Claims, which served in an advisory capacity.[20] Rather than issuing binding decisions, the court simply considered the merits of claims filed against the United States, and recommended appropriations to Congress.[21] At President Lincoln's urging, Congress subsequently empowered the Court of Federal Claims to issue binding decisions, though the Supreme Court found that the Treasury Department could decline enforcement of the decisions.[22] Once Congress repealed this authority, the Supreme Court could hear appeals from the Court of Claims, and the Court of Claims' decisions carried finality and enforcement on par with other Article III courts. Congress also clarified that certifications from the Treasury Department were final and conclusive.[23]

However, in 1921, desiring a tighter hold on the payment of claims, Congress again changed the administration of the settlement process. In the Budget Accounting Act of 1921, Congress transferred authority to the General Accounting Office (GAO)[24] for all claims settlement duties previously held by the Treasury Department.[25] GAO, in turn, sought appropriations from Congress, so that Congress could strengthen controls over expenditures. This allowed Congress to regain structural control over the payments process. However, Congress was left with considerable involvement in appropriating funds for each claim, which encumbered committees and ultimately proved untenable.[26]

Creation of the Judgment Fund

In 1956, Congress passed the Judgment Fund enabling statute, a permanent and indefinite appropriation available to pay all judgments against the United States not covered by a specific appropriation.[27] Congress aimed to reduce the time lapse between judgments entered against the United States and actual payment, so that agencies would pay less post-judgment interest on awards.[28] Originally, the Fund was available only for judgments for claims of less than $100,000 entered in the Court of Federal Claims or a U.S. district court.[29] Congress anticipated that the Fund would cover over 98% of all claims, thereby drastically reducing the need for individual appropriations and also streamlining the payment process.[30] The House Report accompanying the bill indicates that a permanent appropriation "will permit a simplification of the payment procedure, will provide uniformity in interest computation, and will serve to reduce the total amount of interest paid by the government."[31] The Senate report underscored the limitations in the bill on what payments could be made from the Judgment Fund, emphasizing the audit, review, and finality requirements.[32]

Changes in Administration from 1956 to Present

Administration of payments from the Fund changed significantly in the latter 20th century. In 1961, Congress authorized payment from the Judgment Fund for settlements negotiated by the Department of Justice on behalf of the United States, where litigation could have resulted in a monetary judgment.[33] In addition, the Judgment Fund could also pay for judgments against the United States from state and foreign tribunals subject to certification by the Attorney General.[34] By the mid-1970s, the Fund's $100,000 payment ceiling proved too low to cover many settlements and judgments, and Congress raised the allowable damages to avoid making specific appropriations for larger awards.[35] In 1996, Congress transferred certification of payment from the Judgment Fund from GAO to the Financial Management Service in the Department of the Treasury.[36] GAO retained administrative settlement authority for settlement of non-litigative claims. [37] In recent years, Congress has taken an interest in the amount of money that has been spent from the Judgment Fund. Generally, these bills deal with transparency and improved agency accountability, including the Judgment Fund Transparency Act and proposed amendments to the No FEAR Act.[38] In 2011, the Financial Management Service, the bureau in charge of administering the Fund, published a 2011 fiscal report, which included information about payments made from the Judgment Fund.

How Does the Judgment Fund Operate Today?

Overview

The Judgment Fund is a permanent, indefinite appropriation.[39] By definition, it requires no further congressional action and does not expire at the close of any fiscal year. The appropriation makes an unlimited amount of funds available for payment of certain judgments against the United States.[40] Awards are only paid out of the Judgment Fund when payment is not otherwise provided for in a specific appropriation. All judgments must be final, meaning the award will not be overturned on appeal. In addition, all settlements paid out of the Judgment Fund must represent the final and comprehensive award for the actual or threatened litigation, negotiated and agreed to by the Department of Justice.[41] Finally, the Judgment Fund may be used to pay certain costs to the prevailing party in litigation, as enumerated in

28 U.S.C. § 1920.[42] These costs typically include court fees and compensation for court-appointed experts.[43]

When Is the Judgment Fund Appropriately Used?

The Judgment Fund statute sets out four requirements for accessing the Fund. First, the Fund may only be used to pay judgments or settlements involving money judgments.[44] For example, if a court ordered an agency to hire a consultant to implement fair employment practices, the Judgment Fund could not be used to pay costs and fees associated with fulfilling this requirement.

The judgment must also be final, so that payments are not made from the Fund when there is a chance the award could be changed or overturned.[45] This has been interpreted to mean that the judgment must come out of action by the court of last resort or that the parties have declined to seek further review.[46] Most often, the time for appeal simply expires before payment from the Judgment Fund. However, the statute exempts payment for an "irreducible minimum amount," meaning an amount that has been assessed as final.[47] For example, in *Trout v. Garrett*, the D.C. Circuit Court of Appeals found that payment from the Judgment Fund was proper for interim attorneys' fees in a Title VII employment discrimination action against the government.[48] The court found that the Judgment Fund statute was intended to serve as a mechanism for payment rather than to interfere with the ordinary course of litigation.[49]

The Judgment Fund may not be used for payments if the award is otherwise provided for, by appropriation or statute. For example, courts have held that annual appropriations to the Land and Water Conservation Fund must be used where there is a land condemnation judgment against the U.S. Park Service.[50] Courts look for an appropriation that has programmatic specificity, regardless of the agency's use of the funds. The actual funding level is irrelevant; so long as the appropriation exists, it precludes payment from the Judgment Fund.[51] For example, if an agency had already spent an appropriated sum on other litigation or expended the money elsewhere, the Judgment Fund still could not be used. Under these circumstances, the agency would have to seek an additional appropriation from Congress.[52]

Lastly, the Judgment Fund is limited to litigative awards, meaning awards that were or could have been made in a court. Litigative awards are distinguished from administrative awards because the latter are provided for by statute and are paid from the agency's appropriation.[53] These include EEOC claims, awards under the Military Claims Act, and Merit Systems Protection Board matters. The primary exception to this rule is claims under the Federal Tort Claims Act that are over $2,500, which Congress exempted in the statute.[54] Permissible awards include the principal amount, some attorneys' fees, allowable costs, and interest as stated in the judgment or settlement. For settlement awards to be considered litigative, the settlement must be negotiated by the Department of Justice and based on a claim that could have resulted in a monetary judgment in court.[55]

When Is the Judgment Fund Inaccessible?

There are nearly 100 statutes that impact payment from the Judgment Fund, 17 of which specifically dictate denial of payment from the Fund.[56] For example, administrative awards less than $2,500 arising under the Federal Tort Claims Act may not be paid from the Judgment Fund.[57] When there is a specific appropriation, the Judgment Fund may not be used. The most common example of an award against the United States to which the Judgment Fund is inapplicable are tax judgments.[58] Congress makes special, term-limited appropriations to pay tax refunds and judgments, and therefore, they may not be paid out of the Judgment Fund. Neither judgments against the Postal Service, nor those against government corporations, such as the Pension Benefit Guaranty Corporation, are payable from the Judgment Fund.[59] This is in part because government corporations segregate their revenues from the general fund and operate largely without appropriated funds.[60] Therefore, the rationale for using the Judgment Fund, which was intended to reduce the need for Congress to make appropriations, would be inapplicable. In addition, the Judgment Fund may not be used for land condemnation judgments or certain court- awarded contempt citation awards.[61]

Who Administers the Judgment Fund?

Since 1996, the Judgment Fund has been administered by the Financial Management Service (FMS) in the Treasury Department. Once a party has received a final court judgment or negotiated settlement, FMS requires the responsible agency to submit a request for certification of payment from the

Fund.[62] FMS considers the proposed payment in light of the aforementioned rules, determining whether payment out of the Fund is proper or whether it is an obligation chargeable to agency funds.[63] In this respect, FMS is the primary enforcer for the limits on the Judgment Fund's use. FMS also determines whether the judgment is final, and calculates interest subject to the above limitations. If the payee is indebted to the United States, FMS may offset that amount before payment.[64] Generally, unless the claim arises under the Contract Disputes Act (CDA) or the No FEAR Act, the agency does not reimburse the Judgment Fund; therefore, payment ends the process.[65]

The certification and payment is primarily a ministerial function. At no point in the process does FMS consider the nature or merit of the underlying action except to the extent necessary to determine the propriety of payment from the Fund. FMS makes a payment directly to the plaintiff, without an intermediary.[66] This substantially ends the agency's involvement. However, if FMS does not render payment to the correct party, this does not discharge the United States' obligation.[67]

In the event FMS refuses to make payment, the submitting agency is notified, and it may alter and resubmit claims as appropriate. Most commonly, rejections result from errors in the submission forms, absence of underlying documents, or other technical issues. A claim is only denied if, during administration, FMS determines that payment from the Judgment Fund is not proper.[68] Claims are most commonly denied because payment has been provided for by a specific appropriation or the award is less than the legal thresholds for statutes such as the Military Justice Act.[69]

COSTS ALLOWABLE UNDER AWARDS PAID FROM THE JUDGMENT FUND

Federal courts have some discretion when deciding at the end of litigation whether to charge the losing party with costs for the prevailing party. However, the categories of costs that may be awarded are strictly circumscribed and the subject of considerable debate.[70] Under 28 U.S.C. § 1920, the clerk of the court may award costs for court fees, transcripts, fees related to witnesses, materials for presentation in the case, compensation for court-appointed experts, and docket fees.[71] To obtain costs for such items in payment from the Judgment Fund, the submitting agency must include a bill of costs or the court's order awarding costs with the request for payment.[72] Courts have limited payment to the enumerated items in §1920 and the specific exemptions in applicable statutory authority when awarding costs.[73] Payments of interest and attorneys' fees have caused considerable debate with respect to this issue.[74]

Payment of Attorneys' Fees from the Judgment Fund

As a preliminary matter, the U.S. legal system does not generally allow recovery of attorneys' fees by the prevailing party.[75] Termed the "American Rule," this approach distinguishes the U.S. system, making each party responsible for payment of their own legal fees, regardless of the result, unless specifically authorized by statute or contract.[76] In most legal systems around the world, the losing party pays the prevailing party's legal fees as part of the damages award.[77]

The American Rule applies with two major common law exceptions and numerous statutory provisions exempting certain classes of cases.[78] The common benefit rule allows federal courts to award attorneys' fees when a party prevails in a suit at his own expense that benefits a large class of other persons. This shifts the cost of attorneys' fees to those who benefit from the suit, not the opposing party.[79] This allows for so-called private attorney generals to effectuate policy in litigation, benefitting a large class of people, with the added incentive that attorneys' fees will be paid if they prevail.[80] The bad faith exception allows a federal court to award counsel fees to a successful party when his opponent acted vexatious or for oppressive reasons, making the award of fees punitive.[81] This requires proof of malice and a showing that the claim had virtually no chance of success.[82]

Specific statutory exemptions, called fee-shifting provisions, make the federal government responsible for attorneys' fees in a wide variety of suits. Statutes that allow for award of attorneys' fees often do so with an eye towards equalizing two unevenly matched parties, and often apply to environmental and consumer protection litigation. This has the effect of implementing public policy through private litigation.[83] In some instances, statutes specifically limit the awards of attorneys' fees. For example, the Federal Tort Claims Act allows for attorneys' fees up to 20% for administrative settlements and up to 25% for judicial awards.[84] The Freedom of Information Act statute limits attorneys' fees to actual litigation (as opposed to administrative remedies). When attorneys' fees are statutorily authorized, payment may generally be authorized from the Judgment Fund, unless otherwise provided by law.[85] The parties may not alter the source of payment by stipulation or other agreements in the settlement.[86]

Payment of Interest from the Judgment Fund

Payment from the Judgment Fund includes principal awards and, in limited cases, post-judgment interest. However, payment of interest must be considered in light of special considerations for awards entered against the United States. In *Library of Congress v. Shaw*, the Supreme Court held that interest cannot be recovered in a suit against the government unless Congress has expressly waived sovereign immunity for an award,[87] and has specifically contemplated an award of interest on damages.[88] Prejudgment interest is considered in the calculation of damages, and is not awarded separately.[89] Historically, courts have treated post-judgment interest as a separate element of damages unrelated to the substantive claim, and therefore awarded only upon agreement of the parties.[90] Because the United States is immune from suit absent its consent, this rule especially applies in awards against the government.[91] With respect to the Judgment Fund, payment of interest is authorized in certain instances. If a district court award is awaiting appeal by the government, the Judgment Fund statute authorizes payment of interest if the plaintiff sends a trial transcript to the Treasury Department and payment is limited to the period from the date Treasury receives the transcript until judgment is mandated or affirmed.[92]

In *Library of Congress v. Shaw*, the Court also identified two widely recognized exceptions to the no-interest rule, which are not drawn from specific statutes but have been found to be a constitutional waiver of sovereign immunity.[93] The Fifth Amendment provides that private property shall not be taken for public use without "just compensation."[94] Courts have determined that this exception inherently recognizes interest in order to make the person whole. However, courts have not been receptive to the Fifth Amendment as a means to obtain interest when a takings claim is not otherwise involved.[95] The second constitutional exception where interest may be allowed is the commercial venture exception, set out in *Standard Oil Company v. United States*, whereby a plaintiff may recover attorneys' fees from a commercial government enterprise.[96] The commercial venture exception requires that the government entity involved in the suit have a sue-and-be-sued clause.

Therefore, the commercial venture exception is limited to litigation where the agency has been opened to suit by statute and is engaged in a primarily commercial, as opposed to governmental, function.[97]

Therefore, to determine whether interest is payable from the Judgment Fund, a plaintiff bringing suit against the government must engage in a three-step analysis. First, the statute under which suit was brought should first be considered. If the statute authorizes payment of interest, then it may be payable from the Fund. For example, if a plaintiff prevailed under the Back Pay Act, the Fund would pay interest on the claim from the date of the withdrawal or reduction of pay, because this is specifically authorized in the statute.[98] Second, if the case was pending appeal, the plaintiff should consider the interest allowance in 31 U.S.C. § 1304(b).[99] If a plaintiff won in district court, and filed a transcript of judgment with the Treasury Department, interest may be paid in the time between the judgment and when the government decides not to appeal.[100] Finally, a plaintiff should determine whether the cause of action amounts to a taking under the Fifth Amendment or falls under the commercial venture exception.

ILLUSTRATIONS OF THE JUDGMENT FUND

As discussed above, the Judgment Fund enabling statute limits an agency's ability to access the Fund. This section provides examples of statutes that prevent an agency from relying on the Judgment Fund as the source of payment, and briefly outlines the legislative intent of these statutes.

The Equal Access to Justice Act

The Equal Access to Justice Act (EAJA) provides for award of attorneys' fees for individuals and small entities that prevail in cases against the federal government.[101] EAJA applies only when the claimants are the "prevailing party," or when they are successful on a significant issue in the litigation.[102] The party must also show that the result of the lawsuit was not a gratuitous act by the government.[103] The act also contains specific size requirements, so that larger entities may not recover under the act.[104]

Since the passage of EAJA, agencies have disputed whether payments under the act must be made out of their appropriations or whether attorneys' fees may be charged to the Judgment Fund.[105] In *Cienega Gardens v. United*

States, the Federal Circuit ordered an award for the plaintiffs, finding that amendments to the Department of Housing and Urban Development's (HUD) low income housing program constituted a taking.[106] EAJA provides for payment, by directing that a fee award "be paid by any agency over which the party prevails from any funds made available to the agency by appropriation or otherwise."[107] However, the plaintiffs sued the United States, instead of the agency, and HUD argued that they should not be liable because the Department of Justice did not seek review on a facially questionable ruling.[108] HUD proposed that no agency should be responsible under these rare facts, and therefore, payment under EAJA should be made from the Judgment Fund instead of the agency's appropriations.[109] The Treasury Department countered that the Judgment Fund is not responsible for payment when the party prevails over the agency, and denied payment.[110]

In an opinion by its Office of Legal Counsel (OLC), the Justice Department concluded that the Judgment Fund could not pay the award for attorneys' fees, because HUD was the agency over which the party prevailed.[111] OLC had previously concluded that an agency could only seek payment from the Judgment Fund when payment of attorneys' fees would constitute a heavy financial blow to the agency, a loophole that was closed in a subsequent version of EAJA.[112] The opinion looked to congressional intent underlying EAJA, which was in part to create agency accountability when taking a regulatory or adverse action which was not substantially justified.[113] In addition, Congress left no statutory mechanisms for payment of EAJA claims from the Judgment Fund.[114] The opinion did not leave open the possibility that agencies could be reimbursed for awards made pursuant to EAJA from the Judgment Fund and strongly suggested they would have to use their own appropriations.

Contract Disputes Act and No FEAR Act

Congress has passed two statutes that require agencies to reimburse the Judgment Fund for payment of claims. The Contract Disputes Act of 1978 (CDA) allows payment from the Judgment Fund when a contractor for an agency wins a judgment from a court or a contract appeals board, or reaches a settlement with an agency on a contract dispute.[115] The agency must then reimburse the Judgment Fund from its operating appropriations.[116] If the agency has insufficient funds available to reimburse the Funds, CDA requires that the agency seek additional funding from Congress.[117] Congress wanted to incentivize agencies to engage in settlement talks and keep them accountable for the costs of judgments.[118]

The Notification and Federal Employee Antidiscrimination Act of 2002 (No FEAR Act) covers whistleblower and employment discrimination suits for federal employees, creating a cause of action for federal employees who have been subjected to harassment or discrimination in the workplace.[119] The act requires the agency to reimburse the Judgment Fund within a reasonable time.[120]

In 2008, the GAO released a report on reimbursements to the Judgment Fund from CDA and No FEAR payments. The report concluded that, while virtually all agencies have reimbursed the Fund for No FEAR payments since it was made mandatory in 2002, CDA payments are considerably less consistent.[121] Typically, CDA payments are much larger, perhaps keeping agencies from reimbursing the Fund.[122] GAO recommended that the FMS take steps to make agency payments more transparent, and that it report to Congress periodically on the status of payments.[123]

Tribe-Specific Judgment Funds

Congress created a separate but similar system for payment of judgments awarded to tribes under title XXV of the U.S. Code. The Indian Tribal Judgment Funds Use or Distribution Act created a trust to be administered by the Secretary of the Interior, which would distribute all funds appropriated in judgments in favor of tribes. Courts have held this is the exclusive trust for all such payments, and that no additional Congressional action is necessary.[124] The Interior Department holds funds in trust until Congress makes an appropriation to the tribe.[125] When two or more tribes benefit from a single judgment, the Bureau of Indian Affairs submits a plan to Congress recommending a division of the funds, prior to the appropriation.[126]

Recent Legislative Proposals

The Judgment Fund has changed many times in its over 50-year history, and recent legislative proposals in Congress could again alter certain payments and processes. In the 112th Congress, the Judgment Fund Transparency Act of 2011 was introduced to amend the Judgment Fund enabling statute.[127] The act would require the Secretary of the Treasury to post the claimant, agency, fact summary, and payment amount for each claim from the Judgment Fund.[128] Recently, FMS released its 2011 Fiscal Report, which included all of the information from the Transparency Act except for fact summaries,[129] pursuant to the House Appropriations Committee's recommendations that accompanied the Financial Services and General Government Appropriations Act of 2012.[130] The committee instructed FMS to report online each claim paid from the Judgment Fund in the given fiscal year.[131]

The Government Transparency and Recordkeeping Act of 2012 would amend the Judgment Fund enabling statute to require the Secretary of the Treasury to publicly report all Judgment Fund payments since 2003, and report all future payments from EAJA.[132] The disclosures would be made online, and include those required under the Judgment Fund Transparency Act, as well as specific details about attorneys' fees and interest paid from the Judgment Fund.[133]

Legislation in the 110th and 111th Congress would have amended the No FEAR Act to require agencies to reimburse the Judgment Fund for payments for claims within two years of a final finding of discrimination.[134] Claims under the No FEAR Act are paid from the Judgment Fund; however, the law does not specify a definitive period for agencies to reimburse the Fund.[135] The stated purpose of the legislation was to "encourage timely resolution or settlement of complaints."[136] These bills saw no action.

End Notes

[1] Vacketta & Kantor, "Obtaining Payments from the Government's Judgment Fund," Briefing Papers No. 97-3 at 2 (Feb. 1997).

[2] *See* United States v. Sherwood, 312 U.S. 584 (1981).

[3] U.S. CONST. ART. III § 2. *See* Gray v. Bell, 712 F.2d 490, 506 (D.C. Cir. 1983) ("The United States is protected from unconsented suit under the ancient common law doctrine of sovereign immunity.").

[4] *See infra* notes 44-49. *See also* CRS Report R40996, *Contract Liability Arising from the Nuclear Waste Policy Act (NWPA) of 1982*, by Todd Garvey

[5] 28 U.S.C. §§ 1346(b), 2671-2680.

[6] 28 U.S.C. § 1491.

[7] 31 U.S.C. § 3721.

[8] 5 U.S.C. § 8101 *et.seq.*

[9] *See gen*. Donald A. Cyze, *The Federal Tort Claims Act: A Cause of Action for Servicemen*, 14 VAL. U. L. REV. 527 (1980).

[10] *See, e.g.*, Shaw v. Library of Congress, 478 U.S. 310, 317 (1986) ("[W]e must construe waivers strictly in favor of the sovereign.").

[11] Customs Service—Wrongful Acts of Employees, 17 Comp. Gen. 931, A- 92313, May 12, 1938 (explaining that the absence of appropriated funds does not imply the absence of a right of action). *See also* Waiver of Statutes of Limitations in Connection with Claims

Against the Department of Agriculture, 22 Op. Off. Legal Counsel 127, June 18, 1998 ("[N]o money may be paid on a claim against the government unless a statute authorizes payment or mandates compensation.").

[12] *See infra* "Creation of the Judgment Fund."

[13] U.S. GOV'T ACCOUNTABILITY OFFICE, GAO-08-978SP, PRINCIPLES OF FEDERAL APPROPRIATIONS LAW (GAO REDBOOK), Third Edition Volume III, Chapter 14, Claims Against and By the Government, at 14-3.

[14] *Id.*

[15] 31 U.S.C. § 301(a)-(b). Act of Sept. 2, 1789, ch. 12, 1 Stat. 65, originally enacted as the Treasury Bill of 1789, H.R. 9, 1st Congress, text available online: http://www.gwu.edu/~ffcp/mep/displaydoc.cfm?docid=fc061975d1.

[16] *Id.*

[17] GAO Redbook, at 14-5.

[18] *Id.*

[19] *See generally, Appropriate Source for Payment of Judgments and Settlements in United States v. Winstar Corp. and Related Cases*, Memorandum for Neal S. Wilson, Deputy General Counsel, Department of the Treasury, Office of Legal Counsel, July 22, 1998, http://www.justice.gov/olc/winstarfinal.htm.

[20] *See* Act of Feb. 24, 1855, Ch. 122, 10 Stat. 612, 612-13.

[21] *See* Judith Resnik, "Of Courts, Agencies, and the Court of Federal Claims: Fortunately Outliving One's Anomalous Character" (2003). Faculty Scholarship Series Paper 764 at 861. Available Online: http://digitalcommons.law.yale.edu/fss_papers/764/.

[22] Cong. Globe, Dec. 3, 1861, 37th Cong., 2d Sess. app at 2 ("[I]t is as much the duty of Government to render prompt justice against itself in favor of citizens, as it is to administer the same between private individuals," Lincoln urged). *See* 12 Stat. 765, Reprinted at 37 Cong. Ch. 92, March 3, 1863. *See also Muskrat v. United States*, 219 U.S. 346 (1911).

[23] Act of February 24, 1855, Ch. 122, § 1, 33 Cong. Ch. 122, 10 Stat. 612 (1855).

[24] GAO's name was changed in 2004 to the Government Accountability Office, P.L. 108-271, 118 Stat. 811 (2004).

[25] P.L. 67-13, 42 Stat. 20-27, 67 Cong. Ch. 18, June 10, 1921. *See also* Legislative Branch Appropriations Act, P.L. 104-53, 109 Stat. 514 (1995) (transferring authorities to GAO previously held by the Treasury Department).

[26] GAO Redbook, at 14-8.

[27] 31 U.S.C. § 1304. For an example of an instance where the Judgment Fund cannot be used due to a more specific, available appropriation, see Comptroller General of the United States, Letter to the Honorable Pete Hokstra, B-279886, 1998 WL 229292, April 28, 1998 ("The fact that Congress has chosen to bar the use of funds made available in the 1998 Justice and Labor Appropriations Acts to pay the cost of the Election Officer's supervision of the 1996 election rerun should not be viewed as an open invitation to convert the Judgment Fund from an appropriation to pay damage awards against the United States to a program account to circumvent congressional restrictions on appropriations that would otherwise be available to cover these expenses.").

[28] *See infra* notes 30-32, 36.

[29] Vacketta & Kantor, *supra* note footnote 1, at 2 (Feb. 1997) (clarifying that the fund was not originally available for settlements or judgment from other tribunals, such as state or foreign bodies).

[30] H.REPT. 84-2638, at 72 (1956).

[31] *Id.*

[32] S. DOC. 84-146 (1956), reprinted in 1961 U.S.C.C.A. 243.

[33] Albert D. Parker, Comp. Gen. Dec. B-215672, 64 Comp. Gen. 349 (1985). The definition of monetary damages is drawn from Section 702 of the Administrative Procedure Act. 5 U.S.C. § 702.

[34] Pub. L. No. 87-187, § 2, 75 Stat. 415 (Aug. 30, 1961).

[35] Vacketta & Kantor, *supra* note 1, at 3 ("[T]his limitation began to subvert the purpose of the Fund because Congress had to provide a supplemental appropriation for every judgment or compromise settlement that happened to exceed $100,000."). Supplemental Appropriations Act of 1977, P.L. 95-25 § 101, 91 Stat. 61, 96 (May 4, 1977). *See, e.g.*, Tamoak Band of Western Shoshone Indians v. United States, 593 F.2d 994 (Ct. Cl.), *cert. denied*, 444 U.S. 973 (1979).

[36] H.R. REPT. No.104-141, part II at 31. (1996) ("The committee has taken this action because claims and judgment duties are not legislative activities and detract from the essential purposes of the agency."). *See also Legislative Branch Appropriations for Fiscal Year 1996, Hearings on H.R. 1854 Before the Subcomm. of the Senate Comm. on Appropriations*, 104th Cong. 1st sess. 38 (1996) (detailing staff cuts at the Government Accountability Office that would necessarily accompany a reduction in responsibilities for the agency).

[37] P.L. 104-53, Section 211, 109 Stat. 514, 535 (1996). See also GAO Redbook, at 14-10. GAO's settlment authority, however, is limited to accounts and debts unrelated to claims against the United States. See 31 U.S.C. § 3526. GAO may also relieve liable officials and certifying officers. See 31 U.S.C. § 3527. For a full explanation of GAO's authorities after 1996 and examples of agency delegation, see GAO Report B-275605, "Transfer of Claims Settlement and Related Advance Decisions, Waivers, And Other Functions," March 17, 1997, available online: http://www.whitehouse.gov/sites/default/files/omb/assets

[38] *See infra* notes 127-138.

[39] 31 U.S.C. § 1304.

[40] *Id.*

[41] *Id.*

[42] 28 U.S.C. § 2412(a) ("Except as otherwise specifically provided by statute, a judgment for costs, as enumerated in section 1920 of this title, but not including the fees and expenses of attorneys, may be awarded to the prevailing party in any civil action brought by or against the United States or any agency or any official of the United States acting in his or her official capacity in any court having jurisdiction of such action.").

[43] 28 U.S.C. § 1920 (1-6) (enumerating each allowable cost to be taxed). *See infra* "Costs Allowable Under Awards Paid from the Judgment Fund."

[44] *See* Matter of: Availability of Expired Funds for Non-monetary Judicial Awards, 70 Comp. Gen. 225, February 4, 1991. *See also Availability of Judgment Fund in Cases Not Involving A Money Judgment Claim*, 13 Op. Off. Legal Counsel 98, 104 (1989) ("When the Judgment Fund statute was enacted in 1956, only the payment of money judgments was provided for.... Had Congress wished to provide for the payment from the Judgment Fund of all settlements when it amended the Judgment Fund statute in 1961, presumably it would specifically have so indicated. Its failure to do so supports the conclusion that in extending the Judgment Fund statute to reach settlements, Congress believed it was only bringing within the statute's ambit settlements of causes that could have resulted in Judgment Fund disbursements, had such causes resulted in final money judgments rather than settlements.").

[45] McDonald v. Schweiker, 726 F.2d 311, 313 (7th Cir. 1983) (clarifying that "final judgment" does not have a single fixed meaning, but that the case much be situated such that no further action is contemplated).

[46] *See infra* notes 47-52.

[47] 31 U.S.C. § 1304.

[48] Trout v. Garrett, 891 F.2d 332, 335 (D.C. Cir. 1989) (explaining that the Judgment Fund "is auxiliary legislation; its sole office is to furnish 'a mechanism for facilitating payment of judgments' rendered on claims authorized by another statute.").

[49] *Id.*

[50] United States v. 14,770.65 Acres of Land, More or Less, Situated in Richland County, State of S.C., 616 F. Supp. 1235, 1248-1253 (D.S.C. 1985).

[51] 31 U.S.C. § 1304.

[52] GAO Redbook, at 14-7.
[53] 31 U.S.C. § 1304.
[54] *Id.*
[55] P.L. 87-187, § 2, 75 Stat. 415 (Aug. 30, 1961).
[56] Department of the Treasury, Financial Management Services, Judgment Fund: Common Questions, June 20, 2012, http://fms.treas.gov/judgefund/questions.html. *See, e.g.*, 18 U.S.C. § 2712(b)(5); cf 26 U.S.C. § 7432.
[57] 28 U.S.C. § 1346(a)(2).
[58] *See* Financial Management Service, Department of the Treasury, The Judgment Fund: Background, March 11, 2011 http://www.fms.treas.gov/judgefund/background.html.
[59] *Id. See also The Availability of the Judgement Fund for the Payment of Judgments or Settlements in Suits Brought Against the Commodity Credit Corp. Under the Fed. Tort Claims Act*, 13 Op. Off. Legal Counsel 362 (1989) ("The creation of the Judgment Fund therefore did not disturb the prior practice, reflected in GAO decisions, that a government corporation would be required to pay judgments and settlements on personal injury claims where it has express authority to apply its own corporate funds to discharge such debts."). For an overview of government corporations, see CRS Report RL30365, *Federal Government Corporations: An Overview*, by Kevin R. Kosar.
[60] GAO Redbook, at 14-9.
[61] *See infra* note 50 and accompanying text.
[62] See Vacketta & Kantor, *supra* note 1, at 5 (clarifying that for government contract disputes, the responsible agency is always the Department of Justice). *See also* 31 U.S.C. § 1304(a).
[63] *See* Financial Management Service, Department of the Treasury, The Judgment Fund: Overview, March 11, 2011, http://www.fms.treas.gov/judgefund/background.html.
[64] 31 U.S.C. § 3728.
[65] *See* Financial Management Service, Department of the Treasury, The Judgment Fund: Common Questions, March 11, 2011, http://www.fms.treas.gov/judgefund/questions.html. *See infra* "Illustrations of the Judgment Fund."
[66] *See* 31 C.F.R. § 256.10.
[67] *See* Department of the Treasury, Transmittal Letter No. 677, March 28, 2012, http://fms.treas.gov/tfm/vol1/v1p5c150.pdf.
[68] *See* Financial Management Services, The Judgment Fund: Overview, http://www.fms.treas.gov/judgefund.
[69] Financial Management Service, Department of the Treasury, Congressional Report on the Judgment Fund, June 25, 2012, http://www.fms.treas.gov/judgefund/congressSee AFARS 5133.212.90-0(b) and (c)(2) (capping claims under the Military Justice Act to $100,000).
[70] *See* 28 U.S.C. § 1920; cf. Taniguchi v. Kan Pac. Saipan, Ltd., 132. S. Ct. 1997, 2005, 192 L. Ed. 2d 903 (2012) (explaining that courts construe costs under 28 U.S.C. § 1920 narrowly).
[71] 28 U.S.C. § 1920(1-6).
[72] 31 C.F.R. § 256.12.
[73] Obtaining Payments from the Judgment Fund and under Private Relief Bills, 71 FR 60848-01.
[74] *See gen.* James R. Maxeiner, *Cost and Fee Allocation in Civil Procedure*, 58 AM. J. COMP. L. 195 (2010).
[75] Alyeska Pipeline Service Co. v. Wilderness Society, 421 U.S. 240, 247 (1975).
[76] Black's Law Dictionary (9th Ed. 2009) ("The general policy that all litigants, even the prevailing one, must bear their own attorney's fees. The rule is subject to bad-faith and other statutory and contractual exceptions.").
[77] Black's Law Dictionary (9th Ed. 2009) *see* English Rule, Fee-Shifting, Loser-Pays Rule.
[78] CRS Report 94-970, *Awards of Attorneys' Fees by Federal Courts and Federal Agencies*, by Henry Cohen.
[79] Trustees v. Greenough, 105 U.S. 527 (1881) (explaining that this exception is grounded in policy as opposed to a rule or tradition).

[80] Newman v. Piggie Park Enterprises, Inc., 390 U.S. 400, 402 (1968) ("[I]f successful plaintiffs were routinely forced to bear their own attorneys' fees, few aggrieved parties would be in a position to advance the public interest by invoking the injunctive powers of the federal courts. Congress therefore enacted the provision for counsel fees—not simply to penalize litigants who deliberately advance arguments they know to be untenable but, more broadly, to encourage individuals injured by racial discrimination to seek judicial relief ... ").

[81] Hall v. Cole, 412 U.S. 1, 5 (1973) (finding a party acted in bad faith when there was no sound legal basis for the claim and the defendant produced evidence of a pre-existing conflict between the parties).

[82] Copeland v. Martinez, 603 F.2d 981, 991 (D.C. Cir. 1979), *cert. denied*, 444 U.S. 1044 (1980) ("We doubt that such a finding may be supported without some proof of malice entirely apart from interferences arising from the possibly frivolous character of a particular claim. Only in this manner would we assure a sensible distinction between the contents of the equitable and statutory exceptions to the American rule. If, as seems probable, Congress chose to exclude the United States from the statutory 'prevailing party' recovery in all cases, we are obliged to observe closely such a distinction.").

[83] CRS Report 94-970, *Awards of Attorneys' Fees by Federal Courts and Federal Agencies*, by Henry Cohen.

[84] 28 U.S.C. § 2678; *See also* Calculation of Attorneys' Fees under Federal Tort Claims Act, 86 ALR Fed 866 (1988).

[85] Department of the Interior-Funding of Receptions at Arlington House Reconsideration, 61 Comp. Gen. 260 (Comp. Gen.), B-206173 (February 23, 1982).

[86] Office of the Comptroller General, Payment of Refund Ordered by Court of Claims in National Presto Industries, Inc. and *World Aerospace Corp v. United States*, B-164766, June 1, 1979.

[87] Library of Cong. v. Shaw, 478 U.S. 310, 320 (1986) ("The no-interest rule is to the effect that interest cannot be recovered in a suit against the Government in the absence of an express waiver of sovereign immunity from an award of interest. In this case, attorney's fees, as well as interest on those fees, were awarded to a plaintiff who prevailed ... ").

[88] United States ex rel. Angarica v. Bayard, 127 U.S. 251, 260 (1888) ("The only recognized exceptions are where the government stipulates to pay interest, and where interest is given expressly by an act of congress, either by the name of interest or by that of damages. This appears from a succession of the opinions of the attorney general of the United States ... ").

[89] *Library of Cong.*, 478 U.S. at 321. ("Prejudgment interest, however, is considered as damages, not a component of 'costs.'").

[90] *See* Reid v. Rensselaer Glass Factory, 3 Cow. 393 (N.Y. 1824).

[91] Gregory C. Sisk, *The Tapestry Unravels: Statutory Waivers of Sovereign Immunity and Money Claims Against the United States*, 71 GEO. WASH. L. REV. 602, 605 (2003).

[92] *See* Financial Management Services, The Judgment Fund: Overview.

[93] *Library of Cong.*, 478 U.S. at 323 (clarifying that Congress's waiver of immunity as to attorneys' fees did not constitute a waiver as to the government's traditional immunity from interest).

[94] U.S. CONST. AMEND. V.

[95] GAO Redbook, at 14-11.

[96] 267 U.S. 76, 79 (1925).

[97] Loeffler v. Frank, 486 U.S. 549 (1988) ("[I]f the general authority to 'sue and be sued' is to be delimited by implied exceptions, it must be clearly shown that certain types of suits are not consistent with the statutory or constitutional scheme, that an implied restriction of the general authority is necessary to avoid grave interference with the performance of a governmental function, or that for other reasons it was plainly the purpose of Congress to use the 'sue and be sued' clause in a narrow sense.").

[98] *Cf.* Granville House, Inc. v. Dep't of Health, Educ. & Welfare, 813 F.2d 881, 883-884 (8th Cir. 1987) *with* Knight v. United States, 982 F.2d 1573, 1576 (Fed. Cir. 1993).

[99] 31 U.S.C. § 1304(b)(1) ("Interest may be paid from the appropriation made by this section... on a judgment if the Court of Appeals for the Federal Circuit or the United States Court of Federal Claims... only from the date of filing of the transcript of the judgment with the Secretary of the Treasury through the day before the date of the mandate of affirmance.").

[100] *See supra* "Payment of Interest from the Judgment Fund."

[101] 28 U.S.C. § 2412. *See also* CRS Report 94-970, *Awards of Attorneys' Fees by Federal Courts and Federal Agencies*, by Henry Cohen

[102] 28 U.S.C. § 2412(d)(1)(A).

[103] 28 U.S.C. § 2412(d)(1)(B).

[104] 5 U.S.C. § 601 (defining a small entity as a small agency, small organization such as a nonprofit, or small governmental organization).

[105] *See generally* Office of Legal Counsel, Responsibility of Agencies to Pay Attorney's Fee Awards Under the Equal Access to Justice Act, Memorandum Opinion for the Assistant Attorney General, Civil Division, October 16, 2007, http://www.justice.gov/olc/2007/cienega-gardens-final.pdf.

[106] 331 F.3d 1319, 1324 (Fed. Cir. 2003).

[107] 28 U.S.C. § 2412(d)(4).

[108] See Office of Legal Counsel Opinion, *supra* note 105, at 3.

[109] *Id.*

[110] *Id.* at 4.

[111] *Id.* at 6 ("As a general rule, the 'agency over which the party prevails' under EAJA will be the agency whose regulatory interest was at stake in the litigation and whose actions or policies are successfully challenged in the court action. This interest may be identified by the fact that the agency took affirmative action against the prevailing party, in the form of a regulation or administrative ruling, or it may be identified by the fact that the agency had statutory authority over the regulatory program that the prevailing party successfully challenged. In a typical case, that agency may be named as the plaintiff or the defendant, but EAJA does not require that the agency itself be specifically named as a party. These considerations, as we explain, point towards the conclusion that HUD is the agency responsible under EAJA.").

[112] *See* Funding of Attorney Fee Awards Under the Equal Access to Justice Act, 6 Op. O.L.C. 204, 205 (1982).

[113] *Id.* at 205-206

[114] *Id.* at 208-209 ("Contemporaneous discussion on the House floor shows that § 207 [of the EAJA] was specifically intended to ensure that such payments could not be made under the appropriations authority of 31 U.S.C. § 724a (Supp. V 1981), the source of authority for what is commonly known as the judgment fund. The effect of § 207 is, and was intended to be, that the promise of the second sentence may be fulfilled only by additional congressional action in the form of legislation.").

[115] *See* 41 U.S.C. § 601-613. *See generally* CRS Report R41230, *Legal Protections for Subcontractors on Federal Prime Contracts*, by Kate M. Manuel.

[116] 41 U.S.C. § 7108.

[117] 41 U.S.C. § 7108(c).

[118] *See* S. REPT. NO. 95-1118, at 35 (1978). ("Section 13(c) provides that all such payments with be back charged to the procuring agency involved. There may be an incentive in certain cases on the part of the procuring agency to avoid settlements and prolong litigation in order to have the final judgment against the agency occur in court, thus avoiding payment out of agency funds. Second the practice may tend to hid from Congress the true economic costs of some procurements by not requiring the agencies to seek additional appropriations to pay the judgment."). The House Report echoed this sentiment. See H.R. REPT. NO. 95-1556, at 86 ("We favor this approach since it ultimately obligates the agency to account for all awards against it out of its own appropriations... This will also provide visibility to Congress.").

[119] 5 U.S.C. § 2301 note 1. *See also* CRS Report RS21778, *Legal Overview of P.L. 107-174, the Notification and Federal Employee Antidiscrimination and Retaliation Act of 2002*, by Charles V. Dale

[120] For further discussion, see *infra* "Recent Legislative Proposals," see also H.R. 6780 (110th Cong. 2009).

[121] U.S. GOV'T ACCOUNTABILITY OFFICE, GAO-08-295R, THE JUDGMENT FUND: STATUS OF REIMBURSEMENTS REQUIRED BY THE NO FEAR ACT AND CONTRACT DISPUTES ACT 13 (2008).

[122] *Id.* at 8.

[123] *Id.* at 13 ("FMS is taking steps towards implementing its new CDA collection strategy adopted in May 2007, focused on a continued effort to work with agencies and ensure that it has complete information about the status of each agency with regard to CDA reimbursement obligations. However, the strategy does not provide for reporting to Congress the amounts owed by individual departments and agencies for CDA reimbursement obligations. The new FMS strategy could increase transparency regarding federal agencies' obligations to reimburse the Judgment Fund and aid congressional oversight and decision making if it also included notification to Congress of the amounts owed by individual agencies related to CDA cases."). For a discussion of suggested changes to this system, see Recent Legislative Proposals, *infra*.

[124] Wolfchild v. United States, 101 Fed.Cl. 54, 79 (2011) (explaining that Congress allowed the Secretary of the Interior to disperse funds without further Congressional action in most cases because individual appropriations were timely and caused interest to accrue on judgments). *See also* H.REPT. 93–377, at 4 (1973), 1973 U.S.C.C.A.N. 2311, 2313.

[125] Bureau of Indian Affairs, What We Do: Overview, Division of Tribal Government Services, http://www.bia.gov/WhatWeDo/ServiceOverview/TribalGov/index.htm ("[P]ursuant to the Indian Tribal Judgment Funds Use or Distribution Act, 87 Stat. 466, as amended, the BIA prepares a plan for the use or distribution of funds awarded in satisfaction of a judgment of the Indian Claims Commission of the United States Court of Federal Claims in favor of an Indian tribe.").

[126] *Id.*

[127] H.R. 1446 (112th Cong. 2011).

[128] *Id.*

[129] *See* Financial Management Service, 2012 Judgment Fund Transparency Report to Congress, available online: http://www.fms.treas.gov/judgefund/congress

[130] H.R. 2434 (112th Cong. 2012). This bill was enacted in the Consolidated Appropriations Act of 2012, P.L. 112-74, December 23, 2011. The committee's directive appeared in H.Rept. 112-136, at 6 ("The Secretary of the Treasury shall submit to the Committee and make available to the public on its website an annual report about payments made under 31 U.S.C. 1304 for the fiscal year. Unless the disclosure of such information is otherwise prohibited by law or court order, the report shall consist of: (1) the name of the plaintiff or claimant, (2) the name of the counsel for the plaintiff or claimant; (3) the name of the agency that submitted the claim; (4) a brief description of the facts that gave rise to the claim; and (5) the amount paid representing principal, attorney fees, and interest, if applicable. The first report is due within 60 days of enactment of this Act.").

[131] *Id.*

[132] S. 3415 Government Transparency and Recordkeeping Act of 2012 (112th Cong. 2012).

[133] *Id.*

[134] H.R. 6780 (110th Cong. 2008); H.R. 67 (111th Cong. 2009).

[135] *See* H.R. 67, § 102 (110th Cong. 2008) ("[E]stablishing a definitive period for reimbursing the Judgment Fund (as prescribed in section 201 of the No FEAR Act of 2002) should encourage timely resolution or settlement of complaints.").

[136] *Id.*

In: Federal Funds: A Selection of Programs ISBN 978-1-62618-005-5
Editor: Kieran Saccoccio

Chapter 3

THE CRIME VICTIMS FUND: FEDERAL SUPPORT FOR VICTIMS OF CRIME*

Lisa N. Sacco

SUMMARY

In 1984, the Crime Victims Fund (CVF) was established by the Victims of Crime Act (VOCA, P.L. 98-473) to provide funding for state victim compensation and assistance programs. Since 1984, VOCA has been amended several times to support additional victim-related activities. These amendments established within the CVF (1) discretionary grants for private organizations, (2) the Federal Victim Notification System, (3) funding for victim assistance staff within the Federal Bureau of Investigation and Executive Office of U.S. Attorneys, (4) funding for the Children's Justice Act Program, and (5) assistance and compensation for victims of terrorism.

In 1988, the Office for Victims of Crime (OVC) was formally established within the Department of Justice (DOJ) to administer the CVF. As authorized by VOCA, the OVC awards CVF money through grants to states, local units

---

* This is an edited, reformatted and augmented version of the Congressional Research Service Publication, CRS Report for Congress R42672, dated August 22, 2012.

of government, individuals, and other entities. The OVC also distributes CVF money to specially designated programs, such as the Children's Justice Act Program and the Federal Victim Notification System.

Deposits to the CVF come from criminal fines, forfeited appearance bonds, penalties and special assessments collected by the U.S. Attorneys' Offices, federal courts, and Federal Bureau of Prisons. Since 2002, Congress has allowed gifts, bequests, and donations from private entities to be deposited into the CVF.

When the CVF was created in 1984, Congress placed a cap on how much money could be deposited into the CVF each year. Congress eliminated the cap for deposits in 1993. In FY2000, Congress established a cap on the amount that would be available for distribution in a fiscal year to ensure the stability of funds for crime victims programs and activities. Since 2000, Congress has established the yearly CVF cap as a part of DOJ's annual appropriation. For the last several years, Congress has set the CVF distribution cap at $705 million.

In considering the CVF allocation and future caps, there are several issues on which policymakers may deliberate. Congress may consider whether to adjust the manner in which the CVF is allocated, amend VOCA to accommodate additional victim activities or groups, adjust the cap and allow use of the CVF for grant programs other than those explicitly authorized by VOCA, or make other adjustments to the CVF cap—such as eliminate the cap altogether.

INTRODUCTION

In 1984, the Crime Victims Fund (CVF) was established by the Victims of Crime Act (VOCA, P.L. 98-473) to provide funding for state victim compensation and assistance programs.[1] Since 1984, VOCA has been amended several times to support additional victim-related activities.

These amendments established within the CVF

- discretionary grants for private organizations;[2]
- the Federal Victim Notification System;[3]
- funding for victim assistance staff in the Federal Bureau of Investigation (FBI) and Executive Office of U.S. Attorneys (EOUSA);[4]

- funding for the Children's Justice Act Program;[5] and
- assistance and compensation for victims of terrorism.[6]

In 1988, the Office for Victims of Crime (OVC) was formally established within the Department of Justice (DOJ) to administer the CVF.[7] As authorized by VOCA, the OVC awards CVF money through formula and discretionary grants to states, local units of government, individuals, and other entities. The OVC also distributes CVF money to specially designated programs, such as the Children's Justice Act Program and the Federal Victim Notification System (see **Figure 1**).[8]

The OVC mission is to enhance the nation's capacity to assist crime victims and to improve attitudes, policies, and practices that promote justice and help victims. According to the OVC, this mission is accomplished by (1) administering the CVF, (2) supporting direct services for victims, (3) providing training programs for service providers, (4) sponsoring the development of best practices for service providers, and (5) producing reports on best practices.[9] The OVC funds victim-support programs in all 50 states, the District of Columbia, and the territories.[10]

Notably, Congress has amended VOCA several times to provide support for victims of terrorism.[11] These amendments established CVF-funded programs for (1) assistance to victims of terrorism[12] who are injured or killed as a result of a terrorist act outside the United States, (2) compensation and assistance to victims of terrorism within the United States, and (3) an antiterrorism emergency reserve fund to support victims of terrorism.

This report provides background and funding information for VOCA programs and the CVF. It describes the process through which CVF funds are allocated and explains how the CVF impacts the annual budget for DOJ. It then provides an analysis of selected issues that Congress may consider regarding the CVF and the FY2013 federal budget.

FINANCING OF THE CRIME VICTIMS FUND

Deposits to the CVF

The CVF does not receive appropriated funding.[13] Rather, deposits to the CVF come from a number of sources including criminal fines, forfeited bail bonds, penalties, and special assessments collected by the U.S. Attorneys'

Offices, federal courts, and the Federal Bureau of Prisons from offenders convicted of federal crimes.[14] In 2001, the USA PATRIOT Act (P.L. 107-56) established that gifts, bequests, or donations from private entities could also be deposited to the CVF.

The largest source of deposits into the CVF is criminal fines.[15] According to a 2005 report from the National Association of VOCA Assistance Administrators, criminal fines account for approximately 98% of all deposits to the CVF.[16] Large criminal fines, if collected, can have a significant effect on deposits into receipts for the CVF. For example, from FY1996 through FY2004, fines collected from 12 defendants in federal courts accounted for 45% of all deposits to the CVF during this time period.[17] **Table 1** provides the amounts collected into the CVF in each fiscal year from 1985 through 2011.

Caps on the CVF

In 1984, Congress placed a cap on how much could be deposited into the CVF for the first eight years. As shown in **Table 1**, from FY1985 through FY1992, the annual cap on deposits ranged from $100 million to $150 million. In 1993, Congress lifted the cap on deposits, establishing that all criminal fines, special assessments, and forfeited bail bonds could be deposited into the CVF. From FY1985 through FY1999, deposits collected in a fiscal year were distributed in the following fiscal year.[18]

Fluctuation in Deposits

In 2000, Congress established an annual cap on funds available for distribution to reduce the impact of fluctuating deposits and ensure the stability of funds for programs. Since 2000, there has been considerable fluctuation in the amounts deposited each fiscal year. For example, between FY2007 and FY2008, the amount of receipts collected dropped by nearly 12% and then increased by approximately 95% in FY2009. This was followed by a 35% increase in FY2010 and a 15% decrease in FY2011. **Table 1** provides the CVF distribution cap amounts from FY2000 through FY2012.

Since 2000, Congress has established the CVF cap each year as a part of the appropriations for DOJ. For FY2012, Congress set the distribution cap at $705 million under the Consolidated and Further Continuing Appropriations Act, 2012 (P.L. 112-55).

Table 1. Crime Victims Fund: FY1985—FY2012
(dollars in millions)

Fiscal Year	Amount Collected to CVF	Enacted Cap on CVF Deposits	Enacted Cap on CVF Distribution	Funds Made Available for Distribution[a]	Carryover CVF Balance
1985	$68.3	$100	—	$68.3	—
1986	62.5	$110	—	62.5	—
1987	77.5	$110	—	77.5	—
1988	93.6	$110	—	93.6	—
1989	133.5	$125	—	124.2	—
1990	146.2	$125	—	127.2	—
1991	128.0	$150	—	128.0	—
1992	221.6	$150	—	152.2	—
1993	144.7	—	—	144.7	—
1994	185.1	—	—	185.1	—
1995	233.9	—	—	233.9	—
1996	528.9	—	—	528.9	—
1997	362.9	—	—	362.9	—
1998	324.0	—	—	324.0	—
1999	985.2	—	—	500.0	—
2000	777.0	—	500.0	537.5	485.2
2001	544.4	—	537.5	550.0	785.2
2002	519.5	—	550.0	600.0	792.0
2003	361.3	—	600.0	617.6[b]	718.9
2004	833.7	—	621.3[c]	671.3[d]	422.1
2005	668.3	—	620.0	620.0	1,307.4
2006	641.8	—	625.0	625.0	1,333.5
2007	1,018.0	—	625.0	625.0	1,784.0
2008	896.3	—	590.0	590.0	2,084.0
2009	1,745.7	—	635.0	635.0	3,146.5
2010	2,362.3	—	705.0	705.0	4,801.5
2011	1,998.0	—	705.0	705.0	6,099.7
2012	—	—	705.0	705.0	—

Source: U.S. Department of Justice, Office of Justice Programs, Office of Communications.

a. From FY1985-FY1998, deposits collected in each fiscal year were distributed in the following fiscal year to support crime victims services. From FY1985-FY2002, the funds made available for distribution reflect the amounts distributed in the following fiscal year.

b. FY2003 funds include $17.6 million for the Antiterrorism Emergency Reserve.

c. The original cap of $625.0 million was reduced due to congressional rescission.

d. FY2004 funds include $50.0 million for the Antiterrorism Emergency Reserve.

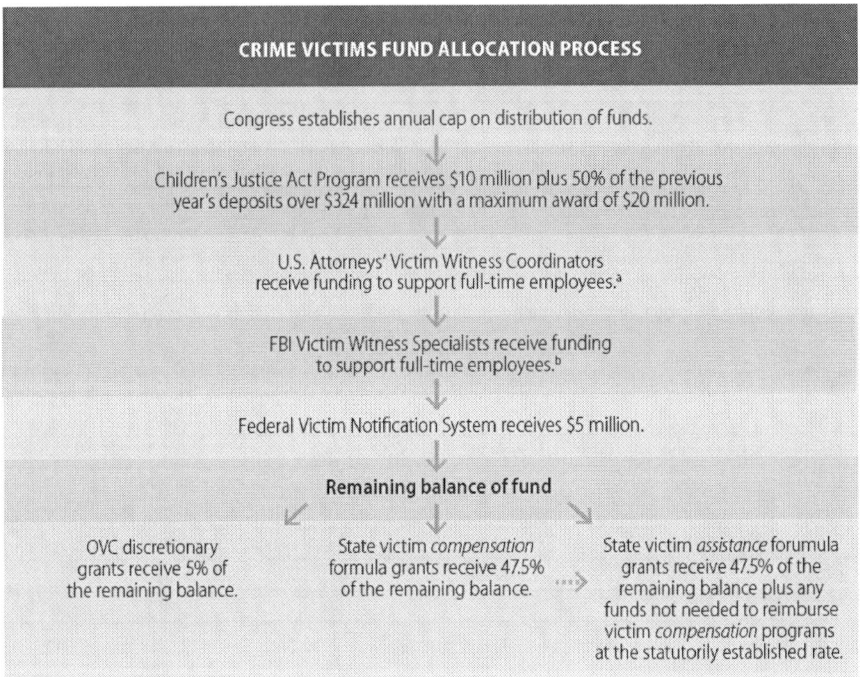

Source: U.S. Department of Justice, Office of Justice Programs, Office for Victims of Crime, Crime Victims Fund, Figure 2, http://www.ojp.usdoj.gov/ovc/pubs/crimevictimsfundfs/intro.html; and U.S. Department of Justice, Federal Bureau of Investigation, FY2013 Congressional Budget Submission.

Notes: In FY2012, OJP assessed management and administrative (M & A) costs for programs funded by the CVF. OJP did not assess M & A costs for the Children's Justice Act Program and state victim compensation grants. State victim assistance grants were assessed 11.6% in M & A costs and all other CVF-funded grants were assessed 8.1% in M & A costs for FY2012.

a. As of FY2012, there are 170 Victim Witness Coordinators supported by the CVF.

b. As of FY2012, there are 134 Victim Witness Specialists supported by the CVF.

Figure 1. Annual Distribution of the Crime Victims Fund.

Carryover Balance of the CVF

Funding for a current year's grants is provided by the previous year's deposits to the CVF, and the OVC is authorized to use the capped amount for grant awards in a given year. After the yearly allocations are distributed, the remaining balance in the CVF is retained for future expenditures. The remaining balance and the capped amount, however, are both counted, or "scored," as part of the DOJ budget total in a given fiscal year. These amounts impact the DOJ appropriation total and are included in the department's overall budget score.[19] As a result, proposals to increase the CVF cap could possibly reduce the available budget for other federal programs by the amount specified in the proposed increase. Thus, congressional proposals to increase the cap may be accompanied by a proposed offset that would reduce the funding of another program.[20]

VOCA law requires that all sums deposited in a fiscal year that are not obligated must remain in the CVF for obligation in future fiscal years.[21] If collections in a previous year exceed the distribution cap, then amounts over the cap are credited to the "rainy day" fund for future program benefits. For example, in FY2000 funding for the year was capped at $500 million despite the fact that collections were over $985 million in FY1999. If the receipts collected in a prior year are not sufficient to reach the cap, the additional amounts are made up from balances credited to the CVF, commonly referred to as the rainy day fund.[22] Approximately $485 million remained in the CVF and was credited for future use.[23] **Table 1** provides the balances that remain credited to the CVF at the end of each fiscal year from FY2000 through FY2011.

DISTRIBUTION OF THE CRIME VICTIMS FUND

As previously stated, the OVC awards CVF money through formula and discretionary grants to states, local units of government, individuals, and other entities. The OVC also awards CVF money to specially designated programs. Grants are allocated according to statute (see **Figure 1**) established by the VOCA.

Children's Justice Act Program

The OVC and the Administration for Children and Families (ACF) within the Department of Health and Human Services manage the Children's Justice Act Program, a grant program designed to improve the investigation, handling, and prosecution of child abuse cases. Up to $20 million must be distributed annually to the Children's Justice Act Program.[24] Of the designated funds, ACF receives up to $17 million to manage this program for the states, while the OVC distributes up to $3 million for tribal populations.[25] In FY2012, the ACF received $17 million from the CVF to fund the Children's Justice Act Program. **Table 2** provides funding data from FY2010 through FY2012.

Executive Office of U.S. Attorneys (EOUSA)

The OVC provides annual funding to support victim-witness coordinators within each of the 93 U.S. Attorney's Offices.[26] In accordance with the *Attorney General Guidelines for Victim and Witness Assistance*,[27] these personnel provide direct support for victims of federal crime by assisting victims in criminal proceedings and advising victims of their rights, such as their right to make oral and written victim impact statements at an offender's sentencing hearing. **Table 3** provides the number of full-time employees supported with CVF funding and the amount of CVF funding that the EOUSA victim-witness coordinator program has received from the OVC from FY2010 through FY2012.

Table 2. Annual Allocation for Children's Justice Act Grants
(dollars in millions)

(Administrative Agency in Parentheses)	FY2010	FY2011	FY2012
State Allocation (ACF)	$17.00	$17.00	$17.00
Tribal Allocation (OVC)	3.00	3.00	3.00

Source: U.S. Department of Health and Human Services, Administration for Children and Families, Office of Legislative Affairs and Budget; and U.S. Department of Justice, Office of Justice Programs, Office of Communications.

Table 3. Annual Allocation and Full-Time Employees for EOUSA Victim Witness Coordinators
(dollars in millions)

	FY2010	FY2011	FY2012
Allocation to EOUSA	$23.33	$23.44	$21.54
Number of FTEs	170	170	170

Source: U.S. Department of Justice, Office of Justice Programs, Office of Communications.

Federal Bureau of Investigation (FBI)

The OVC provides annual funding to support victim witness specialists within the 56 FBI field offices.[28] These specialists, or coordinators, personally assist victims of federal crime and provide information on criminal cases throughout case development and court proceedings.[29] **Table 4** provides the amount of CVF funding that the FBI's Victim Witness Program has received from the OVC in FY2010-FY2012.

The Victim Notification System

The OVC provides annual funding to support the Victim Notification System (VNS), a program administered by the EOUSA and jointly operated by the FBI, EOUSA, OVC, and the Federal Bureau of Prisons.[30] VNS is the vehicle through which victims are notified of major case events relating to the offender, such as the release or detention status of the offender.[31] **Table 5** provides the amount of CVF funding that the FBI's Victim Witness Program has received from the OVC in FY2010-FY2012.

Table 4. Annual Allocation and Full-Time Employees for FBI Victim Witness Specialists
(dollars in millions)

	FY2010	FY2011	FY2012
Allocation to FBI	$14.64	$15.75	$16.21
Number of FTEs	134	134	134

Source: Allocations were provided by U.S. Department of Justice, Office of Justice Programs, Office of Communications. The number of FTEs were taken from the FY2011-FY2013 congressional budget submissions for the FBI.

Table 5. Annual Allocation for Victim Notification System
(dollars in millions)

	FY2010	FY2011	FY2012
Allocation to EOUSA	$5.50	$4.88	$4.49

Source: U.S. Department of Justice, Office of Justice Programs, Office of Communications.

Victim Compensation and Assistance

After the Children's Justice Act, victim witness, and VNS programs are funded, remaining CVF money is distributed as follows: Victim Compensation Formula Grants (47.5%); Victim Assistance Formula Grants (47.5%); and OVC Discretionary Grants (5%).[32] Amounts not used for state compensation grants are made available for state victim assistance formula grants. As shown in **Figure 1**, while both compensation and assistance grants are allotted the same percentage of the remaining balance, the state victim assistance grant program receives 47.5% of the remaining balance *plus* any funds not needed to reimburse victim compensation programs at the statutorily established rate.

Victim Compensation Formula Grant Program

As mentioned, 47.5% of the remaining annual CVF money is for grant awards to state crime victim compensation programs.[33] All 50 states, the District of Columbia, the U.S. Virgin Islands, and Puerto Rico have victim compensation programs.[34] The OVC awards each state 60% of the total amount the state paid (from state funding sources) to victims in the prior fiscal year.[35]

According to VOCA, a state is eligible to receive a victim compensation formula grant if the state program meets the following requirements: (1) promote victim cooperation with requests of law enforcement authorities, (2) certify that grants received will not be used to supplant state funds, (3) ensure that non-resident victims receive compensation awards on the same basis as victims residing within the state, (4) ensure that compensation provided to victims of federal crimes is given on the same basis as the compensation given to victims of state crime, and (5) provide compensation to residents of the state who are victims of crimes occurring outside the state.[36]

The formula grants may be used to reimburse crime victims for out-of-pocket expenses such as medical and mental health counseling expenses, lost wages, funeral and burial costs, and other costs (except property loss) authorized in a state's compensation statute. Victims are reimbursed for crime-related expenses that are not covered by other resources, such as private insurance. Since FY2004, more than half of annual compensation expenses paid have been for medical and dental services.[37]

According to the OVC, assault victims represent the highest percentage of victims receiving compensation each year.[38] In FY2011, there were 80,344 claims made by victims of assault, representing nearly half of all claims filed during the reporting period for FY2011. Nearly 40% of assault claims for FY2011 were domestic violence-related.[39]

Table 6 provides the amount of CVF funding that was allotted to OVC's Victim Compensation Program from FY2010 through FY2012.

Victim Assistance Formula Grant Program

The other 47.5% of the remaining annual CVF money (see **Figure 1**) is for the Victim Assistance Formula Grants Program. Amounts not used for state compensation grants are made available for the Victim Assistance Formula Grants Program. This program provides grants to state crime victim assistance programs to administer funds for state and community-based victim service program operations.[40] The grants support direct services to crime victims including information and referral services, crisis counseling, temporary housing, criminal justice advocacy support, and other assistance needs.

Assistance grants are distributed by states according to guidelines established by VOCA. States are required to prioritize the following groups: (1) underserved populations of victims of violent crime,[41] (2) victims of child abuse, (3) victims of sexual assault, and (4) victims of spousal abuse.[42] States may not use federal funds to supplant state and local funds otherwise available for crime victim assistance.

VOCA establishes the amount of funds allocated to each state and territory. Each of the 50 states, the District of Columbia, the U.S. Virgin Islands, and Puerto Rico receive a base amount of $500,000 each year.[43] The territories of the Northern Mariana Islands, Guam, and American Samoa receive a base amount of $200,000 each year.[44] The remaining funds are distributed based on U.S. census population data. **Table 7** provides the amount of CVF funding that the OVC allotted for the Victim Assistance Grant Program from FY2010 through FY2012.

Table 6. Annual Allocation for Victim Compensation Grant Program
(dollars in millions)

	FY2010	FY2011	FY2012
Allocation for Compensation Grants	$198.04	$180.89	$180.73

Source: U.S. Department of Justice, Office of Justice Programs, Office of Communications.

Table 7. Annual Allocation for Victim Assistance Grant Program
(dollars in millions)

	FY2010	FY2011	FY2012
Allocation for Assistance Grants	$412.13	$428.08	$377.09

Source: U.S. Department of Justice, Office of Justice Programs, Office of Communications.

Notes: The reduction in allocation for FY2012 reflects a new OJP management and administrative cost assessment for CVF programs, with the exception of the Children's Justice Act Program and victim compensation grants, were assessed $55.59 million in FY2012.

According to the OVC, victims of domestic violence make up the largest number of victims receiving services under the Victim Assistance Formula Grants Program. In 2011, approximately 45% of the 3,760,235 victims served by these grants were victims of domestic violence.[45] This figure has remained relatively stable since 2000, when 50% of all victims served by the victim assistance grants were victims of domestic violence.[46]

Discretionary Grants

Five percent of the CVF money available after the specially designated program allocations have been made (see **Figure 1**) is for discretionary grants.[47] According to VOCA, discretionary grants must be distributed for (1) demonstration projects, program evaluation, compliance efforts, and training and technical assistance services to crime victim assistance programs; (2) financial support of services to victims of federal crime; and (3) nonprofit victim service organizations and coalitions to improve outreach and services to victims of crime.[48] The OVC awards discretionary grants each year through a competitive application process.[49]

Table 8. Annual Allocation for Discretionary Grants
(dollars in millions)

	FY2010	FY2011	FY2012
Allocation for Discretionary Grants	$32.12	$32.05	$29.36

Source: U.S. Department of Justice, Office of Justice Programs, Office of Communications.

Table 8 provides the amount of CVF funding that the OVC allotted for discretionary grants from FY2010 through FY2012.

Antiterrorism Emergency Reserve

The Antiterrorism Emergency Reserve was established in P.L. 104-132 to meet the immediate and long-term needs of victims of terrorism and mass violence.[50] The OVC accomplishes this mission by providing supplemental grants to states for victim compensation and assistance and also by providing direct compensation to victims (U.S. nationals or officers or employees of the U.S. government, including Foreign Service Nationals working for the U.S. government) of terrorist acts that occur abroad.

The Director of the OVC is authorized to set aside $50 million of CVF money in the Antiterrorism Emergency Reserve to respond to the needs of victims of the September 11 terrorist attacks, and subsequently, to replenish any amounts expended so that not more than $50 million is reserved in any fiscal year for any future victims of terrorism.[51] After funding all other program areas, as listed above, the funds retained in the CVF may be used to replenish the Antiterrorism Emergency Reserve.[52] This reserve fund supports the following programs:

- Antiterrorism and Emergency Assistance Program,
- International Terrorism Victim Expense Reimbursement Program,
- Crime Victim Emergency Assistance Fund at the FBI, and
- Victim Reunification Program.

Assistance for Victims of 9/11

In the aftermath of the terrorist attacks on September 11, 2001, the OVC used money available in the Antiterrorism Emergency Reserve account to immediately respond to the needs of victims. The OVC awarded $3.1 million in victim assistance funding and $13.5 million in victim compensation funding[53] to the states of New York, Virginia, and Pennsylvania.[54] The funds were used by these states to coordinate and provide emergency assistance to victims in the form of crisis counseling and other direct services, and to offset out-of-pocket expenses for medical and mental health services, funeral costs, and lost wages.

In addition to providing funds to states, the OVC provided other assistance and services to victims, including the following:

- OVC staff worked to identify the short- and long-term needs of victims and related costs, as well as to coordinate its efforts with other federal agencies such as the Federal Emergency Management Agency (FEMA).
- Immediately following the attacks, the OVC set up a call center that offered a 24- hour, toll-free telephone line for collecting victim information and providing referrals for financial, housing, and counseling assistance. Approximately 37,000 victims and family members received assistance and referrals through the call center.[55]
- The OVC also established a Victim and Family Travel Assistance Center, which handled all logistical arrangements and paid travel and lodging costs for 1,800 family members traveling to funerals and memorial services.[56]
- The OVC designed and operated a special "Hope and Remembrance" website to provide victims with answers to frequently asked questions, official messages from U.S. government sources, news releases, etc.[57]

The OVC continues to assist those affected by 9/11 through the Healing and Remembrance Program. In FY2010, the Mental Health Association of New York City received CVF money to operate a website to assist and support those affected by 9/11 and provide travel support for 9/11 anniversary events.[58]

Selected Issues

Congress may confront several issues when considering the annual distribution cap on the CVF and possible amendments to VOCA. These issues include using the CVF for programs other than those explicitly authorized by VOCA, making adjustments to the CVF cap such as eliminating the cap, and amending VOCA to accommodate new programs or to adjust the allocation formula.

Issues in Considering the CVF Cap

One issue Congress might consider is whether to use receipts from the CVF to fund grant programs that are not authorized by VOCA. In the past, Congress has passed legislation that made CVF money available to support programs authorized outside of VOCA.[59] For example, the National Defense Authorization Act (P.L. 110-181) included a provision mandating that the Attorney General transfer from the emergency reserve of the CVF "such funds as may be required" to cover the costs of special masters appointed by U.S. district courts in civil cases brought against state sponsors of terrorism.

Thus far, CVF money has not been used to fund *grant programs* outside of those authorized by VOCA. In the *Budget of the United States Government, Fiscal Year 2013*, the Administration requests to raise the CVF cap by $365 million and specifies that the additional money should be transferred to other accounts administered by DOJ, including the Office on Violence Against Women (OVW) and the Office of Justice Programs (OJP). Both the Senate and the House Committee on Appropriations rejected the Administration's proposal to fund OVW and OJP grant programs through the CVF for FY2013. While it could be argued that the non-VOCA grant programs the Administration proposed to fund with receipts from the CVF would assist crime victims in some manner, the Administration's proposal raises a question about whether this might pave the way for the CVF to be used to support other DOJ grant programs that might not be victim-focused. On the other hand, as mentioned above, the CVF has a balance of more than $6 billion, which indicates that receipts to the fund are exceeding the congressionally specified cap. In a time of fiscal constraint, the CVF might provide an avenue to fund some DOJ grant programs while reducing DOJ's discretionary appropriation; however, there is no guarantee that receipts going into the CVF will be consistent from one year to the next. Therefore, if Congress were to increase the cap and use funding from the CVF for non-VOCA programs, it is not possible to ensure that there will be a consistent level of funding to support these programs in future budget cycles.

Congress could decide to eliminate the cap on the Crime Victims Fund altogether. If Congress should decide to eliminate the cap and allow all collected funds to be distributed in a given fiscal year, it could possibly have significant consequences for the DOJ budget. As mentioned, the capped amount and remaining balance in the CVF are considered part of the DOJ budget total. These amounts impact the DOJ appropriation, are used to offset spending limits for DOJ programs, and are included in the overall budget score for DOJ. If Congress were to eliminate the cap, it would have to make up the amount of the CVF through offsets. Moreover, Congress may wish to consider whether VOCA programs would be able to use all money in the fund if the distribution cap were eliminated.

Issues in Considering Amendments to VOCA

While VOCA may be amended in many possible ways, this report presents two options that Congress may choose to consider. Congress may wish to reassess the allocation formula of the CVF (see **Figure 1**) or consider the addition of new programs to be supported through the CVF.

VOCA Assistance Administrators have voiced concern that fluctuations in annual obligations can directly impact fund availability for victim assistance formula grants and, to a lesser extent, discretionary grants. The addition of new programs, increases in funding to other programs funded by the CVF, and new management and administration costs cause a reduction in funding available for victim assistance formula grants and discretionary grants.[60] Congress may choose to review the allocation formula to determine if changes should be made to reduce the impact of fluctuations in obligated funds on these grants.

Since 1984, VOCA has been amended several times to support additional victim-related activities and accommodate the needs of specific groups of victims, such as child abuse victims and victims of terrorist acts. Congress may choose to continue amending VOCA to accommodate the needs of additional special populations, such as victims of elder abuse. As the so-called "baby boom" generation ages, it is possible that elder abuse will grow as a social concern.[61] Likewise, other populations with unique risks and needs may present themselves, and Congress may choose to use VOCA as one potential vehicle to address those risks and needs.

End Notes

[1] P.L. 98-473, Title II, Chapter XIV, Victims of Crime Act of 1984, October 12, 1984, 98 Stat. 2170. VOCA is codified at 42 U.S.C. §10601 et seq.

[2] P.L. 109-162, Title XI, Subtitle B, §1132, January 5, 2006, 119 Stat. 3107.

[3] P.L. 107-77, Title I, §111, November 28, 2001, 115 Stat. 765.

[4] P.L. 106-553, §1(a)(2), Title I, §113, December 21, 2000, 114 Stat. 2762, 2762A-68; P.L. 106-554, §1(a)(4), Division A, §213(a)(2), December 21, 2000, 114 Stat. 2763, 2763A-179; and P.L. 106-113, Division B, §1000(a)(1) [H.R. 3421, Title I, §119], November 29, 1999, 113 Stat. 1535, 1501A-22.

[5] P.L. 106-177, Title I, §104(a), Child Abuse Prevention and Enforcement Act, March 10, 2000, 114 Stat. 36.

[6] P.L. 104-132, Antiterrorism and Effective Death Penalty Act of 1996, Title II, Subtitle C; P.L. 107-56, USA PATRIOT Act, Title VI, §621(a) to (d).

[7] P.L. 100-690, Title VII, Subtitle D.

[8] Grants are distributed according to a formula established by VOCA.

[9] For more information on OVC and its mission, see http://www.ojp.usdoj.gov/ovc/.

[10] For information on OVC grant allocations, see http://www.ojp.usdoj.gov/ovc/grants

[11] P.L. 104-132, Justice for Victims of Terrorism Act of 1996, April 24, 1996, 110 Stat. 1243; P.L. 106-386, Victims of Trafficking and Violence Protection Act of 2000, October 28, 2000, 114 Stat. 1543; and P.L. 107-56, USA PATRIOT Act, Title VI, §621(a) to (d), October 26, 2001, 115 Stat. 370.

[12] Victims who are eligible for assistance include nationals of the United States and employees of the U.S. government.

[13] In January 2002, Congress enacted a one-time appropriation of $68.1 million for the Crime Victims Fund to assist in providing relief to 9/11 victims (P.L. 107-117, 115 Stat. 2294).

[14] See 42 U.S.C. §10601.

[15] U.S. Department of Justice, Office of Justice Programs, Office for Victims of Crime, *2011 OVC Report to the Nation*, p. 2, http://www.ovc.gov/pubs/reporttonation2011/ReporttoNation2011.pdf (hereinafter, 2011 OVC Report to the Nation).

[16] Steve Derene, *Crime Victims Fund Report: Past, Present, Future*, National Association of VOCA Assistance Administrators, March 2005, p. 6, http://www.navaa.org/budget/CVFReport/CrimeVictimsReport.pdf (hereinafter, *Crime Victims Fund Report*).

[17] *Crime Victims Fund Report*, p. 3.

[18] *2011 OVC Report to the Nation*, p. 3.

[19] For the DOJ *FY2013 Summary of Budget Authority by Appropriation*, see http://www.justice.gov/jmd/2013summary/pdf/budget-authority-appropriation.pdf.

[20] While some may assume that the program that has its funding reduced would be a DOJ program, this report does not assume this and recognizes that the program could also be from another department aside from DOJ.

[21] 42 U.S.C. §10601(c).

[22] U.S. Department of Justice, Office of Justice Programs, Office for Victims of Crime, *2009 OVC Report to the Nation*, p. 11, https://www.ncjrs.gov/ovc_archives/reporttonation2009/ReporttoNation09Part1.pdf.

[23] *Crime Victims Fund Report*, p.16.

[24] 42 U.S.C. §10601(d)(2).

[25] For more information regarding the Children's Justice Act Program, see CRS Report R40899, *The Child Abuse Prevention and Treatment Act (CAPTA): Background, Programs, and Funding*, by Emilie Stoltzfus.

[26] 42 U.S.C. §10601(d)(3).

[27] U.S. Department of Justice, *Attorney General Guidelines for Victim and Witness Assistance*, http://www.justice.gov/olp/pdf/ag_guidelines2012.pdf.

[28] 42 U.S.C. §10601(d)(3).

[29] For more information on the FBI Victim Assistance Program, see http://www.fbi.gov/stats-services/victim_assistance/overview/field-office-victim-assistance-program.

[30] 42 U.S.C. §10601(d)(3).

[31] For more information on VNS, see https://www.notify.usdoj.gov/.

[32] 42 U.S.C. §10601(d)(4).
[33] Ibid.
[34] Territories and the District of Columbia are treated as states for grant eligibility and distribution purposes. See 42 U.S.C. §10602(d)(4).
[35] 42 U.S.C. §10602(a).
[36] 42 U.S.C. §10602(b).
[37] Medical and dental services do not include mental health services. OVC records these mental health costs in a separate category. For additional compensation data, as well as the number of victims served, by victim types and service categories, see U.S. Department of Justice, U.S. Department of Justice, Office of Justice Programs, Office for Victims of Crime, *VOCA Nationwide Performance Reports*, http://www.ojp.usdoj.gov/ovc/grants
[38] Ibid.
[39] U.S. Department of Justice, Office of Justice Programs, Office for Victims of Crime, *2011 Victims of Crime Act Performance Report, State Assistance Program*, http://www.ojp.usdoj.gov/ovc/grants
[40] 42 U.S.C. §10603(c).
[41] States have flexibility in determining the populations of victims of violent crimes that may be underserved in their respective states.
[42] 42 U.S.C. §10603(a).
[43] 42 U.S.C. §10603(a)(5)(A).
[44] 42 U.S.C. §10603(a)(5)(B).
[45] U.S. Department of Justice, Office of Justice Programs, Office for Victims of Crime, *2011 Victims of Crime Act Performance Report, State Assistance Program*, http://www.ojp.usdoj.gov/ovc/grants
[46] U.S. Department of Justice, Office of Justice Programs, Office for Victims of Crime, *2000 Victims of Crime Act Performance Report, State Assistance Program*, http://www.ojp.usdoj.gov/ovc/grants For additional annual reports on the Victim Assistance Formula Grants Program, see http://www.ojp.usdoj.gov/ovc/grants/ vocareps.html.
[47] 42 U.S.C. §10601(d)(4).
[48] 42 U.S.C. §10603(c).
[49] For more information on discretionary programs, see http://www.ojp.usdoj.gov/ovc/grants/types.html#discretionarygrants.
[50] P.L. 104-132, Title II, Subtitle C.
[51] 42 U.S.C. §10601(d)(5). The OVC also received a one-time $68.1 million appropriation in the FY2002 Department of Defense Appropriations Act (P.L. 107-117, 115 Stat. 2294) to assist in its work of providing relief to 9/11 victims (USA PATRIOT Act, P.L. 107-56, 115 Stat. 371).
[52] These funds do not fall under the annual cap of the CVF.
[53] Emergency funds were disbursed under the authority of the 2001 Emergency Supplemental Appropriations Act for Recovery from and Response to Terrorist Attacks on the United States (P.L. 107-38). The Antiterrorism Emergency Reserve was later reimbursed under the Department of Defense Appropriations Act (P.L. 107-117).
[54] U.S. Department of Justice, Office for Victims of Crime, *Meeting the Needs of the Victims of the September 11th Terrorist Attacks: Department of Defense Appropriations Act of 2002, Report to Congress*, April 2003, p. 4, https://www.ncjrs.gov/ovc_archives/reports/911victimsreptocongress03/meetingneedssept11.pdf.
[55] Ibid, p. 5.
[56] Ibid, p. 5.
[57] Ibid, p. 5.
[58] For additional information regarding the Healing and Remembrance Program, see http://www.9-11healingandremembrance.org/ovc/FamilySupportCenters/Default.aspx.
[59] For expenditure guidelines, see 42 USC §10601(d).

[60] Ibid; National Association of VOCA Assistance Administrators, *Victims of Crime Act (VOCA) Crime Victims Fund: Briefing Background*, p. 4, http://www.navaa.org/budget/13/docs/VOCA_Backgrounder%202013.pdf.

[61] Martin J. Gorbien and Amy R. Eisenstein, "Elder Abuse and Neglect: An Overview," *Clinics in Geriatric Medicine*, vol. 2 (May 21, 2005).

In: Federal Funds: A Selection of Programs ISBN 978-1-62618-005-5
Editor: Kieran Saccoccio

Chapter 4

THE HOUSING TRUST FUND: BACKGROUND AND ISSUES*

Katie Jones

SUMMARY

On July 30, 2008, President Bush signed into law the Housing and Economic Recovery Act of 2008 (P.L. 110-289), which included the establishment of a national Housing Trust Fund. In general, affordable housing trust funds provide dedicated, permanent sources of funding for affordable housing that do not require annual appropriations. Several states and many localities across the United States already have their own affordable housing trust funds, and for years affordable housing advocates had worked to get such a fund created on a national level. Opponents of a national affordable housing trust fund argued that it would be duplicative of other affordable housing programs.

The Housing Trust Fund created by P.L. 110-289 would provide formula-based grants to states to use for affordable housing activities. By statute, most of the funding would have to be used for rental housing; states could use up to 10% of their grants for homeownership activities. Furthermore, all of the funds

* This is an edited, reformatted and augmented version of the Congressional Research Service Publication, CRS Report for Congress R40781, dated January 18, 2012.

would have to benefit very low- or extremely low-income households, with at least 75% of the funding for rental housing being used exclusively for the benefit of extremely low-income households.

P.L. 110-289 directed Fannie Mae and Freddie Mac to annually contribute a percentage of the dollar volume of mortgages that they purchased to the Housing Trust Fund as the fund's dedicated funding source. However, the law also gave the director of the Federal Housing Finance Agency (FHFA), Fannie and Freddie's regulator, the authority to suspend those contributions if he determined that they were contributing to financial trouble at the agencies. On September 7, 2008, Fannie and Freddie were placed in conservatorship, and in November 2008, the director of FHFA suspended their contributions to the Housing Trust Fund. The Fund had not yet received any funding at the time the contributions were suspended.

It is unclear whether contributions from Fannie Mae and Freddie Mac to the Housing Trust Fund will ever be reinstated. Advocates have begun searching for a new source of funds for the program. Several pieces of legislation have been introduced in the 112th Congress that include funding for the Housing Trust Fund, and similar legislation had been introduced in previous Congresses. However, no funding has been provided to the program as of the date of this report. Legislation has also been introduced in the 112th Congress that would eliminate the Housing Trust Fund entirely.

INTRODUCTION

Many states and localities across the nation have created housing trust funds that provide dedicated sources of state or local funding for affordable housing activities. For several years, affordable housing advocates campaigned for a national affordable housing trust fund to provide a permanent federal source of funding for affordable housing that would not be subject to the annual appropriations process. In July 2008, Congress passed the Housing and Economic Recovery Act of 2008 (P.L. 110-289), which was signed into law by President Bush on July 30, 2008. P.L. 110-289 included a national Housing Trust Fund that would be funded through contributions from Fannie Mae and Freddie Mac. However, Fannie and Freddie were both placed in conservatorship in September 2008, and their contributions to the Housing

Trust Fund were suspended before they had begun. To date, no new funding source has been identified for the Housing Trust Fund.

This report briefly describes the structure and eligible uses of the Housing Trust Fund as authorized in P.L. 110-289, and discusses current proposals for new funding sources for the Fund.

BACKGROUND ON EFFORTS TO CREATE A NATIONAL AFFORDABLE HOUSING TRUST FUND

For several years, a coalition of low-income housing organizations has advocated for the establishment of a national affordable housing trust fund. The idea of an affordable housing trust fund is not new; several states and localities have already adopted their own state and local trust funds. In general, affordable housing trust funds are permanent funding streams that are not reliant on annual appropriations, and are dedicated to affordable housing activities for low- income households. According to the Center for Community Change, nearly 700 state, city, and county housing trust funds have been established in 45 states across the nation.[1]

Advocacy organizations such as the National Low Income Housing Coalition, one of the leading proponents of a national affordable housing trust fund, have long argued that a federal fund should be established to complement these state and local efforts.[2] These advocates want this fund to be capitalized with new resources devoted to affordable housing activities, rather than from current appropriations for other affordable housing programs.

Opponents of a national housing trust fund argue that the federal government already provides funding for affordable housing through other programs, and that a national housing trust fund is duplicative of these programs. In recent years, opponents have also pointed to concerns about growing federal budget deficits as an argument against a national affordable housing trust fund.

Legislation to establish a national affordable housing trust fund was introduced several times, beginning in the 106th Congress.[3] One major question surrounding the creation of an affordable housing trust fund was how the program would be funded. Early legislation proposed using a portion of receipts from the Federal Housing Administration (FHA), but diverting FHA receipts to a housing trust fund would count as new spending and would be subject to annual spending limits, including the Pay-As-You-Go rule (PAYGO).[4]

Later legislation proposed using contributions from Fannie Mae and Freddie Mac, two government-sponsored enterprises (GSEs), as a potential funding source. Because of the GSEs' status as private entities, contributions from Fannie Mae and Freddie Mac would not have counted as new government spending. There was some disagreement over whether it was appropriate for the government to require the GSEs to contribute to affordable housing funds. Opponents of GSE contributions argued that the GSEs should not be asked to balance public policy objectives against the interests of their shareholders. Proponents pointed to the special privileges that GSEs received, and the housing goals that they already had, to justify their contributions to the Housing Trust Fund.[5] Ultimately, GSE contributions were identified as the funding source for the Housing Trust Fund created in P.L. 110-289.

THE HOUSING TRUST FUND

P.L. 110-289 created a national Housing Trust Fund within the Department of Housing and Urban Development (HUD). The Housing Trust Fund was to be funded by contributions from Fannie Mae and Freddie Mac.[6] However, P.L. 110-289 also required the head of the Federal Housing Finance Agency (FHFA), Fannie's and Freddie's regulator, to suspend their contributions to the Housing Trust Fund if he found that the contributions (1) were contributing or would contribute to financial instability, (2) were causing or would cause a GSE to be classified as undercapitalized, or (3) were preventing or would prevent a GSE from successfully completing a capital restoration project.

Fannie Mae and Freddie Mac were placed in conservatorship on September 7, 2008. In November 2008, FHFA informed Fannie Mae and Freddie Mac that they should suspend their contributions to the Housing Trust Fund until further notice.[7] Neither GSE had begun making contributions to the Housing Trust Fund at the time that the contributions were suspended.

The suspension of the GSEs' contributions left the Housing Trust Fund without a source of funding. Without a funding source, the Housing Trust Fund is not yet operational.

It is unclear if or when GSE contributions to the Housing Trust Fund will be resumed, and affordable housing advocates have been pursuing additional sources of revenue to capitalize the Fund (see discussion under "Current Funding Issues"). Although funding for the Housing Trust Fund is uncertain, HUD has moved forward with implementing regulations governing the program. HUD published a proposed rule governing the allocation formula on December 4, 2009,[8] and a proposed program rule on October 29, 2010.[9] This section describes how the Housing Trust Fund would operate if it received funding, according to the statutory authority in P.L. 110-289 and HUD's proposed rules.

Formula Allocation

The Housing Trust Fund is intended to provide formula-based grants for states to increase housing opportunities for extremely low- and very low-income renters and homeowners. P.L. 110-289 required the Secretary of HUD to develop a formula for allocating the monies in the Housing Trust Fund among the states,[10] and, as mentioned above, HUD has published a proposed rule governing the allocation formula. By statute, the formula is based in part on the following factors:

- the relative number of affordable standard rental units available to extremely low-income renter households in the state (this factor is given "priority emphasis");
- the relative number of affordable standard rental units available to very low- income renter households in the state;
- the relative number of extremely low-income renter households living with incomplete kitchen or plumbing facilities, more than one person per room, or spending more than 50% of income on housing costs in the state; and
- the relative number of very low-income renter households spending more than 50% of income on rent in the state.

The sum of these factors is then to be multiplied by the relative cost of construction in the state to arrive at a grant amount.[11] Each state is to receive a minimum annual grant of $3 million.[12]

Funding Distribution

Grants from the Housing Trust Fund are to be awarded to states based on the formula described above. States can designate entities such as housing finance agencies, housing and community development agencies, or tribally designated entities to administer the funds. The state-designated agency can administer the grant itself, or it can allow subgrantees to administer the funds; subgrantees must be state agencies or units of local government that have submitted Consolidated Plans to HUD.[13] Grantees and subgrantees ultimately provide funds to recipients, which are for- profit or nonprofit entities that receive Housing Trust Fund funds as owners or developers of affordable housing.

Recipients of Housing Trust Fund grant amounts must have relevant experience. More specifically, an organization receiving funding for a rental housing project must have experience owning, constructing, rehabilitating, managing, or operating affordable multifamily rental projects. An organization receiving funding for homeownership activities is required to have experience in designing, constructing, rehabilitating, or marketing affordable homeownership housing, or in providing assistance with down payments, closing costs, or interest rate subsidies. Recipients also have to demonstrate general financial experience and expertise and familiarity with the requirements of any related federal, state, or local housing programs that will be used in conjunction with grants from the Housing Trust Fund.

Eligible Uses

States must use most of their grants from the Housing Trust Fund to support rental housing, although they can use a portion of their funding for homeownership housing. Similarly, most of the funding is required to be used for extremely low-income families or families with incomes below the poverty line, but some funding can be used for very low-income families as well.[14]

Rental Housing

Grants from the Housing Trust Fund can be used for the production, preservation, rehabilitation, or operation of rental housing. By law, all funding used for rental housing must benefit families that are extremely low- or very low-income. At least 75% of the grant amounts for rental housing must be used for the sole benefit of extremely low-income families or families with incomes at or below the poverty line for a family of its size. No more than 25% of the grant amounts for rental housing can be used for the sole benefit of very low-income families.

Owner-Occupied Housing

Up to 10% of a state's grants from the Housing Trust Fund may be used for the production, preservation, and rehabilitation of homeownership housing, or for related homeownership costs such as down payment assistance, closing cost assistance, and interest-rate buy-downs. By law, both the home and the homebuyer must meet certain requirements,[15] and the funds must be used to benefit families who are extremely low- or very low-income.

Restrictions and Requirements

Restriction on Eligible Activities

Money from the Housing Trust Fund cannot be used for political activities, advocacy, lobbying, counseling services, travel expenses, or preparing or providing advice on tax returns. The Secretary can set a limit of up to 10% of a state or state-designated entity's Housing Trust Fund grant amount that can be used for the cost of administering the programs funded by the grant; using funds for other outreach or other administrative costs of the grantee or fund recipient is prohibited.

Oversight

P.L. 110-289 requires states or the state-designated entities that administer grants from the Housing Trust Fund to develop allocation plans describing how the grant money will be distributed. An allocation plan must explain how the allocation of funds will be based on priority housing needs, and it must include performance goals. The states and state-designated entities are to make their allocation plans available for public comment and consider any public comments they receive.

Any funds not committed for use by a grantee within two years will be recaptured by the Housing Trust Fund and reallocated.

The states or state-designated entities that receive grants from the Housing Trust Fund are responsible for overseeing the proper use of the funds and obtaining reimbursement for improperly used funds. Future grants are to be reduced by the amount of any improperly used money that is not reimbursed.

CURRENT FUNDING ISSUES

As described earlier, the Housing Trust Fund's original funding source was suspended when Fannie Mae and Freddie Mac encountered financial trouble in the fall of 2008. Advocates have continued to search for both a new dedicated source of permanent funding for the Housing Trust Fund and an initial appropriation to capitalize the Housing Trust Fund. P.L. 110-289 allows other funds to be "appropriated, transferred, or credited" to the Housing Trust Fund. However, to date, no new funding source has been identified for the Housing Trust Fund.

Some affordable housing advocates have suggested a range of other potential sources of either permanent or initial funding, including using Ginnie Mae receipts (which was proposed in some of the bills that would have created national housing trust funds prior to the passage of P.L. 110-289), dividends from the Troubled Assets Relief Program (TARP), or receipts generated from other housing programs.

The President's FY2012 budget request included $1 billion in mandatory funding for the Housing Trust Fund, but did not identify a funding source.[16] No funding for the Housing Trust Fund was included in the Consolidated and Further Continuing Appropriations Act, 2012 (P.L. 112-55), which included FY2012 HUD appropriations.

Recent Legislative Proposals

111th Congress

Several legislative proposals in the 111th Congress included funding for the Housing Trust Fund. For example, the House-passed version of H.R. 4213, the American Jobs and Closing Tax Loopholes Act of 2010, would have provided $1.065 billion for the Housing Trust Fund.[17] Of this amount, $1 billion would have been used for formula grants to states, and the remaining $65 million would have been used for project-based rental assistance associated with those grants. The bill also would have made some changes to the underlying statute that governs the Housing Trust Fund. The version of the bill enacted into law did not include any provisions related to the Housing Trust Fund.

There were also several other legislative proposals to provide funding for the Housing Trust Fund in the 111th Congress. The House-passed version of the Jobs for Main Street Act of 2009 included funding for the Housing Trust Fund. Like the version of H.R. 4213 that was passed by the House, the House-passed version of the Jobs for Main Street Act included $1.065 billion for the Housing Trust Fund, including $65 million for project-based rental assistance to be used in conjunction with projects funded by the Housing Trust Fund. The funding for the Housing Trust Fund was not included in the version of the bill that was signed into law (P.L. 111-147).

Additionally, Representative Barney Frank introduced two bills that would have used TARP funds to fund the Housing Trust Fund in the 111th Congress. The first (H.R. 3068) would have provided $1 billion for the Housing Trust Fund from dividends paid to the Treasury by financial institutions that received funds under TARP. The second (H.R. 3766) would have provided $1 billion for the Housing Trust Fund by diverting TARP funds directly to the Housing Trust Fund, rather than using dividends paid to the Treasury by TARP recipients. The latter bill also would have limited the rents paid by tenants living in housing assisted with monies from the Housing Trust Fund to no more than 30% of the family's adjusted income. Senator Jack Reed also introduced a bill (S. 1731) that would have provided $1 billion for the Housing Trust Fund, using funds from the sale of warrants under TARP. No laws that included funding for the Housing Trust Fund were enacted by the end of the 111th Congress.

112th Congress

In the 112th Congress to date, the Preserving Homes and Communities Act has been introduced in both the House and the Senate (H.R. 1477 and S. 489, respectively). Both of these bills would provide $1 billion to the Housing Trust Fund, with the funding coming from the sale of warrants under TARP.

There has also been legislation introduced in the 112th Congress to eliminate the Housing Trust Fund. The GSE Bailout Elimination and Taxpayer Protection Act has been introduced in both the House and the Senate (H.R. 1182 and S. 693, respectively) and would repeal the section of HERA that established the Housing Trust Fund. The Housing Trust Fund Elimination Act of 2011 (H.R. 2441) would eliminate the Housing Trust Fund and transfer any amounts available in the fund to the Treasury, to be used solely for the purpose of reducing the federal budget deficit.

Appendix. Legislative History of Housing Trust Fund Bills

Prior to the establishment of the Housing Trust Fund in P.L. 110-289, proposals to create an affordable housing trust fund had been included in legislation since the 106th Congress. This report has described the Housing Trust Fund as it was authorized by P.L. 110-289. This appendix discusses the major features of previous housing trust fund proposals.

106th Congress

In the 106th Congress, Senator John Kerry and 10 cosponsors introduced S. 2997, the National Affordable Housing Trust Fund Act of 2000. This bill would have both established a National Affordable Housing Trust Fund within the Department of the Treasury and provided a dedicated funding source for the Fund. The dedicated funding source would have come from FHA Mutual Mortgage Insurance Fund (MMI Fund) funds above a capital adequacy level of 3%, as well as any excess funds from Ginnie Mae. Hearings on the bill were held by the Subcommittee on Housing and Transportation of the Committee on Banking, Housing, and Urban Affairs.

107th Congress

In the 107th Congress, Senator John Kerry and 28 cosponsors introduced S. 1248, the National Affordable Housing Trust Fund Act of 2001. Like S. 2997, this bill would have authorized a trust fund and proposed the same dedicated funding source of FHA MMI Fund funds above a capital adequacy level set at 3% and any excess funds from Ginnie Mae. Again, subcommittee hearings were held, but the bill was never sent to the full committee. In the House, Representative Bernie Sanders and 199 cosponsors introduced H.R. 2349, also called the National Affordable Housing Trust Fund Act of 2001. This bill proposed using the same dedicated funding source of excess Ginnie Mae funds and FHA MMI Fund funds above a capital adequacy level, but it set the capital adequacy level at 2% rather than 3%. The bill was referred to the Subcommittee on Housing and Community Opportunity, but hearings were never held.

108th Congress

In the 108th Congress, Senator John Kerry and 21 cosponsors introduced S. 1411, the National Affordable Housing Trust Fund Act of 2003. The bill proposed the same dedicated source of funding as S. 2997 and S. 1248. S. 1411 was referred to the Committee on Banking, Housing, and Urban Affairs, but the Committee never held hearings on it. Also in the 108th Congress, the Reed Affordable Housing Fund amendment to S. 1508, a GSE reform bill, was unanimously adopted by the Senate Banking Committee. This amendment proposed a dedicated funding source of 5% of Fannie Mae's and Freddie Mac's pretax profits. In the House, Representative Bernie Sanders and 214 cosponsors introduced H.R. 1102, also called the National Affordable Housing Trust Fund Act of 2003. This bill also included both authorizing and appropriating language and specified a dedicated source of funding that was the same as H.R. 2349 (and the same as the Senate bills, except for setting the FHA MMI Fund capital adequacy level at 2% rather than 3%). The bill was referred to the Subcommittee on Housing and Community Opportunity, but hearings were never held.

109th Congress

In the 109th Congress, proponents of an affordable housing fund concentrated their efforts on including an affordable housing fund in H.R. 1461, the Federal Housing Finance Reform Act of 2005. The bill would have required each GSE to create an affordable housing fund and to contribute either 3.5% or 5% of the prior year's after-tax income, depending on the year. The bill included a sunset provision after five years, after which the GSEs would no longer have been required to make contributions. The bill was referred to the Senate Committee on Banking, Housing, and Urban Affairs.

110th Congress

In the 110th Congress, Representative Barney Frank and three cosponsors introduced H.R. 1427, the Federal Housing Finance Reform Act of 2007, on March 9, 2007. The bill authorized the creation of a trust fund and directed the GSEs to contribute 1.2 basis points for each dollar of their average total mortgage portfolio for five years, at which point the funding requirement would have ended. H.R. 1427 passed the House and was referred to the Senate Committee on Banking, Housing, and Urban Affairs.

Representative Maxine Waters and 13 cosponsors introduced H.R. 1852, the Expanding American Homeownership Act of 2007, on March 29, 2007. The bill passed the House and was referred to the Senate Committee on Banking, Housing, and Urban Affairs. H.R. 1852 would have set aside a portion of FHA savings for a housing trust fund.

Representative Barney Frank and 16 cosponsors introduced H.R. 2895, the National Affordable Housing Trust Fund Act of 2007, on June 28, 2007. H.R. 2895 was passed by the House and referred to the Senate Committee on Banking, Housing, and Urban Affairs. The bill would have created a permanent affordable housing trust fund and included guidance on how trust fund grantees should use the funds, but it did not create a permanent funding source.

Senator Jack Reed introduced S. 2391, the Government Sponsored Enterprise Mission Improvement Act, on November 16, 2007. The bill would have established an affordable housing block grant program and a Capital Magnet Fund, and would have funded both through GSE contributions of 4.2 basis points for each dollar of the unpaid principal balance of their total new business purchases. The bill did not include a sunset provision. S. 2391 was referred to the Committee on Banking, Housing, and Urban Affairs.

Senator John Kerry and 23 cosponsors introduced S. 2523, the National Affordable Housing Trust Fund Act of 2007, on December 19, 2007. The bill would have established a national affordable housing trust fund but would not have created a dedicated funding source. S. 2523 was referred to the Committee on Banking, Housing, and Urban Affairs.

Representative Nancy Pelosi and 18 cosponsors introduced H.R. 3221, the Housing and Economic Recovery Act of 2008, on July 30, 2007. This is the legislation that eventually became P.L. 110-289, and both authorized the affordable housing funds and created a permanent source of money for those funds. The version of the affordable housing trust fund that was created by P.L. 110-289 most resembles the proposed fund in S. 2391.

End Notes

[1] For more information on the Center for Community Change's research on housing trust funds, see http://housingtrustfundproject.org/housing-trust-funds

[2] For details on efforts to create a national affordable housing trust fund, see the National Low Income Housing Coalition's website, "National Housing Trust Fund Campaign," available at http://www.nlihc.org/template/page.cfm? id=40.

[3] For a legislative history of affordable housing trust fund proposals, see the National Low Income Housing Coalition's website, "Details about the National Housing Trust Fund Campaign," January 31, 2007, available at http://www.nlihc.org/detail/article.cfm?article_id =3834#prop, or see the **Appendix**.

[4] See CRS Report RL34300, *Pay-As-You-Go Procedures for Budget Enforcement,* by Robert Keith, for more information on Congressional budgeting rules, including PAYGO.

[5] For more information on the GSEs and the privileges that they have historically enjoyed, see CRS Report RL33756, *Fannie Mae and Freddie Mac: A Legal and Policy Overview*, by N. Eric Weiss and Michael V. Seitzinger.

[6] A new Capital Magnet Fund, to be administered by the Department of the Treasury, was to share the contributions. For a fuller discussion of the original funding mechanism, and how that funding was to be divided between the Housing Trust Fund and the Capital Magnet Fund, see archived CRS Report RL34158, *The New GSE Affordable Housing Funds: The Housing Trust Fund and the Capital Magnet Fund*, by N. Eric Weiss and Katie Jones.

[7] United States Securities and Exchange Commission filing, Form 8-K, Federal National Mortgage Association, November 18, 2008, available at http://www.sec.gov/Archives/ edgar/data/310522/000129993308005442/ htm_30041.htm, and United States Securities and Exchange Commission Filing, Form 10-Q, Federal Home Loan Mortgage Corporation, November 14, 2008, p. 66, available at http://ir.10kwizard.com/files.php?source=1372.

[8] Department of Housing and Urban Development, "Housing Trust Fund; Allocation Formula; Proposed Rule," 74 *Federal Register* 63938-63942, December 4, 2009. This proposed rule would create a new Part 93 to Title 24 of the Code of Federal Regulations.

[9] Department of Housing and Urban Development, "Housing Trust Fund; Proposed Rule," 75 *Federal Register* 66978-67009, October 29, 2010. This proposed rule would create a new Subpart N to Part 92 of Title 24 of the Code of Federal Regulations. Part 92 of Title 24 contains the regulations governing HUD's Home Investment Partnerships Program.

[10] The term "states" includes the 50 states, the District of Columbia, and the territories and possessions of the United States, including Puerto Rico, the Northern Mariana Islands, Guam, the Virgin Islands, American Samoa, and the Trust Territory of the Pacific Islands.

[11] HUD's Office of Policy Development and Research has released preliminary estimates of the amount of funding that each state could receive from $1 billion allocated to the Housing Trust Fund, based on the proposed formula. These estimates are available at http://www. huduser.org/portal/periodicals/cityscpe/vol12num1/ch7.pdf.

[12] The $3 million minimum grant amount applies only to the 50 states and the District of Columbia.

[13] HUD requires jurisdictions to submit a Consolidated Plan in order to receive funds from its block grant programs, such as the Community Development Block Grant (CDBG) program and the HOME Investment Partnerships Program. The Consolidated Plan describes a jurisdiction's affordable housing needs and explains how funds received from HUD and other sources will be used to meet those needs.

[14] Very low-income households are households that have an income at or below 50% of area median income. Extremely low-income households have an income at or below 30% of area median income.

[15] The home must be available for purchase by extremely low- or very low-income families who will use the home as a principal residence and are first-time home buyers, meaning that they have not owned a home in the prior three years. Home buyers must also complete a pre-purchase financial counseling requirement. The home is subject to initial purchase price and resale restrictions.

[16] The President's FY2010 and FY2011 budget requests also included $1 billion in mandatory funding for the Housing Trust Fund, but did not identify a funding source. Neither the Consolidated Appropriations Act, 2010 (P.L. 111-117), which appropriated FY2010 funding for HUD, nor the Department of Defense and Full-Year Continuing Appropriations Act, 2011 (P.L. 112-10), which appropriated HUD funding for FY2011, included any funding for the Housing Trust Fund.

[17] The version of H.R. 4213 that passed the House on May 28, 2010, was a House amendment to the Senate amendment to H.R. 4213.

In: Federal Funds: A Selection of Programs ISBN 978-1-62618-005-5
Editor: Kieran Saccoccio

Chapter 5

UNIVERSAL SERVICE FUND: BACKGROUND AND OPTIONS FOR REFORM*

Angele A. Gilroy

SUMMARY

The concept that all Americans should be able to afford access to the telecommunications network, commonly called the "universal service concept" can trace its origins back to the 1934 Communications Act. Since then, the preservation and advancement of universal service has been a basic tenet of federal communications policy, and Congress has historically played an active role in helping to preserve and advance universal service goals. The passage of the Telecommunications Act of 1996 (P.L. 104-104) not only codified the universal service concept, but also led to the establishment, in 1997, of a federal Universal Service Fund (USF or Fund) to meet the universal service objectives and principles contained in the 1996 act. According to Fund administrators, from 1998 through end of year 2010, $73.7 billion was distributed, or committed, by the USF, with all 50 states, the District of Columbia, and all territories receiving some benefit.

* This is an edited, reformatted and augmented version of the Congressional Research Service Publication, CRS Report for Congress RL33979, dated October 25, 2011.

The Federal Communications Commission (FCC) is required to ensure that there be “specific, predictable and sufficient ... mechanisms to preserve and advance universal service.” However, changes in telecommunications technology and the marketplace, while often leading to positive benefits for consumers and providers, have had a negative impact on the health and viability of the USF, as presently designed. These changes have led to a growing imbalance between the entities and revenue stream contributing to the fund and the growth in the entities and programs eligible to receive funding. The desire to expand access to broadband and address what some perceive as a “digital divide” has also placed focus on what role, if any, the USF should take to address this issue. The FCC’s national broadband plan, *Connecting America: The National Broadband Plan*, calls for a major restructuring of the USF to enable it to take a major role in achieving the goal of nationwide broadband access and adoption. The FCC has initiated a series of proceedings to achieve this goal.

There is a growing consensus among policy makers, including some in Congress, that significant action is needed not only to ensure the viability and stability of the USF, but also to address the numerous issues surrounding its appropriate role in a changing marketplace. How this concept should be defined, how these policies should be funded, who should receive the funding, and how to ensure proper management and oversight of the Fund are among the issues framing the debate.

The current policy debate has focused on five concerns: the scope of the program; who should contribute and what methodology should be used to fund the program; eligibility criteria for benefits; concerns over possible program fraud, waste, and abuse; and the impact of the Antideficiency Act (ADA) on the USF.

It is anticipated that Universal Service Fund reform will continue to be a topic of congressional interest. The House Energy and Commerce Committee and the Senate Commerce, Science, and Transportation Committee have included USF reform on their agendas of issues for consideration and oversight. Three stand-alone measures (H.R. 2163, H.R. 3118, S. 297) relating to USF have been introduced to date.

INTRODUCTION

The concept that all Americans should be able to afford access to the telecommunications network is commonly called the “universal service concept." This concept can trace its origins back to the 1934 Communications Act.[1] Since then the preservation and advancement of universal service has been a basic tenet of federal communications policy, and Congress has historically played an active role in helping to preserve and advance universal service goals. In 1996 Congress passed the Telecommunications Act of 1996 (P.L. 104-104), which not only codified the universal service concept, but also led to the establishment of a federal Universal Service Fund (USF or the Fund) to meet the universal service objectives and principles contained in the 1996 act. According to Fund administrators, since 1998 almost $73.7 billion in support has been disbursed by the USF, with all 50 states, the District of Columbia, and all territories receiving some benefit.[2]

Over the past decade the telecommunications sector has undergone a vast transformation fueled by rapid technological growth and subsequent evolution of the marketplace. A wide range of new services have become available, offered by a growing list of traditional as well as nontraditional providers. One of the results of this transformation is that the nation's expectations for communications services have also grown. In the past, access to the public switched network through a single wireline connection, enabling voice service, was the standard of communications. Today the desire for simple voice connectivity has been replaced by the demand, on the part of consumers, business, and government, for access to a vast array of multifaceted fixed and mobile services. Consumers are also demanding greater flexibility and may choose to gain access to the same content over a variety of technologies, whether it be a computer, a television, or a mobile telephone. The trend towards sharing information, such as music, movies, or photographs, is also growing, making it necessary to ensure that network upload speeds match download capabilities. These advances require that networks transition into converged next-generation wireline and wireless broadband networks capable of meeting these demands. One of the challenges facing this transition is the desire to ensure that all citizens have access to an affordable and advanced telecommunications infrastructure so that all members of American society may derive the benefits.[3]

Technological advances such as the ability of the Internet to provide data, voice, and video, the bundling of service offerings, the advancement of wireless services, and the growing convergence of the telecommunications sector have, according to many policy makers, made it necessary to reexamine traditional policy goals such as the advancement of universal service mandates. These changes in technology and the marketplace, a declining funding base, and significant increases in the amount of support disbursed by the Fund, have led to concerns that the USF is in need of reform. There is a growing consensus among policy makers, including some in Congress, that significant action is needed not only to ensure the viability and stability of the USF, but also to address the numerous issues surrounding such reform. How this concept should be defined, how these policies should be funded, who should receive the funding, and how to ensure proper management and oversight of the Fund are among the issues expected to frame the policy debate.

THE UNIVERSAL SERVICE CONCEPT

Since its creation in 1934 the Federal Communications Commission (FCC, or Commission) has been tasked with "mak[ing] available, so far as possible, to all the people of the United States ... a rapid, efficient, Nation-wide, and world-wide wire and radio communications service with adequate facilities at reasonable charges."[4] This mandate led to the development of what has come to be known as the universal service concept.

The universal service concept, as originally designed, called for the establishment of policies to ensure that telecommunications services are available to all Americans, including those in rural, insular and high cost areas, by ensuring that rates remain affordable. During the 20th century, government and industry efforts to expand telephone service led to the development of a complex system of cross subsidies to expand the network and address universal service goals. The underlying goal of the cross-subsidization policy was to increase the number of subscribers to the network by shifting costs among network providers and subscribers. Profits from more densely populated, lower cost urbanized areas helped to subsidize wiring and operation costs for the less populous, higher cost rural areas. Higher rates and equipment charges for business and long distance customers helped to subsidize the charges for residential local calling. The funding for universal service objectives was built into the rate structure, and effectively most telephone subscribers have contributed to universal service goals for decades.[5]

With the advent of competition and the breakup of the Bell System, the complex system of cross subsidies that evolved to support universal service goals was no longer tenable. The Telecommunications Act of 1996 (P.L. 104-104; 47 USC) codified the long-standing commitment by U.S. policymakers to ensure universal service in the provision of telecommunications services (§254). The 1996 act also required that every telecommunications carrier that provides interstate telecommunications services be responsible for universal service support [§254(d)] and that such charges be made explicit [§254(e)].[6] The 1996 act also expanded the concept of universal service to include, among other principles, that elementary and secondary schools and classrooms, libraries, and rural health care providers have access to telecommunications services for specific purposes at discounted rates [§254(b)(6) and 254(h).]

The Federal Universal Service Fund

Over the years this concept fostered the development of various FCC policies and programs to meet this goal. A new federal Universal Service Fund (USF or Fund) was established in 1997 to meet the specific objectives and principles contained in the 1996 act. The USF is administered by the Universal Service Administrative Company (USAC), an independent-not-for-profit organization, under the direction of the FCC. The FCC, through the USF, offers universal service support through a number of direct mechanisms that target both providers of and subscribers to telecommunications services.[7] The USF provides support and discounts for providers and subscribers through four programs: high-cost support; low-income support; schools and libraries support; and rural health care support.[8]

High-Cost Program

High-cost support, provided through the high cost program, is an example of provider-targeted support. Under the high cost program, eligible telecommunications carriers, usually those serving rural, insular, and high cost areas, are able to obtain funds to help offset the higher than average costs of providing telephone service.[9] This mechanism has been particularly important to rural America where the lack of subscriber density leads to significant costs.

Low-Income Program

FCC universal service policies have been expanded to target low-income subscribers. Two income-based programs, Lifeline and Link Up, established in the mid-1980s, were developed to assist economically needy individuals. The Link Up program, established in 1987, assists low- income subscribers pay the costs associated with the initiation of telephone service, and the Lifeline program, established in 1984, assists low-income subscribers pay the recurring monthly service charges incurred by telephone subscribers.[10] Discounts are eligible for one connection, either wired or wireless, per household.

Schools and Libraries or "E-Rate" Program

Under universal service provisions contained in the 1996 act, elementary and secondary schools and classrooms, and libraries are designated as beneficiaries of universal service discounts. Universal service principles detailed in Section 254(b)(6) state that "Elementary and secondary schools and classrooms ... and libraries should have access to advanced telecommunications services." The act further requires in Section 254(h)(1)(B) that services within the definition of universal service be provided to elementary and secondary schools and libraries for education purposes at discounts, that is at "rates less than the amounts charged for similar services to other parties."

The FCC established the Schools and Libraries Division within the Universal Service Administrative Company (USAC) to administer the schools and libraries or "E (education)-rate" program to comply with these provisions. Under this program, which became effective, January 1, 1998, eligible schools and libraries receive discounts ranging from 20% to 90% for telecommunications services depending on the poverty level of the school's (or school district's) population and its location in a high cost telecommunications area. Three categories of services are eligible for discounts: internal connections (e.g., wiring, routers and servers); Internet access; and telecommunications and dedicated services, with the third category receiving funding priority. Unlike the high-cost and low-income programs, the FCC established a yearly ceiling, or cap, of $2.25 billion, adjusted for inflation prospectively beginning with funding year 2010, for this program.[11]

Rural Health Care Program

Section 254(h) of the 1996 act requires that public and non-profit rural health care providers have access to telecommunications services necessary for the provision of health care services at rates comparable to those paid for similar services in urban areas. Subsection 254(h)(1) further specifies that "to the extent technically feasible and economically reasonable" health care providers should have access to advanced telecommunications and information services. The FCC established the Rural Health Care Division (RHCD) within the USAC to administer the universal support program to comply with these provisions. Under FCC-established rules only public or non-profit health care providers are eligible to receive funding. Eligible health care providers, with the exception of those requesting only access to the Internet, must also be located in a rural area.[12] Similar to the Schools and Libraries program, this support program went into effect on January 1, 1998, and a funding ceiling, or cap, was established, in this case at $400 million annually. The primary use of the funding is to provide reduced rates for telecommunications and information services necessary for the provision of health care. In addition, in 2007 the FCC established the "Rural Health Care Pilot Program" to help public and non-profit health care providers build state and region-wide broadband networks dedicated to the provision of health care services.[13]

Funding

The USF receives no federal monies but is funded by mandatory contributions from telecommunications carriers that provide interstate service.[14] Under current rules, a carrier's contributions are assessed based on a percentage of its interstate and international end-user telecommunications revenues. This percentage is called the contribution factor. The FCC calculates the contribution factor based on anticipated funding needs of the USF in the upcoming quarter. This information is submitted quarterly, to the FCC, by USAC's universal service administrator. The contribution factor is calculated four times a year, on a quarterly basis, and may increase, decrease, or remain the same depending on the needs of the universal service programs drawing on the USF. The FCC's Wireline Competition Bureau releases a public notice stating the proposed factor. After 14 days, absent any FCC action, the factor becomes final. As shown in **Table A-1**, from 2003 to the first half of 2005 the contribution factor generally saw a steady increase. During that period the contribution factor varied from a low of 7.3% in the first quarter of 2003 to a high of 11.1% in the second quarter of 2005. Since reaching that high, the factor had begun to moderate; however, the contribution factors for the second and third quarters of 2007, at 11.7% and 11.3% respectively, were a strong reversal of this trend, resulting in a significant increase from the first quarter 2007 contribution factor of 9.7%. Since reaching a high of 11.7% the contribution factor began to moderate with a first quarter 2008 factor of 10.2%. The contribution factor once again began to climb and reached an historic high of 15.5% for the first quarter of 2011. The contribution factor for the second quarter of 2011 at 14.9% and the third quarter at 14.4% represented a slight moderate downward trend. The contribution factor for the fourth quarter of 2011, however, had a significant increase to 15.3 % and represents the second highest rate on record. The overall growth in the factor over this decade remains a significant policy concern. (See "Policy Options" section, below, for a discussion of some of the reasons attributed to this increase.)

There are some exceptions to this funding process. Under the FCC's rules telecommunications providers are not required to contribute in a given year to universal service if their annual contributions to the program would be de minimis, that is less than $10,000 in that year, or if they provide only international services. Filers are also not required to contribute based on international revenues if their interstate end-user revenues meet the 12% rule, that is, if their interstate end-user revenues represent less than 12% of their combined interstate and international end-user revenues. In other cases the FCC has determined that selected categories of providers, for example, wireless carriers and interconnected VoIP providers, may, but are not required to, base their contributions on an FCC-established revenue percentage, or "safe harbor," that attempts to estimate the percentage of the provider's total revenues that are interstate and international end-user revenues.[15] The current (effective June 2006) safe harbor for wireless carriers and VoIP providers is set at 37.1% and 64.9% of total revenues, respectively.[16]

Many assessed providers have chosen, but are not required, to recover USF contributions directly from their customers. They pass through universal service payments directly to consumers and earmark a universal service charge on subscriber's bills. This is legal and a common industry practice. However, if an assessed provider does choose to collect USF fees directly from their customers the provider is not permitted to recover, through a federal universal service line item on a customer's bill, an amount that exceeds the universal service charge contribution factor.[17]

Disbursements

According to USAC, universal service support disbursements for calendar year 2010 totaled $8.0 billion.[18] **Figure 1**, below, shows the breakdown of calendar year 2010 USF disbursements as a percentage by individual program. High Cost support accounted for 53.7% of total disbursements, or $4.3 billion. Schools and Libraries support represented 28.7% of disbursements, totaling $2.3 billion. Low Income support was 16.5% of disbursements, totaling $1.3 billion. Disbursements for Rural Health Care support were $86.0 million, or 1.1% of disbursements. (It should be noted that "commitments" for the schools and libraries support program and the rural health care program are not the same as "disbursements." Commitments authorize beneficiaries to spend up to a total dollar figure of USF money committed for procuring telecommunications services, while disbursements pay for specific activities actually carried out and for which beneficiaries have received "commitments" of USF support. In the aggregate, applicants end up spending less than the total amounts of dollars committed. Commitments operate on a school year calendar, July 1-June 30, and disbursements are reported on a calendar year basis.) Although subscribers benefit from the USF, only companies that provide the services draw money directly from the fund.

Table A-2 provides data on USF payments and contributions broken down by state and program for 2009. The data show that service providers (and their subscribers) in every state, territory, and commonwealth received, to varying degrees, some 2009 USF payments. For example, all received at least some payments from the Low Income program, all received support from the Schools and Libraries program, and all with the exception of the District of Columbia and Connecticut received payments from the High Cost program. Payments from the Rural Health Care program were received by 45 states and 3 territories. The allocation of benefits varies depending on which individual program is examined. However, when overall net dollar flow[19] is examined 25 states and the District of Columbia were net contributors to the 2009 USF program as a whole. The service providers in the remaining 25 states and 5 territories were net receivers, that is they received more payments from the USF, for 2009, than estimated contributions. Although there is some variation within programs and among states in any given year, on the whole whether a particular state is a net receiver of, or contributor to, the USF program, is a fairly stable pattern.[20] In general, rural states with low population density typically tend to benefit most as they receive significant funding from the High Cost program, but tend to contribute less to the USF program overall, since they tend to generate lower telecommunications revenues.

POLICY OPTIONS

The FCC is required to ensure that there be "specific, predictable and sufficient ... mechanisms to preserve and advance universal service."[21] However, changes in telecommunications technology and the marketplace, while often leading to positive benefits for consumers and providers, have had a negative impact on the health and viability of the USF, as presently designed. These changes have led to a growing imbalance between the entities and revenue stream contributing to the fund and the growth in the entities and programs eligible to receive funding. The desire to expand access to broadband and address what some perceive as a "digital divide" has also placed focus on what role, if any, the USF should take to address this issue.[22]

The current policy debate surrounding USF reform has focused on four major concerns: the scope of the program; who should contribute and what methodology should be used to fund the program; eligibility criteria for benefits; and concerns over possible program fraud, waste, and abuse. A separate and more narrowly focused issue, the impact of the Antideficiency Act (ADA) on the USF, also has become an issue of concern.

Program Scope

One of the major policy debates surrounding universal service is whether access to advanced telecommunications services (i.e., broadband) should be incorporated into universal service objectives. The term universal service, when applied to telecommunications, refers to the ability to make available a basket of telecommunications services to the public, across the nation, at a reasonable price. As directed in the 1996 Telecommunications Act [Section 254(c)], a federal- state Joint Board was tasked with defining the services which should be included in the basket of services to be eligible for federal universal service support; in effect using and defining the term "universal service" for the first time. The Joint Board's recommendation, which was subsequently adopted by the FCC in May 1997, included the following in its universal services package: voice grade access to, and some usage of, the public switched network; single line service; dual tone signaling; access to directory assistance; emergency service such as 911; operator services; access and interexchange (long distance) service.

Some policy makers have expressed concern that the FCC-adopted definition is too limited and does not take into consideration the importance and growing acceptance of advanced services such as broadband and Internet access. They point to a number of provisions contained in the Universal Service section of the 1996 act to support their claim. Universal service principles contained in Section 254(b)(2) state that "Access to advanced telecommunications services should be provided to all regions of the Nation." The subsequent principle (b)(3) calls for consumers in all regions of the Nation including "low-income" and those in "rural, insular, and high cost areas" to have access to telecommunications and information services including "advanced services" at a comparable level and a comparable rate charged for similar services in urban areas. Such provisions, they state, dictate that the FCC expand its universal service definition.

The 1996 act does take into consideration the changing nature of the telecommunications sector and allows for the universal service definition to be modified if future conditions warrant. Section 254(c) of the act states that "universal service is an evolving level of telecommunications services" and the FCC is tasked with "periodically" reevaluating this definition "taking into account advances in telecommunications and information technologies and services." Furthermore, the Joint Board is given specific authority to recommend "from time to time" to the FCC modification of the definition of the services to be included for federal universal service support. The Joint Board, in July 2002, concluded such an inquiry and recommended that at that time no changes be made in the list of services eligible for universal service support. The FCC, in a July 10, 2003, order (FCC 03 170) adopted the Joint Board's recommendation, thereby leaving unchanged the list of services supported by Federal universal service. More recently, however, the Joint Board was once again called upon to reexamine this issue and came up with a different conclusion. The Joint Board, on November 19, 2007, recommended that the FCC change the mix of services eligible for universal service support and concluded that "the universal availability of broadband Internet services" be included in the Nation's communications goals and hence be supported by Federal universal service funds.[23] The FCC in its national broadband plan, *Connecting America: the National Broadband Plan*, released March 16, 2010, to Congress, has recommended that access to and adoption of broadband be a national goal and has proposed that the USF be restructured to become a vehicle to help reach this goal. (See the "FCC National Broadband Plan" section of this report, below, for more details on how the USF could be transformed to help achieve this recommendation.)

Other policy makers caution that a more modest approach is appropriate given the "universal mandate" associated with this definition. Also at issue is the uncertainty and costs associated with mandating nationwide deployment of such advanced services as a universal service policy goal. Some have expressed concern that given the pressures currently facing the Fund, and their impact on the contribution factor, the inclusion of broadband services, at this time, is taking on too large a mandate. Current policy concerns regarding both the contribution and distribution mechanisms should be addressed first, they state, prior to any expansion of the USF definition. Furthermore, they state, the USF has already taken on limited broadband deployment responsibilities through the E-rate and Rural Health Care programs, and indirectly through the High Cost program, as funding is used to upgrade existing telephone networks. If ubiquitous broadband deployment is a national policy goal, they state, policymakers should not place further stress on the USF program but should seek out other means of achieving this goal which may be more effective, such as providing economic incentives, easing economic regulation, encouraging municipal ownership, expanding other existing programs or establishing a new program.[24]

Contribution Methodology

One of the major policy questions surrounding USF reform is to what degree, if any, there should be a change in the way the program is funded. A consensus has been forming that some reform to broaden the contribution base is needed. How this should be accomplished, however, remains open to debate. Proposals range from modest options to expand the existing funding base, to broadening the base to include *intrastate* revenues, to calling for a complete restructuring of the contribution methodology.

Expanding the Base

One option is to broaden the base of entities that must contribute to the Fund, by calling for technology neutral funding. The FCC has taken a number of actions, over the years, to expand the pool of contributors, thereby broadening the base of entities supporting the Fund.[25] For example, in 1998 the FCC established a revenue percentage, or safe harbor, of 15% of revenues for determining the USF contribution for wireless carriers. That percentage has been increased twice since and is currently set at 37.1%. In a June 2006 decision, the FCC further expanded the pool of contributors by requiring that providers of interconnected VoIP contribute to the USF and established a safe harbor of 64.9%.[26] Some policy makers have recommended that the list of providers be expanded to include broadband providers which were removed from the base when the FCC ruled that Internet access services are information services, not telecommunications services. However, they generally recommend that this expansion be contingent on the understanding that USF support be used to upgrade the telecommunications infrastructure to include broadband capabilities.

Intrastate Revenues

Another proposal calls for broadening the revenue base by assessing fees on *intrastate* as well as interstate/international revenues. Although this would provide an additional source for USF funds, many state that this option may not be available absent congressional action to specifically designate intrastate revenues as a source for federal USF contributions. The recommendation for specific congressional clarification is based, to a large part, on a successful court challenge of an earlier attempt by the FCC to collect support for the E-rate program based on combined interstate and intrastate revenues. In the case of *Texas Office of Public Utility Counsel v. FCC* (183F.3d; 393;1999) the United States Court of Appeals, 5th Circuit concluded that "the agency (FCC) exceeded its jurisdictional authority when it assessed contributions for Section 254(h), 'schools and libraries' programs based on combined intrastate and interstate revenues of interstate telecommunications providers and when it asserted its jurisdictional authority to do the same on behalf of high-cost support." Proponents of including intrastate revenues cite technological and marketplace changes which have eroded the distinction between interstate and intrastate services as well as the growth of combined calling plans in support of such action. Some, however, have expressed concern over the potential negative impact that the inclusion of intrastate revenues may have on state-supported USF programs since many are funded by intrastate telecommunications revenues.

Numbers or Connections

Another proposal calls for a shift in the basis of support away from revenues to a completely new methodology based on working numbers or connections. Under this proposal contributions for USF would be assessed based on a monthly flat fee, or charge, per working telephone number. Since users need a discrete number to connect to the public switched network, supporters claim this proposal would lead to a more stable assessment, would be technologically neutral, would spread contributions over a broader base, and would be easier to administer.[27] Opponents, however, state that using a numbers-based approach shifts the burden of USF from high volume users directly to all subscribers as a regressive fixed charge. This, they state, not only adds a financial burden on low volume subscribers, who may be elderly, and/or on low and fixed incomes, but could possibly lead to subscriber drop-off, thereby defeating the purpose of the USF program.[28]

Distribution Methodology

Another major issue facing USF reform concerns the eligibility criteria used to distribute USF funds. Over the past 12 years (1998-2010) annual USF receipts have grown from $2.3 billion to an estimated $8.0 billion and the contribution factor needed to support this growth has almost tripled to reach an all time high of 15.5% for the first quarter of 2011. While this factor had experienced a slight moderation the current (fourth quarter 2011) contribution factor is 15.3%,the second highest rate on record. This significant rise in the funding level, and subsequently the contribution factor, has led to an examination of the Fund's eligibility criteria and distribution methodology. More specifically concerns have been voiced over the long-term sustainability of the Fund and the cost burden it imposes on contributors.

Examination of USF program revenue flows, since 2003, shows that three of the four programs— Low Income, Schools and Libraries, and Rural Health Care—have been relatively stable.

However, the High Cost program has experienced significant growth (30.4%), with disbursements increasing from $3,273.2 million to $4,267.7 million over the most recent seven year (2003-2010) period; and as a result, is the major factor contributing to the USF's recent overall growth. Within the High Cost program the growth can be traced to support given to competitive eligible telecommunications carriers. For example, payments for competitive eligible telecommunications carriers, which are largely wireless carriers, increased from $1 million in 2000 to $126.7 million in 2003, but are estimated by USAC to total slightly more than $1.2 billion for 2010. On the other hand, while incumbent eligible telecommunications carriers still receive a significant majority of funds from the High Cost program, revenues disbursed in 2003 and 2010 decreased from $3.2 billion to $3.1 billion.[29] The FCC's May 2008 decision to place an interim cap on High Cost payments to competitive eligible telecommunications carriers has helped to mitigate this trend. (See "Capping" section, below, for a further discussion.) A more recent trend which has added to the overall increase in the USF has been the growth, after years of relative stability, in the Low Income program. Disbursements to the Low Income program have increased from $822 million in 2008 to an estimated $1.3 billion in 2010. This recent growth can be attributed, to some degree, to the entrance of pre-paid wireless providers to the Lifeline program. According to the FCC, pre-paid wireless eligible telecommunications carriers now account for one-third of all Lifeline reimbursements.[30] An increase in eligible households, due to the recession, is also a likely contributing factor. Whether this will become a growing trend, placing further pressure on the Lifeline program, or is a limited uptick, is yet to be determined.

Hence, most policy discussions regarding the distribution methodology focus on proposals to stem the growth of the High Cost Program by limiting eligibility criteria and/or controlling the amount of funding disbursed. A variety of proposals, to be used on their own or in combination, are being discussed including limiting USF support to a single line per household, eliminating the "identical support rule," using reverse auctions to determine eligibility, placing a cap (or ceiling) on funds, and improving targeting. Improving management of all four funds to eliminate any fraud, waste, or abuse, has also been a focus of reform efforts.

Primary or Single Line Limitation

As presently designed, USF support is available to multiple lines per household. Some policy makers have proposed that one way to curb the increase in funding requirements is to limit eligibility criteria. USF funding, they state, should be limited to a single or primary line, not multiple access.[31] The universal service mandate, they claim, is not to artificially construct a competitive marketplace with multiple carriers in areas that are not able to support a single carrier, but to ensure that high cost areas receive service at a reasonable rate. The use of USF funds to support multiple carriers in high cost areas, they claim, is an abuse of funds and places unnecessary strain on those supporting the program. Others, however, have argued that limiting USF support to a single provider relegates those areas to a lower standard, which does not fulfill the universal service principle to afford consumers in rural, insular and high cost areas, access to telecommunications and information services that are "reasonably comparable to those services provided in urban areas" (§254 [b] [3]). High cost areas, they state, should have the benefits and choices of competition and the opportunity to select from a variety of providers just like other regions of the nation. Line limitations, opponents state, will only discourage investment in rural infrastructure.

Reverse Auctions

One proposal under consideration for selecting an eligible carrier is the use of reverse auctions, or competitive bidding. Under this method a geographic area would be designated as high cost, providers interested in offering service would be asked how little universal service support they would need to provide service and the provider that submits the *lowest* bid, all else equal, would receive the funds.[32] This approach, in theory, would result in a decrease in funding for High Cost support since it would be based on low bids submitted by providers instead of on the current method that is based on the embedded costs of the incumbent telecommunications provider in the area. This, supporters claim, will lead to the use of the most efficient technology and will relieve the growing pressure on USF funds. However, there is no single methodology that must be used and the reverse auction concept could be designed in a number of ways and impose a variety of requirements and obligations. For example, some support a phased-in approach to reverse auctions where it is used solely to select a competitive carrier for an area while the designated incumbent eligible telecommunications carrier remains under the present system indefinitely, or for a specific time period. Others suggest that an auction system could reward the lowest bidder with the most support, but still give other participants some limited support. Still others suggest the establishment of a pilot program to test for successes and/or unintended consequences. On the other hand, others have expressed reservations about adopting reverse auctions stating that many questions remain about how to implement reverse auctions, how to administer the costs associated with their adoption, and the long-term impact they would have on consumers as well as providers. Concerns were also expressed that a reverse auction would not create a favorable environment for network investment possibly resulting in stranded investment, erratic funding, and ultimately inferior networks.

Identical Support Rule

The criteria used for the distribution of funds for the High Cost program has also come under scrutiny. High Cost program fund distribution is based on what is known as the "identical support rule." Under this rule funds are distributed to competitive eligible telecommunications carriers based on the embedded costs, or per line support, of the incumbent carrier. Typically the incumbent carrier is a wireline carrier while the competitive carrier is a wireless carrier. The infrastructure costs associated with the investment and maintenance of a wireline system are generally significantly higher than those associated with a wireless system. Therefore some have questioned whether basing funding levels on the incumbent carrier's costs, particularly when support is based on a more expensive infrastructure, is reasonable, or even fair. Switching to a more refined distribution methodology, more reflective of a carrier's actual costs they claim, would help to alleviate some of the pressure facing funding of the High Cost program. Furthermore they state, it is anticipated that the growth in competitive eligible telecommunications carriers will be increasing based on the number of applications pending at the FCC, and that therefore addressing this issue is of growing significance.

Capping

Some have also proposed placing a cap, as a temporary or permanent measure, on the funds available for distribution to competitive eligible telecommunications carriers through the High Cost program. Supporters of capping claim that it will prevent the uncontrolled growth of this part of the High Cost program, which is the major contributor to the overall growth in the USF. In turn, they state, this will bring stability to the Fund and the USF contribution factor. They note that both the E-rate and the Rural Health Care programs operate under yearly caps, and with the exception of the Low Income program which has been relatively stable, the High Cost program is the only program with no built-in restraints on its growth. Others, however, are opposed to implementing a cap. They point out that placing a cap on an existing program, such as the High Cost program, could lead to confusion and be very disruptive. The dynamic, they state, is very different than capping programs, such as the E-rate and Rural Health Care, at their inception. The High Cost program, they claim, is an ongoing program responsible for providing basic voice service and connection to the network, a fundamental tenet of the universal service mandate. The placing of a cap on this program, they claim, could have significant unintended consequences which could undermine universal service goals.

The federal-state Joint Board recommended that the FCC immediately impose an interim cap on a portion of the high cost fund.[33] More specifically the Joint Board, in a May 1, 2007, action, issued a recommendation that the FCC place an interim, emergency cap on the amount of high-cost support that competitive eligible telecommunications carriers receive for each state from the High Cost program. The Joint Board recommended that the support be based on the average level of competitive eligible telecommunications carrier support distributed in that state in 2006 and that the interim cap apply until one year from the date that it makes its recommendation regarding comprehensive USF reform. This is seen as a temporary measure to curb the growth of the High Cost program until more permanent action can be taken to reform the USF. The FCC, in a May 11, 2007, action, adopted a notice of proposed rulemaking[34] seeking comment on this recommendation; comments and reply comments were received in June 2007.

On May 1, 2008, the FCC adopted, by a 3-2 vote, an interim cap on payments to competitive eligible telecommunications carriers to the High Cost fund. Total annual support is capped, with some limited exceptions,[35] at the level of support received in each state, during March 2008, on an annualized basis. The decision went into effect August 1, 2008, and will remain in place only until the FCC adopts comprehensive high cost universal service reform.[36]

Improved Targeting

An additional proposal calls for making a better effort to target areas of need by using better mapping technology (geographic information systems or GIS) or modeling to determine support for eligible telecommunications carriers. Some claim that the designated areas for support are too large and cover areas which might not be in need of USF support. Designating areas for USF support that do not need such subsidies only encourages the influx of eligible carriers into areas that they might choose to enter absent such support, they claim, and leads to the use of funds which may be more appropriately used elsewhere. Taking a more refined and precise approach, they state, will result in using funds more effectively in areas that truly need support. While most support such efforts, and see such proposals to be more long-term efforts, progress is being made. Provisions in the American Recovery and Reinvestment Act (P.L. 111-5) called for the development and maintenance of a national broadband inventory map, which was released in February 2011, and additional efforts are also underway to improve and refine data collection.[37]

Fraud, Waste, and Abuse

Directly related to the funding issue are concerns expressed by policy makers over the potential for possible fraud, waste, or abuse of the program. While all USF programs have the potential for mismanagement, the E-rate program, "due to its materiality and an initial assessment of its potential for waste, fraud, and abuse,"[38] was initially singled out for particular attention. The ability to ensure that only eligible services are funded, that funding is disbursed at the proper level of discount, that alleged services have been received, and the integrity of the competitive bidding process is upheld have been questioned. A series of Government Accountability Office (GAO) reports raising concerns about the financial oversight of the E-rate program prompted additional congressional scrutiny.[39] The USAC, as the administrator responsible for the management and oversight of the USF, initiated a number of measures to address specific E-rate concerns and extended them to all USF programs. These measures include establishing a whistleblower hotline to report violations and conducting random and targeted audits of USF program participants and contributors.

In August 2007 the FCC adopted a series of measures to safeguard the USF to deter fraud, waste, and abuse. Included in the measures taken are those that extend the debarment rules (three years) and sanctions for criminal and civil violations beyond the Schools and Libraries Program to cover all four programs; tighten rules requiring timely payments and assessing penalties or interest for late payments on USF contributors; and increase record keeping requirements for both contributors and beneficiaries. In addition the FCC, as recommended by the GAO, adopted performance measures, for all four programs and for USAC.[40]

A GAO report focusing on the USF's High Cost Program was released in July 2008. The report, *FCC Needs to Improve Performance Management and Strengthen Oversight of the High-Cost Program*, noted that the "FCC has not established performance goals or measures [for the Program]." Furthermore, the GAO stated "In the absence of performance goals and measures, the Congress and the FCC are limited in their ability to make informed decisions about the future of the high-cost program." Although the GAO acknowledged that "the FCC has begun preliminary efforts to address these shortcomings," problems with these efforts still exist.[41]

The FCC, in an August 15, 2008, action, adopted a Notice of Inquiry (NOI) seeking public "comment on ways to further strengthen management, administration, and oversight of the USF ... define more clearly the goals of the USF ... identify any additional quantifiable performance measures" and "comment on whether, and if so, to what extent the Commission's oversight of the USF can be improved."[42] Citing the steps the FCC has already taken to strengthen its oversight and management of the Fund, and the recent benefits and improvements that have been made, the FCC, however, acknowledged both the demand for "constant scrutiny and assessment of the Commission's oversight efforts" as well as the GAO's July 2008 recommendation that the FCC take steps to improve its oversight of the USF. This NOI has been initiated, according to the FCC, to continue to assess and solicit public input to develop additional rules and safeguards to protect the Fund.

The FCC's Office of the Inspector General (OIG) has also been active in pursuing oversight of the USF focusing initially on the E-rate program. Since 2002 the OIG has included in its semi- annual reports coverage of its specific efforts to oversee E-rate program activity, including audits, to ensure program integrity.[43] More recently, however, the OIG has also expanded its audit efforts to include the remaining three USF programs and audits of USF contributors.

In 2006, USAC took additional action by initiating with the OIG "a large-scale beneficiary audit program" covering all four USF programs and planned to "conduct more than 450 audits of program beneficiaries and contributors."[44] The result of this audit, which was comprised of 459 audits of USF program participants for beneficiaries of all four programs and contributors to the USF, was released by the OIG in October 2007. According to the preliminary OIG analysis of the audits, using estimates extrapolated from incomplete audits which covered beneficiaries of all four programs as well as contributors,

> in general the audits indicated compliance with the [FCC's] rules, although erroneous payment rates exceeded 9% in most USF program

segments. The audit resulted in the following erroneous payment rates: contributors payments, 5.5% ($385,000,000); Low Income, 9.5% ($75,500,000); Schools and Libraries, 12.9% ($210,000,000); High Cost, 16.6% ($618,000,000) and Rural Health Care, 20.6% ($4,450,000).[45]

USAC has completed all the audit work left unfinished in the first three rounds of the OIG USF audits and found that the actual improper payment rate was significantly lower than early estimates. For example, the "improper" payment rate in the High Cost Program dropped to 2.7% from the earlier reported 16.6% and the Schools and Libraries Program improper payment rate dropped to 8.6% form the earlier estimate of 12.8%.[46] It should also be noted that an "erroneous payment" as defined by OMB, is "any payment that should not have been made or that was made in an incorrect amount," which includes overpayments, underpayments, and the inappropriate denial of a payment or service.[47]

Despite this activity, however, the OIG continues to cite the need for additional resources, stating that "Although we have made progress in achieving the goal of establishing a more effective oversight program, we need significant increases in audit, investigative, and legal resources to achieve the goal of having a truly effective oversight program."[48] The FCC's Enforcement Bureau is the primary entity within the FCC tasked with enforcing the provisions of the Communications Act, including those related to Section 254 (universal service). The Enforcement Bureau pursues violators and initiates enforcement actions including notices of liability, suspensions, consent decrees, and debarments.[49]

The Department of Justice (DOJ) has also taken an active role in pursuing instances of deliberate fraud related, in particular, to the E-rate program. The Antitrust Division of the DOJ has established a task force to investigate E-rate fraud and has prosecuted a number of individuals and companies leading to fines, restitution, program debarments, and imprisonment.[50]

As was the case in the 110th and 111th Congresses, the 112th Congress is expected to continue its review of the USF, and all four of the programs will be subject to oversight to prevent any fraud, waste, or abuse. (See "Congressional Activity," below, for a discussion of congressional oversight activities.) Concerns about fraud and abuse are shared by both critics and supporters of the program. For example, critics of the E-rate program have used examples of fraud, waste, and abuse to call for a halt to the program or at a minimum, its suspension until additional safeguards are in place. Supporters also want to ensure the integrity of all four programs since the misuse of funds or unreasonable administrative costs not only leave the program vulnerable to critics, but would only decrease available funding to meet the program's goals.

Antideficiency Act Compliance

A more narrowly focused policy issue relating to the operation of the USF deals with Antideficiency Act (ADA) compliance. With the guidance of the Office of Management and Budget (OMB) the FCC decided, in August of 2004, that the accounting requirements contained in the ADA should be applied to the operation of the USF. Under this accounting methodology, the government is precluded from incurring obligations prior to the funds being available. E-rate fund commitment letters, which are issued far in advance of actual funds payment, were considered to be obligations. Therefore ADA compliance requires that the funds be on hand to cover obligations and the program was required to have the cash on hand to cover all of the commitment letters. USAC changed the timing of its funds distribution in order to meet this requirement, leading to a temporary four-month suspension (from August through November 2004) of E-rate funding commitments. The temporary halt in the disbursement of E-rate funding commitments, the concern that funding for other USF programs might be disrupted and that compliance might necessitate a significant increase in USF revenues, brought this issue to congressional attention.

The 108th Congress enacted legislation to provide for a one-year exemption (through December 31, 2005) from the ADA for the USF (P.L. 108-494). Since then the temporary one-year exemption has been extended six times, once to December 31, 2006, in conjunction with the Science, State, Justice, and Commerce appropriations measure (P.L. 109-108); again for an additional one-year exemption (until December 31, 2007) as part of the CR2007 (H.J.Res. 20; P.L. 110-5); once again a one-year extension (until December 31, 2008) as part of the Consolidated Appropriations Act of 2008 (H.R. 2764; P.L. 110-161); again an extension until December 31, 2009, as part of the 2009 Omnibus Appropriations bill (H.R. 1105; P.L. 111-8), again until December 31, 2010, as part of the 2010 Consolidated Appropriations Act (H.R. 3288; P.L. 111-117), and most recently until December 31, 2011, as part of the Continuing Appropriations and Surface Transportation Extensions Act, 2011 (H.R. 3082;P.L. 111-322). Whether the USF program should be required to comply with the accounting provisions contained in the ADA and if so what consequences that may have for USF programs is expected to continue to be an issue. Once again this exemption will expire at the close of the first session of the 112th Congress and Congress may choose to address this issue in a variety of ways. It may continue to enact legislation to provide short-term relief by extending the temporary exemption. Also it could choose to enact legislation, such as S. 297 pending in the 112th Congress, to provide the USF program with a permanent exemption from ADA requirements, or it may choose to take no further action allowing the temporary exemption to expire, thereby requiring the FCC to ensure, through whatever steps it deems necessary, that the USF is in full compliance with ADA requirements.

The FCC has resolved, at least temporarily, any compliance problems. Former FCC Chairman Martin, in response to questioning during his September 2006 Senate confirmation hearing, stated that the Commission has concluded that the ADA does apply to the USF. However, he assured Commerce Committee members that funds will be sufficient and that E-rate program commitment letters will not be delayed.[51] Some, however, have continued to express concern that the actions taken by the FCC are only temporary and that ADA compliance may jeopardize disbursements for not only the E-Rate program, but possibly other USF programs, and may cause a significant increase in the contribution factor.

FCC National Broadband Plan

Provisions contained in the American Recovery and Reinvestment Act of 2009 (ARRA) called for the FCC to develop, and submit to Congress, a national broadband plan (NBP) to ensure that every American has "access to broadband capability."[52] This plan, *Connecting America: The National Broadband Plan*,[53] submitted to Congress on March 16, 2010, calls for the USF to play a major role in achieving this goal. The NBP calls for the USF to be transformed, in three stages over a 10-year period, from a mechanism to support voice telephone service to one that supports the deployment, adoption, and utilization of broadband. More specifically, two new funds, the Connect America Fund and a Mobility Fund, are created, the High Cost program is phased-out, while the Low Income, E-rate, and Rural Health Care programs are modified and assume wider responsibilities. Before these transitions should occur, however, the NBP recommends that the FCC continue to take steps to improve USF performance and accountability through stronger oversight and management and enhanced data collection and reporting.[54]

High-Cost Program

The goal of the reform of the High Cost program is to transition it from one that primarily supports voice communications to one that supports a broadband platform that enables multiple applications, including voice. Although some carriers that receive high-cost funding do use it to deploy broadband capable infrastructure, currently there is no requirement that recipients of high- cost funding provide any households in their service areas with broadband. The NBP recommends that the High-Cost program be phased-out and replaced in stages, over the next 10 years, to directly support high-capacity broadband networks through a newly created Connect America Fund and a Mobility Fund.[55] More specifically, the NBP recommends that the legacy High-Cost program cease operation by 2020 and support be given solely to providers who offer broadband that offers high-quality voice through the Connect America Fund.[56]

Connect America and Mobility Funds

The NBP recommends the creation of two new funds: the Connect America Fund (CAF) and the Mobility Fund (MF). The CAF is created to support the provision of affordable broadband and voice with at least 4 Mbps actual download speed and 1 Mbps of actual upload speed. The NBP recommends that the FCC adhere to the following principles in developing the CAF: funding should only be provided in geographic areas where there is no private sector business case to provide broadband and high-quality voice grade service; there should be at most one subsidized provider of broadband per geographic area; eligibility criteria should be company and technology agnostic; ways to drive funding to efficient levels, including market-based mechanisms where appropriate, to determine the firms selected for and the levels of support given should be identified by the FCC; recipients of funding must be subject to accountability requirements and subject to enforceable timelines for achieving access as well as a broadband provider-of-last resort obligation.[57]

The MF is created to provide targeted funding to ensure that all states achieve the national average for 3G wireless coverage used for both voice and data. The MF will provide one-time support for deployment of 3G networks.

3G availability, according to the NBP, will improve the business case for the development of 4G networks in harder-to-serve areas and potentially benefit public safety users. The NBP further recommends that the FCC "... select an efficient method, such as a market-based mechanism, for supporting mobility in targeted areas."[58]

Low-Income Program

According to an FCC conducted broadband consumer survey 36% of non-adopters of broadband cited a financial reason as the main reason they do not have broadband service at home.[59] To address this barrier the NBP recommends that both Low-Income programs, Lifeline and Link Up, be expanded to increase broadband adoption levels for low-income households.[60] The NBP recommends that the FCC require that ETC's receiving funds permit Lifeline customers to apply Lifeline discounts to any service or package that includes basic voice service. In this way Lifeline customers can apply their discounts to bundled offerings (i.e., voice and data) making broadband service more affordable.[61]

The NBP also recommends that the FCC integrate the expanded Lifeline and Link Up programs with state and local e-government efforts as well as facilitate pilot programs to obtain information to determine what program design elements most effectively increase adoption rates. Upon completion of the pilot programs the FCC is directed to report to Congress on these results and begin a "... full scale implementation of a low-income program for broadband."[62]

Schools and Libraries and Rural Health Care Programs

The NBP contains almost a dozen recommendations to modernize and improve the E-rate program.[63] These recommendations focus on three goals: improve flexibility, deployment, and use of infrastructure; improve program efficiency; and foster innovation. Among these recommendations are those that call for the FCC to initiate rulemakings to streamline the applications process, raise the yearly cap on funding to account for inflation, and set goals for minimum broadband connectivity for schools and libraries; adopt the pending notice of proposed rulemaking to remove barriers to off-hours community use of E-rate funded resources; expand E- rate support for internal connections to more schools and libraries; improve data collection efforts on use of E-rate funds; provide more flexibility to purchase the lowest-cost broadband solutions; and make overall broadband-related E-rate program expenses more cost-efficient.

Citing the importance of health care to the lives of consumers and its importance to the national economy the NBP calls for reform of the Rural Health Care Program. The NBP calls for the restructuring and expansion of its program components.[64] The NBP recommends that the existing Internet Access Fund be replaced with a Health Care Broadband Access Fund, subsidy support be increased beyond the current 25%, the application process be simplified, and, unlike the present Fund, eligibility be expanded beyond rural health care providers to include both rural and urban health care providers, based on need.[65] It also recommends that the FCC establish a Health Care Broadband Infrastructure Fund, based on lessons learned from the Pilot Program, to subsidize network deployment to health care delivery locations where existing network infrastructure is insufficient.[66] Additional recommendations for the Rural Health Care Program include those that suggest the FCC expand the definition of eligible health care provider to include long-term care facilities, off-site administrative offices, data centers and other similar locations and suggest that Congress consider expanding the definition for eligibility to include providing support of certain for-profit entities.[67] To help protect against, fraud, waste, and abuse the NBP recommends that the FCC require that participating institutions meet outcomes-based performance measures to measure the efficient use of health IT to ensure that funds are used to not only build and deploy broadband infrastructure, but to improve the country's health delivery system.[68]

The NBP also recommends that federal and state policies, including USF policies, should facilitate demand aggregation for broader community use and not develop policies that result in dedicated, single purpose networks, such as school networks funded by E-rate, or hospitals funded through the Rural Health Care program. Citing the extremely low connection rates and other unique challenges facing Tribal lands, the NBP specifically recommends that Congress amend the 1934 Communications Act to provide the FCC with the discretion to permit anchor institutions on Tribal lands to share broadband network capacity funded through the E-rate and rural health care programs with other community institutions designated by Tribal governments.[69] The NBP also recommends that Congress consider amending the 1934 Communications Act to help Tribal libraries overcome barriers to E-rate eligibility arising from state laws.[70]

Funding

The NBP calls for a major restructuring of the USF, but recommends that the funding level be maintained close to its current size (in 2010 dollars). The NBP recommends that $15.5 billion (present value in 2010 dollars) be shifted, through selected reforms, over the next decade from the existing USF High Cost program to support the transition to broadband.[71] However, the NBP also recommends that if Congress wishes to accelerate this transition it could allocate to the CAF additional general funds of "... a few billion dollars per year over a two to three year period."[72]

The NBP also recommends that the USF contribution base be broadened and the FCC "... adopt revised contribution methodology rules to ensure that USF remains sustainable over time."[73] It does not, however, provide specific guidance on how this should be accomplished. Furthermore, the NBP acknowledges the relationship between its broadband goals and the USF contribution factor and seeks to "... minimize the burden of increasing universal service contributions on consumers."[74]

Implementation

The NBP contains over 208 recommendations involving a wide range of Executive Branch agencies, Congress, nonfederal and nongovernmental entities as well as the FCC; approximately 60 of these recommendations call for FCC action. The FCC has initiated a series of proceedings which will provide further guidance regarding how the FCC-specific recommendations will be implemented. These proceedings will flush out the details and give all stakeholders an opportunity to provide input into how the FCC should proceed to implement the recommendations contained in the NBP. The FCC also announced, on June 14, 2010, the establishment of a Universal Service Working Group, an in-house multi-bureau group to facilitate collaboration between the bureaus to further the universal service goals established in the National Broadband Plan.[75]

High Cost Program

The FCC took two major steps towards implementing the NBP recommendations to reform the USF High Cost program by adopting two Notices of Proposed Rulemaking: one to create a Mobility Fund to address access to advanced wireless services; and the other to create a Connect America Fund to promote the development of broadband services. The FCC is scheduled to vote on these rulemakings on October 27, 2011.

Mobility Fund

The FCC adopted, on October 14, 2010, a Notice of Proposed Rulemaking (NPRM) to seek comment on proposals to create a Mobility Fund (MF) to improve the coverage of 3G wireless, or better, services.[76] Under this proposal the MF would provide one-time support, ranging from a total of $100 million to $300 million, to areas that currently do not have access to advanced wireless services, defined as those that offer mobile wireless voice telecommunications services, e-mail, and Internet access. The NPRM proposes using a reverse auction mechanism to make the support to service providers to extend 3G or better mobile voice and Internet service coverage in specified unserved areas.[77] The NPRM also seeks comment on a range of additional proposals, including whether to make support available to any unserved area in the nation or target support by making it available to limited areas; minimum performance and coverage requirements for MF support; suggested administrative, management, and oversight functions to deter fraud, waste, and abuse; and whether the MF initiative should be repeated. The comment and reply periods are now closed.

Connect America Fund

The FCC proposed, in a Notice of Proposed Rulemaking (NPRM) and Further Notice of Proposed Rulemaking (FNPRM), to eliminate and shift the money from the current High Cost program by establishing a new Connect America Fund. Coupled with this action will be a shift in focus from voice to subsidize broadband, which would include voice access. The NPRM and FNPRM, adopted on February 8, 2011, call for this transition to occur in three phases over the next 10 years.[78] Numerous steps are proposed, to complete the transition of the current High Cost program to a "new, more efficient, broadband-focused Connect America Fund," to accelerate broadband deployment. The USF concept is broadened to include the adoption of the principle "that universal service support should be directed where possible to networks that provide advanced services, as well as voice services" and suggests that broadband and mobility should be added to the definition of supported services. The proposal calls for the use of a reverse auction to provide broadband to unserved areas by awarding a "significant amount of funding" (from $500 million to more than $1 billion) in 2012 as a one-time infusion, with the potential for future auctions. Recipients could be either fixed (wireline or wireless) or mobile wireless providers.

The notices seek comment on a wide range of proposals, some more immediate and others more long term, to complete this transition. Included among these proposals, which are open for comment by all stakeholders, are whether the use of reverse auctions, or another mechanism, is appropriate to bring broadband to underserved areas; whether the per-line subsidy should be capped at $3,000 per year in high-cost areas in the continental United States, absent exceptional circumstances; whether existing carriers should be given the first option to continue serving a given area, or whether some other option should be pursued; whether the minimum broadband speed should be set at 4 megabits per second actual downstream and 1 megabit per second actual upstream, or 3 megabits/768 kilobits per second, or a different speed requirement; how often broadband speed requirements should be reevaluated; what public interest obligations should apply to eligible telecommunications carriers; ending the identical support rule; adopting performance goals and metrics; the appropriate role of the states in preserving and advancing universal service, and the expected level of financial commitment from the states. The comment and reply periods are closed.

Low Income Program

The FCC adopted, on March 3, 2011, a notice of proposed rulemaking (NPRM) seeking comment on a set of reforms to "modernize and drive tougher accountability measures" for the Lifeline and Link Up components of the Low Income program.[79] The FCC is soliciting comments on proposed changes that will better position the program to, among other concerns, take on the expanded role, detailed in the NBP, as a provider of broadband service. The NPRM seeks to modernize the program to accommodate broadband while still controlling program size, strengthen program administration and accountability, increase protections against fraud, waste, and abuse, and improve enrollment and outreach efforts. More specifically the proposed reforms include those to create a National Accountability Database to verify consumer eligibility and a uniform national framework for validating ongoing eligibility; eliminate funding for services that go unused for more than 60 days; evaluate the need for a temporary or permanent cap to control program growth; permit eligible households to use Lifeline discounts on bundled voice and broadband service offerings; address the unique situations facing residents on Tribal lands; and establish pilot programs, from savings from reforms, to test strategies for supporting broadband services. Comments were due April 21, 2011, and replies May 10 and 25, 2011.

Separately, the FCC adopted, on June 17, 2011, a report and order to address "potential waste" in the Lifeline and Link Up programs by strengthening rules to prevent support payments for multiple services to the same individual.[80] The FCC clarified that an eligible consumer may only receive support for "a single telephone line in their principle residence" and codified that "... no qualifying consumer is permitted to receive more than one Lifeline subsidy concurrently."[81] This clarification is necessary, according to the FCC, since consumers now have multiple Lifeline options, through wireless carriers, in contrast to the past when most consumers only had one option for telephone service through their incumbent telephone company's wireline service. To further insure that no duplication occurs the FCC has required that: USAC notify consumers that are receiving multiple benefits that they are allowed only one Lifeline-subsidized phone service; consumers in violation be given 30 days to select which subsidized service they wish to keep; and companies not chosen must de-enroll the consumer from the Lifeline service within five days after notification by USAC that they have been deselected by the consumer. The expectation is that the dollars saved by removing duplicative Lifeline support will be used to help cover costs associated with a yet-to-be-established pilot program to help expand the Low Income program to provide broadband services.

Schools and Libraries Program

Reform of the Schools and Libraries Program (E-Rate Program) is also underway. The FCC adopted, September 23, 2010, an order to "upgrade(d) and modernize(d)" the E-rate program.[82] While significant these new rules are viewed by the FCC as "a first stage in a multi-stage upgrade of the E-rate program."[83]

Included among the proposals that were adopted are those that allow applicants to lease broadband from a wider range of options, including dark fiber; permit schools to allow community use of E-rate funded services outside of school hours; index the yearly $2.25 billion funding cap to account for inflation as of the FY2010 funding year; support eligible services to the residential portion of schools that serve students in special circumstances (e.g., schools on Tribal lands, schools that meet special medical needs; juvenile justice facilities); permit schools and libraries to receive consideration when disposing of and/or recycling E-rate-funded obsolete equipment; streamline the application process; increase protections against fraud, waste, and abuse by codifying the competitive bidding requirements and clarifying ethics obligations; and establish a limited pilot program to support off-campus wireless connectivity for portable learning devices outside of regular school or library learning hours.[84]

Rural Health Care Program

A NPRM initiating reforms to the Rural Health Care Program to expand the reach and use of broadband connectivity by health care providers was adopted on July 15, 2010.[85] The FCC maintains the existing $400 million funding cap but proposes three major changes to the existing program: creation of a new health infrastructure program that would support up to 85% of the new regional or statewide network broadband project construction costs to serve public and non- profit healthcare providers (a 15% private funding match would be required); creation of a health broadband services program that would subsidize 50% of the monthly recurring costs for access to broadband services for eligible entities; and expansion of the definition of "eligible health care provider" to include such entities as skilled nursing facilities, renal dialysis centers and facilities, data centers, and administrative offices. Comment is also sought on issues such as prioritizing funding requests; establishing performance measures; and whether there are any "unique circumstances" in Tribal lands or insular areas "that would necessitate a different approach." Comments and replies on the NPRM have already been filed.

Congressional Activity

112th Congress

It is anticipated that Universal Service Fund reform will continue to be a topic of congressional interest. Both the House Energy and Commerce Committee and the Senate Commerce, Science, and Transportation Committee have included USF reform on their agendas of issues for consideration and oversight. The Senate Commerce Committee held a hearing on October 12, 2011, on reforming the USF, with a particular focus on the High Cost Fund. The chairman and ranking members of the House Energy and Commerce Committee and the Subcommittee on Telecommunications and Technology have requested, in a June 22, 2011, letter to the FCC, USF data focusing on the High Cost and Low Income programs to assist them to better understand the USF and its operations.

Three stand-alone measures (H.R. 2163, H.R. 3118, S. 297) relating to USF have been introduced to date. Representative Matsui introduced, on June 14, 2011, H.R. 2163, the "Broadband Affordability Act of 2011." This measure expands the USF's low-income Lifeline program to include subscribership to broadband services at reduced rates. Eligibility requirements are the same as those used for the current Lifeline telephone program. Provisions require the FCC to establish regulations to prevent eligible households from receiving more than a single subsidy per household. The FCC is tasked with establishing the amount of support and determining whether state matching funds will be required for participation as well as determining how broadband service is defined. Broadband service providers are required to obtain FCC authorization to participate in the program, but the program is neutral as to what type of technology is used and does not require a provider to be classified as eligible telecommunications carrier to participate.

H.R. 3118, introduced on October 6, 2011, by Representative Farenthold, contains provisions to freeze USF funding at 2011 levels and reform the Low Income program More specifically the bill will: rescind the forbearance authority which is used by eligible carriers to offer prepaid wireless Lifeline service; freeze USF funding at 2011 levels and transfer, on a yearly basis, $500 million of those funds to the General Fund of the Treasury; and implement reforms to the Low Income Program, including the establishment of a database, to help prevent fraud, waste, and abuse.

S. 297, introduced February 7, 2011, by Senator Rockefeller, amends Section 254 of the Communications Act of 1934 to provide for a permanent exemption for the USF from the Antideficiency Act.

111th Congress

The House Subcommittee on Communications, Technology, and the Internet and the Senate Commerce Committee are among the committees that held hearings on USF reform and the FCC's national broadband plan. Former House Communications Subcommittee Chairman Boucher and Representative Terry released, on July 22, 2010, a bill (H.R. 5828) which addressed comprehensive reform of the USF. H.R. 5828, the "Universal Service Reform Act of 2010," provided for a major restructuring of the USF. Included among its provisions were those that expanded the USF to include support for broadband services; widened the contribution base to support the USF; required the FCC to develop new cost models for calculating USF support; limited fund eligibility; prohibited the FCC from adopting a primary line restriction; and directed the FCC to establish performance goals and measures for each program to strengthen accountability. The House Communications Subcommittee held a hearing, September 16, 2010, on the measure, but no further action was taken.

Then-House Energy and Commerce Committee Chairman Waxman and other committee members also expressed interest in examining USF reform and released USF data requested by committee and subcommittee members from the FCC, focusing on USF support, that is being used to better understand the USF and its operations.[86]

Legislation (H.R. 3646, H.R. 4619, S. 2879) to expand the role of the USF was introduced. In a move to address the issue of affordability of broadband for low-income households Representative Matsui introduced, on September 24, 2009, H.R. 3646, the "Broadband Affordability Act of 2009." This measure expanded the USF's low-income Lifeline program to include subscribership to broadband services at reduced rates. Eligibility requirements were the same as those used for the current Lifeline telephone program. The FCC was tasked with establishing the amount of support and determining whether state matching funds will be required for participation. Broadband service provider were required to obtain FCC authorization to participate in the program, but the program was neutral as to what type of technology is used and did not require a provider to be classified as eligible telecommunications carrier. H.R. 4619, the "E-Rate 2.0 Act of 2010," introduced February 9, 2010, by Representative Markey, expanded the E-rate program to address access to broadband. This bill created three temporary pilot programs to expand access to broadband by: extending funding to qualifying low-income students for vouchers to be used for monthly service fees for broadband services at home; expanding the E- rate program to include discounts for community colleges and head start programs; and funding an electronic books project. H.R. 4619 also called for the FCC to take steps to "streamline and simplify" the E-rate program application process and adjusted the current $2.25 billion annual program cap to account for inflation.

S. 2879, the "Broadband Opportunity and Affordability Act," introduced on December 11, 2009, by Senator Rockefeller, directed the FCC to conduct a two-year pilot program by expanding the Lifeline program, to include broadband services. The FCC was tasked with establishing the amount of support, determining whether state matching funds would be required for participation, and ensuring that the program is technologically neutral in terms of providers. After 18 months of operation the FCC was required to submit a report to the Senate Commerce and the House Energy and Commerce committees on the status of the pilot program. S. 2879 also required the FCC to initiate a notice of inquiry to determine whether the Link Up program should be expanded to reduce the cost of initiating broadband service and report its findings to the Senate Commerce and House Energy and Commerce committees.

Action to address the Antideficiency Act (ADA) exemption was also undertaken. In keeping with previous Congressional efforts legislation to extend the ADA exemption for one year periods was enacted. The Consolidated Appropriations Act, 2010, which was enacted into law (P.L. 111-117), contained a provision to extend the USF ADA exemption until December 31, 2010; this exemption was extended once again, until December 31, 2011, as part of the Continuing Appropriations and Surface Transportation Extensions Act, 2011 (H.R. 3082; P.L. 111-322). S. 348, introduced January 29, 2009, by Senate Commerce Committee Chairman Rockefeller, and H.R. 2135, introduced April 28, 2009, by Representative Rehberg, as well as provisions contained in H.R. 5828, provided for a permanent ADA exemption for the USF, but none of these measures received further consideration.

An additional provision pertinent to the USF is also contained in P.L. 111-117. This provision prohibits the FCC from using its FY2010 funds to limit USF support to a primary, or single, line.

APPENDIX A. USF CONTRIBUTION FACTORS AND STATE SUPPORT

Table A-1. Universal Service Fund Contribution Factors

Year	Quarter	Factor
2004	First	8.7%
	Second	8.7
	Third	8.9
	Fourth	8.9
2005	First	10.7%
	Second	11.1
	Third	10.2
	Fourth	10.2
2006	First	10.2%
	Second	10.9
	Third	10.5
	Fourth	9.1
2007	First	9.7%
	Second	11.7
	Third	11.3
	Fourth	11.0
2008	First	10.2%
	Second	11.3
	Third	11.4
	Fourth	11.4
2009	First	9.5%
	Second	11.3
	Third	12.9
	Fourth	12.3
2010	First	14.1%
	Second	15.3
	Third	13.6
	Fourth	12.9
2011	First	15.5%
	Second	14.9
	Third	14.4
	Fourth	15.3

Source: Quarterly Public Notices on universal service contribution factors. Federal Communications Commission.

Table A-2. USF Support by State 2009

Universal Service Support Mechanisms by State: 2009
(Annual Payments and Contributions in Thousands)

State or Jurisdiction	Payments from USF to Service Providers [1]						Estimated Contributions [2]		Estimated Net Dollar Flow [3]
	High-Cost Support	Low-Income Support	Schools & Libraries	Rural Health Care	Total				
					Amount	% of Total	Amount	% of Total	
Alabama	$100,061	$25,652	$28,922	$229	$154,864	2.13%	$118,935	1.60%	$35,929
Alaska	168,272	24,480	22,542	29,122	244,417	3.37%	19,511	0.26%	224,906
American Samoa	3,939	39	4,282	141	8,400	0.12%	516	0.01%	7,885
Arizona	67,204	21,813	49,278	1,954	140,249	1.93%	146,289	1.97%	-6,040
Arkansas	148,253	4,019	14,974	401	167,647	2.31%	68,063	0.91%	99,584
California	107,508	194,238	281,161	942	583,849	8.05%	822,527	11.05%	-238,678
Colorado	79,397	2,905	14,452	234	96,989	1.34%	132,967	1.79%	-35,979
Connecticut	-390	5,389	22,255	0	27,253	0.38%	99,000	1.33%	-71,746
Delaware	226	661	831	0	1,719	0.02%	27,334	0.37%	-25,615
Dist. of Columbia	0	1,077	8,440	0	9,518	0.13%	34,291	0.46%	-24,773
Florida	70,396	74,720	75,933	854	221,903	3.06%	495,839	6.66%	-273,936
Georgia	136,139	33,514	67,875	1,989	239,517	3.30%	243,770	3.27%	-4,253
Guam	16,650	307	334	101	17,392	0.24%	3,904	0.05%	13,488
Hawaii	58,416	495	1,930	196	61,037	0.84%	36,936	0.50%	24,101
Idaho	50,779	3,603	4,750	257	59,389	0.82%	37,003	0.50%	22,386
Illinois	74,939	13,649	63,987	1,389	153,964	2.12%	307,767	4.13%	-153,803
Indiana	74,418	4,917	22,702	822	102,858	1.42%	145,484	1.95%	-42,626
Iowa	127,435	4,314	9,899	571	142,218	1.96%	67,353	0.90%	74,865
Kansas	230,301	3,128	15,278	327	249,034	3.43%	65,855	0.88%	183,179
Kentucky	101,805	9,802	28,136	708	140,451	1.94%	97,031	1.30%	43,420
Louisiana	156,494	12,011	35,427	40	203,972	2.81%	106,388	1.43%	97,584
Maine	27,443	6,798	6,159	63	40,463	0.56%	31,580	0.42%	8,883
Maryland	3,966	858	9,850	0	14,673	0.20%	163,148	2.19%	-148,475
Massachusetts	2,413	21,043	22,729	150	46,335	0.64%	169,539	2.28%	-123,204
Michigan	63,193	30,329	51,300	941	145,763	2.01%	212,378	2.85%	-66,615
Minnesota	127,037	7,043	17,168	2,637	153,885	2.12%	118,125	1.59%	35,760
Mississippi	281,267	9,880	29,982	148	321,278	4.43%	66,750	0.90%	254,528
Missouri	108,639	8,198	26,168	578	143,583	1.98%	143,845	1.93%	-262
Montana	79,855	3,875	4,201	843	88,774	1.22%	25,215	0.34%	63,560
Nebraska	116,611	2,157	9,004	1,391	129,163	1.78%	41,711	0.56%	87,452
Nevada	25,570	2,906	4,295	73	32,845	0.45%	69,280	0.93%	-36,435
New Hampshire	8,576	746	2,285	11	11,617	0.16%	36,248	0.49%	-24,631
New Jersey	1,058	15,053	37,106	0	53,218	0.73%	248,888	3.34%	-195,671
New Mexico	71,391	14,595	26,912	386	113,284	1.56%	48,248	0.65%	65,036
New York	44,967	60,082	237,857	62	342,968	4.73%	480,589	6.46%	-137,621
North Carolina	85,635	33,899	57,744	312	177,591	2.45%	225,632	3.03%	-48,041
North Dakota	94,452	3,101	3,560	1,201	102,314	1.41%	16,438	0.22%	85,877
Northern Mariana Is.	1,309	168	1,142	0	2,619	0.04%	806	0.01%	1,813
Ohio	33,856	36,707	63,578	426	134,569	1.85%	259,335	3.48%	-124,767
Oklahoma	142,547	71,141	35,314	809	249,812	3.44%	78,444	1.05%	171,368
Oregon	78,826	5,413	15,057	312	99,608	1.37%	89,978	1.21%	9,629
Pennsylvania	57,770	21,603	69,524	109	149,006	2.05%	307,789	4.13%	-158,783
Puerto Rico	74,387	28,854	8,735	0	111,977	1.54%	69,074	0.93%	42,902
Rhode Island	34	3,425	5,466	0	8,925	0.12%	24,456	0.33%	-15,531
South Carolina	98,376	9,629	37,412	47	145,463	2.00%	110,601	1.49%	34,863
South Dakota	97,338	3,334	5,536	1,388	107,595	1.48%	19,168	0.26%	88,427
Tennessee	58,896	31,349	49,110	242	139,598	1.92%	157,946	2.12%	-18,349
Texas	262,049	101,914	155,009	889	519,860	7.16%	518,620	6.97%	1,241
Utah	19,221	3,808	15,628	666	39,323	0.54%	55,550	0.75%	-16,226
Vermont	21,208	2,576	1,382	115	25,282	0.35%	18,062	0.24%	7,220
Virgin Islands	15,986	77	2,014	74	18,152	0.25%	5,136	0.07%	13,016
Virginia	72,933	15,198	29,056	731	117,918	1.63%	209,307	2.81%	-91,389
Washington	94,459	17,704	27,850	80	140,092	1.93%	155,701	2.09%	-15,609
West Virginia	58,640	1,189	10,647	308	70,784	0.98%	49,119	0.66%	21,665
Wisconsin	139,287	9,341	22,569	5,281	176,478	2.43%	125,210	1.68%	51,268
Wyoming	50,740	469	3,559	148	54,917	0.76%	15,103	0.20%	39,813
Total	$4,292,180	$1,025,194	$1,878,295	$60,698	$7,256,367	100.00%	$7,443,781	100.00%	-$187,414

Source: Universal Service Monitoring Report, Table 1.12, Federal Communications Commission. December 2010.

Notes: Figures may not add due to rounding. Support payments do not include quarterly true-ups. USF is an abbreviation for the Universal Service Fund.

[1] Data from USAC's Annual Report.

[2] Estimated contributions include administrative cost of approximately $187 million, as shown in USAC's Annual Report. Allocations of contributions among states is an FCC staff estimate.

[3] Net dollar flow is positive when payments from USF to carriers exceed contributions to USF. Total is negative because of administrative expenses

APPENDIX B. CONGRESSIONAL ACTIVITY: 110TH CONGRESS

The 110th Congress took an active role regarding USF oversight and reform. Legislative measures to address the reform, restructuring, and expansion into broadband of the USF were introduced (S. 101, S. 711, S. 3491, H.R. 42, H.R. 2054, H.R. 5806, H.R. 6320, H.R. 6356, H.R. 7000), but not enacted. The Senate Commerce Committee held a March 1, 2007, hearing on the challenges facing the USF and the House Telecommunications Subcommittee held a June 24, 2008, hearing focusing on the future of universal service including the role of broadband and its role in the future of the program. FCC oversight hearings held by the Senate Commerce Committee and the House Telecommunications Subcommittee, as well as hearings on broadband deployment held by the House Small Business Committee included examination of USF issues. Furthermore, the Senate Commerce Committee held a June 12, 2007, hearing to examine the federal-state Joint Board's recommendation that the FCC place an interim, emergency cap on the amount of high- cost support that competitive eligible telecommunications carriers receive for each state from the High Cost program. (For a further discussion of this proposal see the section on "Capping," above.)

The House Oversight and Government Reform Committee under the direction of then-Chairman Waxman requested information from industry recipients as part of an oversight investigation of the USF. The inquiry focused on the High Cost Fund portion of the program and requested information from 24 companies that, according to the FCC, are the top 10 recipients of federal high cost funds from 2006 through 2008 as well as the those that have received the 10 highest per-line subsidies, by location, for 2006 and 2007. According to a memorandum[87] Chairman Waxman sent to the committee, he was not accusing any of these companies of wrongdoing, but felt that the gathering of additional information about and committee oversight of the USF program will "benefit" the program and "may offer useful information to the state and federal policymakers as they formulate proposals for USF reform." This inquiry, he further stated, "is consistent with the Committee's strong interest in ensuring accountability in both the government and private sector."[88]

A provision to extend for one year (until December 31, 2007) the USF exemption from the Antideficiency Act (ADA) was passed as part of the FY2007 continuing resolution (H.J.Res. 20) and was signed into law (P.L.

110-5). Another one-year extension (until December 31, 2008) was passed as part of the Consolidated Appropriations Act of 2008 (H.R. 2764; P.L. 110-161). Two stand-alone measures (H.R. 278, S. 609) as well as provisions contained in S. 101 and H.R. 2054 calling for a permanent ADA exemption were introduced, but not enacted. Two additional provisions pertinent to the USF are also contained in P.L. 110-161. One provision prohibits the FCC from using its FY2008 funds to limit USF support to a primary, or single, line. The other provision permits the transfer of up to $21,480,000 of FY2008 funds from the USF to monitor the USF to prevent and remedy fraud, waste, and abuse, and to conduct audits and investigations by the OIG.

P.L. 110-161 (H.R. 2764)

Consolidated Appropriations Act, 2008. For the USF extends for one year (until December 31, 2008) the USF exemption for the Antideficiency Act (Title V, §510); prohibits the FCC from using its FY2008 funds to limit USF support to a primary, or single, line (Title V, §511); permits the transfer of up to $21,480,000 of FY2008 funds from the USF to monitor the Program to prevent and remedy fraud, waste, and abuse, and to conduct audits and investigations by the OIG (Title V, FCC Salaries and Expenses). Signed by President, December 26, 2007.

P.L. 110-5 (H.J.Res. 20)

Revised Continuing Appropriations Resolution, 2007. Extends for one year (until December 31, 2007) the USF exemption for the Antideficiency Act (§20946). Signed by President, February 15, 2007.

H.R. 42 (Velázquez)

The Serving Everyone with Reliable, Vital Internet, Communications, and Education Act of 2007. A bill to amend the Communications Act of 1934 to continue in effect and expand the Lifeline Assistance Program and the Link Up Program, and for other purposes. Introduced January 4, 2007; referred to the Subcommittee on Telecommunications and the Internet February 2, 2007.

H.R. 278 (Cubin)

A bill to amend section 254 of the Communications Act of 1934 to provide that the funds received as universal service contributions and the universal service support programs established pursuant to that section are not subject to certain provisions of Title 31, United states Code, commonly known as the Antideficiency Act. Introduced January 5, 2007; referred to the Subcommittee on Telecommunications and the Internet February 2, 2007.

H.R. 2054 (Boucher)

The Universal Service Reform Act of 2007. A bill to reform the universal service provisions of the Communications Act of 1934, and for other purposes. Introduced April 26, 2007; referred to the Committee on Energy and Commerce.

H.R. 2829 (Serrano)

The Financial Services and General Government Appropriations Bill, 2008. A bill to provide for FY2008 appropriations for selected agencies including the FCC.

The House-passed version contained a provision to authorize the FCC to transfer up to $20.98 million from the USF to monitor and conduct audits of the USF to prevent fraud, waste, and abuse; passed (240-179) the House, June 28, 2007. The Senate Appropriations Committee-passed version contains language that extends for one year (December 31, 2008) the exemption of the USF from the Antideficiency Act (Title V, §501) and prohibits limiting USF funding to a single, or primary line (Title V, §502). Reported out of committee July 13, 2007 (S.Rept. 110-129).

H.R. 5806 (Rush)

The School Emergency Notification Deployment Act. A bill to permit universal support (E-rate funds) to public and nonprofit elementary and secondary schools under the Communications Act of 1934 to be used for enhanced emergency notification services. Introduced April 15, 2008; referred to the Committee on Energy and Commerce.

H.R. 6320 (Markey)

The Twenty-first Century Communications and Video Accessibility Act of 2008. A bill to ensure that individuals with disabilities have access to emerging Internet Protocol-based communication and video programming technologies in the 21st Century. Introduced June 19, 2008; referred to the Committee on Energy and Commerce.

H.R. 6356 (Barton)

The Universal Service Reform, Accountability, and Efficiency Act of 2008. A bill to reform the collection and distribution of universal service support under the Communications Act of 1934. Introduced June 24, 2008; referred to the Committee on Energy and Commerce.

H.R. 7000 (Waxman)

The Universal Roaming Act of 2008. A bill to require any eligible carrier receiving universal service support for the provision of services for rural, insular, and high cost areas to offer automatic roaming services to any technically compatible carrier upon request. Introduced September 23, 2008; referred to the Committee on Energy and Commerce.

S. 101 (Stevens)

The Universal Service for Americans Act, or USA Act. A bill to update and reinvigorate universal service provided under the Communications Act of 1934 and to exempt universal service contributions and disbursements from the Antideficiency Act. Introduced January 4, 2007; referred to the Committee on Commerce, Science, and Transportation January 4, 2007.

S. 609 (Rockefeller)

A bill to amend Section 254 of the Communications Act of 1934 to provide that funds received as universal service contributions and the universal service support programs established pursuant to that section are not subject to certain provisions of Title 31, United States Code, commonly known as the Antideficiency Act. Introduced February 15, 2007; referred to the Committee on Commerce, Science, and Transportation February 15, 2007.

S. 711 (Smith)

The Universal Service for the 21st Century Act. A bill to amend the Communications Act of 1934 to expand the contribution base for universal service, establish a separate account within the universal service fund to support the deployment of broadband service in unserved areas of the United States, and for other purposes. Introduced February 28, 2007; referred to the Committee on Commerce, Science, and Transportation.

S. 3491 (Stevens)

The Telehealth for America Act of 2008. A bill to amend the Communications Act of 1934 to improve the effectiveness of rural health care support under section 254(h) of that act. Introduced September 16, 2008; referred to the Committee on Commerce, Science, and Transportation.

End Notes

[1] Communications Act of 1934, as amended [47 U.S.C.151 et seq.].

[2] See http://www.usac.org/about/universal-service/fund-facts/fund-facts.aspx.

[3] For a discussion of issues relating to broadband deployment, access, and regulation see CRS Report R40230, *The Evolving Broadband Infrastructure: Expansion, Applications, and Regulation*, by Patricia Moloney Figliola, Angele A. Gilroy, and Lennard G. Kruger.

[4] Communications Act of 1934, as amended, Title I §1[47 U.S.C. 151].

[5] Specific federal programs such as the Rural Telephone Bank and Rural Utilities Service loan programs were also developed to assist high cost rural areas.

[6] Section 254 (d) also states that other providers of interstate telecommunications may be required to contribute to the preservation and advancement of universal service if it is in the public interest.

[7] Many states participate in or have programs that mirror FCC universal service mechanisms to help promote universal service goals within their individual states.

[8] For further information on the FCC's universal service support mechanisms see http://www.fcc.gov/cgb/consumerfacts/universalservice.html.

[9] The High-Cost Fund consists of five sub-funds which address specific needs: High-Cost Loop Support; High-Cost Model Support; Local Switching Support; Interstate Common Line Support; and Interstate Access Support.

[10] Support is not given directly to the subscriber but to their designated telecommunications service provider, who in turn charge these subscribers lower rates, or in the case of some wireless options no charge for the basic package.

[11] In a September 23, 2010, order modifying the E-rate program the FCC included among its modifications the indexing of the $2.25 billion cap of the program to account for inflation starting with funding year 2010 of the program; during periods of deflation the funding cap will remain at the level from the previous funding year. *In the Matter of Schools and Libraries Universal Service Support Mechanism; A National Broadband Plan For Our Future, CC Docket No. 02-6*; GN Docket No. 09-51 (paras. 34-40). Available at http://hraunfoss.fcc.gov/edocs-public/attachmatch/FCC-10-175A1.pdf.

[12] Any health care provider that does not have toll-free access to the Internet can receive support. Support is available for limited long distance charges for accessing the Internet. This has become an increasingly rare occurrence, however, and the last time such support was given was in 2001.

[13] For additional information on this program, including funding commitments, see the RHCD website: http://www.universalservice.org/rhc/.

[14] These companies include wireline telephone companies, wireless telephone companies, paging service providers and interconnected Voice over Internet Protocol (VoIP) providers.

[15] These providers have expressed concern over their inability to distinguish between their interstate and intrastate revenues. However, in lieu of using the safe harbor percentage they do have the option to submit traffic study data to show that they should contribute less.

[16] *FCC Updates Approach for Assessing Contributions to the Federal Universal Service Fund.* Available at http://hraunfoss.fcc.gov/edocs_public/attachmatch/DOC

[17] It should also be noted that an assessed provider is not permitted to collect any fees from a lifeline or link-up subscriber, unless that subscriber has incurred long-distance charges.

[18] These figures are based on USAC 2009 unaudited financial data. Detailed data, including state-specific information, on USF support can be found in the Universal Service Company 2009 Annual Report at http://www.usac.org/_res/documents/about/pdf/USAC-annual-report-2009.pdf.

[19] Contribution allocation among states is an FCC staff estimate. Net dollar flow is annual payments minus estimated contributions.

[20] For a breakdown of USF distributions and contributions by state for previous years see Table 1.12 of the FCC's Universal Service Monitoring Report. Monitoring reports issued since 1991 are available at http://www.fcc.gov/wcb/ iatd/monitor.html.

[21] 47 U.S.C. §254 (b)(5).

[22] For a discussion of the issues surrounding the "digital divide" see CRS Report RL30719, *Broadband Internet Access and the Digital Divide: Federal Assistance Programs*, by Lennard G. Kruger and Angele A. Gilroy.

[23] For a summary of the Joint Board's recommendations see http://hraunfoss.fcc.gov/edocs_public/attachmatch/FCC-07J-4A1.pdf.

[24] For example, provisions contained in the American Recovery and Reinvestment Act (P.L. 111-5) call for the disbursement of $7.2 billion in broadband funding, and the USDA's Rural Utilities Service has a broadband loan and grant program for rural areas. For information on these programs see CRS Report R40436, *Broadband Infrastructure Programs in the American Recovery and Reinvestment Act*, by Lennard G. Kruger, CRS Report R41164,

Distribution of Broadband Stimulus Grants and Loans: Applications and Awards, by Lennard G. Kruger, and CRS Report RL33816, *Broadband Loan and Grant Programs in the USDA's Rural Utilities Service*, by Lennard G. Kruger.

[25] However, it should be noted that in a reversal of this trend, the FCC, in an August 2005 decision, exempted digital subscriber line (DSL) service from USF assessments on the basis of its August 2005 "information service" classification.

[26] See *FCC Updates Approach For Assessing Contributions To The Federal Universal Service Fund*, available at http://hraunfoss.fcc.gov/edocs_public/attachmatch/DOC

[27] For a more detailed discussion supporting this proposal see The USF by the Numbers Coalition, *The Benefits of a Numbers-Based Collection for Universal Service*. Available at http://files.ctia.org/pdf/ PositionPaper_numberscoalition_USF.pdf.

[28] For a more detailed discussion opposing a numbers-based proposal see *Losing Numbers: How America's Most Vulnerable Consumers Could Suffer Under Universal Service Fund Reform*. Available at http://keepusffair.org/ KeepUSFFair/resources.html.

[29] More specifically, High Cost program revenues disbursed between 2003 and 2010 to incumbents decreased from $3,234.9 million to $3,055.1 million. USF fund data taken from USAC annual reports available at http://www.usac.org/about/governance/annual-reports/.

[30] *In the Matter of Lifeline and Link Up Reform and Modernization, Federal-State Joint Board on Universal Service, Lifeline and Link Up*. WC Docket No. 11-42, CC Docket No. 96-45, WC Docket No. 03-109, Notice of Proposed Rulemaking, released March 4, 2011,(para 27). Available at http://hraunfoss.fcc.gov/edocs_public/attachmatch/FCC11-32A1.pdf.

[31] It should be noted, however, that the 109th, 110th, and 111th Congresses enacted legislation prohibiting the FCC from using any of its appropriated funds to change its rules, or regulations, to limit USF support payments to a single connection, or primary line (P.L. 109-108, Title VI, §622; P.L. 110-161, Title V, §511; P.L. 111-8, Title V, §502; and P.L. 111-117, Division C, Title V §502).

[32] The provider would be required to meet certain "carrier of last resort" obligations, which would be detailed when the bids are solicited. For example, the carrier would be required to offer a specific package of services and provide that service to the entire designated service area (regardless of cost), and would have to meet interconnection mandates.

[33] *Joint Board Recommends Cap On High-Cost Fund*. Available at http://hraunfoss.fcc.gov/ edocs_public/attachmatch/ DOC-272806A1.pdf.

[34] *In the Matter of High-Cost Universal Service Support and Federal-State Joint Board on Universal Service*, WC Docket No. 05-337, CC Docket No. 96-45, Notice of Proposed Rulemaking, released May 14, 2007. Available at http://hraunfoss.fcc.gov/edocs_public/ attachmatch/FCC-07-88A1.pdf.

[35] Competitive eligible telecommunications carriers that serve tribal lands or Alaska Native regions and competitive telecommunications carriers that file their own cost data will not be subject to a cap.

[36] For further information see the FCC's adopted order available at http://hraunfoss.fcc.gov/ edocs_public/attachmatch/ FCC-08-122A1.pdf. For a summary and discussion of this order see Federal Register, Vol. 73, No. 128, July 2, 2008, p. 37882.

[37] For information on broadband mapping and data collection efforts see CRS Report RL30719, *Broadband Internet Access and the Digital Divide: Federal Assistance Programs*, by Lennard G. Kruger and Angele A. Gilroy.

[38] Federal Communications Commission Office of the Inspector General, Semiannual Report to Congress, April 1, 2006—September 30, 2006, p.8. Available at http://www.fcc.gov/oig/ oigreportssemiannual.html.

[39] For example, see *Schools and Libraries Program: Actions Taken to Improve Operational Procedures Prior to Committing Funds* (March 1999) GAO/RCED-99-51; *Schools and Libraries Program: Application and Invoice Review Procedures Need Strengthening* (December 2000) GAO-01-105; *Schools and Libraries Program: Update on E-Rate*

Funding (May 2001) GAO-01-672; *Greater Involvement Needed by FCC in the Management and Oversight of the E- Rate Program* (February 2005) GAO-05-151. Available at http://www.gao.gov/docsearch/topic.php.

[40] For a summary of this final rule see *Federal Register*, Vol. 72, No.184, September 24, 2007, p. 54214.

[41] This report is available at http://www.gao.gov/new.items/do8633.pdf.

[42] See *In the Matter of Comprehensive Review of the Universal Service Fund Management, Administration, and Oversight*, released on September 12, 2008, available at http://hraunfoss.fcc.gov/edocs_public/attachmatch/FCC-08-189A1.pdf.

[43] Semiannual Reports issued by the FCC's OIG are available at http://www.fcc.gov/oig/oigreportssemiannual.html.

[44] USAC 2006 Annual Report, p.11. Available at http://www.usac.org/_res/documents/about/pdf/usac-annual-report-2006.pdf.

[45] FCC Office of the Inspector General Semiannual Report to Congress, April 1, 2007 - September 30, 2007, p. 17. Available at http://hraunfoss.fcc.gov/edocs_public/attachmatch/DOC For a detailed analysis of the OIG audit see FCC Office of the Inspector General, *Initial Statistical Analysis of Data from the 2006/2007 Compliance Audits*, October 3, 2007. Available at http://www.fcc.gov/oig/ under release date October 3, 2007.

[46] USAC 2009 Annual Report, pp.2, 6, 12. Available at http://www.usac.org/_res/documents/about/pdf/usac-annual- report-2009.pdf.

[47] See p. 17, OIG Semiannual Report to Congress, April 1, 2007-September 30, 2007, for the full OMB definition of an "erroneous payment" Available at http://hraunfoss.fcc.gov/edocs_public/attachmatch/DOC

[48] FCC Office of the Inspector General Semiannual Report to Congress, April 1, 2007 - September 30, 2007, p. 16. Available at http://hraunfoss.fcc.gov/edocs_public/attachmatch/DOC

[49] A brief overview of the Enforcement Bureau's USF enforcement responsibilities and a list of recent enforcement actions is available at http://www.fcc.gov/eb/usfc/.

[50] For example, see *Six Corporations And Five Individuals Indicted In Connection With Schemes To Defraud The Federal E-Rate Program*. Available at http://www.usdoj.gov/opa/pr/2005/April/05_at_169.htm; and *Two New Jersey Executives Agree to Plead Guilty in Nationwide Scheme to Defraud the Federal E-Rate Program*. Available at http://www.usdoj.gov/opa/pr/2008/April/08_at_334.html.

[51] Remarks by former Chairman Martin during confirmation hearings before the Senate Commerce, Science and Transportation Committee, September 12, 2006.

[52] American Recovery and Reinvestment Act of 2009, P.L. 111-5, §6001 (k)(2)(D).

[53] A copy of this plan is available at http://hraunfoss.fcc.gov/edocs_public/attachmatch/DOC

[54] NBP, Chapter 8, *Availability*, recommendation 8.1.

[55] Much of this transition is detailed in Chapter 8, *Availability*, of the NBP.

[56] NBP, Chapter 8, *Availability*, recommendation 8.13.

[57] NBP, Chapter 8, *Availability*, recommendation 8.2.

[58] NBP, Chapter 8, *Availability*, recommendation 8.3.

[59] NBP, Chapter 9, *Adoption and Utilization*, 9.1, Understanding Broadband Adoption.

[60] Details of this expansion are addressed in, Chapter 9, *Adoption and Utilization*, of the NBP.

[61] NBP, Chapter 9, *Adoption and Utilization*, recommendation 9.1.

[62] NBP, Chapter 9, *Adoption and Utilization*, recommendation 9.1.

[63] A detailed discussion of all of these recommendations is contained in NBP Chapter 11, *Education.Section 11.3, Modernizing Educational Broadband Infrastructure*.

[64] A detailed discussion on the Rural Health Care Program recommendations is contained in NBP Chapter 10, *Health Care*.

[65] NBP, Chapter 10, *Health Care*, recommendation 10.6

[66] NBP, Chapter 10, *HealthCare*, recommendation 10.7.

[67] NBP, Chapter 10, *Health Care*, recommendation 10.8.

[68] NBP, Chapter 10, *Health Care*, recommendation 10.9.
[69] NBP, Chapter 8, *Availability*, recommendations 8.20 and 8.21.
[70] NBP, Chapter 11, *Education*, recommendation 11.22
[71] NBP, Chapter 8, *Availability*, recommendation 8.6.
[72] NBP, Chapter 8, *Availability*, recommendation 8.15.
[73] NBP, Chapter 8, *Availability*, recommendation 8.10.
[74] NBP, chapter 8, *Availability*, recommendation 8.12.
[75] *FCC Chairman Julius Genachowski Announces Launch of Universal Service Working Group*. Released June 14, 2010. Available at http://hraunfoss.fcc.gov/edocs_public/attachmatch/ DOC
[76] *In the Matter of Universal Service Reform, Mobility Fund*. WT Docket No. 10-208, Notice of Proposed rulemaking, adopted October 14, 2010. Available at http://hraunfoss.fcc.gov/ edocs_public/attachmatch/FCC-10-182A1.pdf.
[77] It should be noted that the Obama Administration's FY2012 budget calls for a "national wireless initiative," with a one-time infusion of $5 billion into the USF, to extend 4G wireless coverage to at least 98% of the population, within five years.
[78] *In the Matter of Connect America Fund; A National Broadband Plan for Our Future; Establishing Just and Reasonable Rates for Local Exchange Carriers; High-Cost Universal Service Support; Developing a[n] Unified Intercarrier Compensation Regime; Federal-State Joint Board on Universal Service; Lifeline and Link-Up*. WC Docket No. 10-90, GN Docket No. 09-51, WC Docket No. 07-135, WC Docket No. 05-337, CC Docket No. 01-92, CC Docket No. 96-45, WC Docket No. 03-109, Notice of Proposed Rulemaking and Further Notice of Proposed Rulemaking, adopted February 8, 2011. Available at http:// www.fcc.gov/Daily_Releases/Daily_Business/2011/db0209/FCC-11-13A1.pdf.
[79] *In the Matter of Lifeline and Link Up Reform and Modernization, Federal-State Joint Board on Universal Service, Lifeline and Link Up*. WC Docket No. 11-42, CC Docket No. 96-45, WC Docket No. 03-109, Notice of Proposed Rulemaking, released March 4, 2011. Available at http://www.fcc.gov//Daily_Releases/Daily_Business/2011/db0304/ FCC-11-32A1.pdf.
[80] In the Matter of Lifeline and Link Up Reform and Modernization, Federal-State Joint Board on Universal Service, Lifeline and Link Up, WC Docket no. 11-42, CC Docket No. 96-45, WC Docket No. 03-109. Available at http://transition.fcc.gov/Daily_Releases/Daily_Business/ 2011/db0621/FCC-11-97A1.pdf.
[81] *In the Matter of Lifeline and Link Up Reform and Modernization*, para 3 and para 8.
[82] *In the Matter of Schools and Libraries Universal Service Support Mechanism, A National Broadband Plan For Our Future*, CC Docket No. 02-6, GN Docket No. 09-51. Available at http://hraunfoss.fcc.gov/edocs_public/attachmatch/ FCC-10-175A1.pdf.
[83] The FCC notes in paragraph 5 that the proposals adopted in this order do not address all of the proposals raised in the E-rate NPRM adopted May 20, 2010. A copy of the NPRM, *In the Matter of Schools and Libraries Universal Service Support Mechanism; A National Broadband Plan* CC Docket No. 02-6; GN Docket No. 09-51 is available at http:// hraunfoss.fcc.gov/edocs_public/attachmatch/FCC-10-83A1.pdf.
[84] The FCC announced on March 9, 2011, the selection of 20 schools and libraries as part of a wireless pilot program, "*Learning On-The-Go*," to be funded from $9 million from the E-rate program. The pilot program will help K-12 students connect to the Internet at home and increase access to digitized materials, and help library patrons find and apply for jobs. Qualified pilot programs will be funded, assuming compliance with all program requirements, in the 2011-12 school year. For a list of selectees see *FCC Chairman Julius Genachowski Announces Recipients Of Innovative Wireless Pilot Projects At Digital Roundtable in New York City*, released March 9, 2011. Available at http://www.fcc.gov/ Daily_Releases/Daily_Business/2011/db0309/DOC
[85] *In the Matter of Rural Health Care Support Mechanism*, WC Docket No. 02-06. Available at http://www.fcc.gov/ Daily_Releases/Daily_Business/2010/db0715/FCC-10-125A1.pdf.

[86] This data was similar to that which was formerly requested in the 110th Congress by Representative Waxman who at the time was Chairman of the House Oversight and Government Reform Committee. For a further discussion of this activity in the 110th Congress see **Appendix B**.

[87] Memorandum to Members of the Committee on Oversight and Government Reform, from Chairman Henry A. Waxman, regarding Universal Service Fund High Cost Program Subsidies, July 28, 2008. Available at http://oversight

[88] Examples of the letters sent to the companies are available at http://oversight

In: Federal Funds: A Selection of Programs ISBN 978-1-62618-005-5
Editor: Kieran Saccoccio

Chapter 6

THE RECLAMATION FUND: A PRIMER*

Charles V. Stern

SUMMARY

The Reclamation Fund was established in 1902 to fund the development of irrigation projects on arid and semiarid lands of the 17 western states. It originated as a revolving fund for construction projects and was supported by the proceeds of the sale of land and water in the western United States. Over time, it was amended to receive proceeds from a number of other sources. It is currently derived from repayments and revenues associated with federal water resources development as well as the sales, rentals, and leases (including natural resource leasing) of federal land in the western United States. Portions of the fund's balance are appropriated annually by Congress for multiple purposes, including some of the operational expenditures of the Bureau of Reclamation (Reclamation) and the Power Marketing Administrations. Through FY2011, collections deposited into the Reclamation Fund totaled more than $40 billion, while total appropriations from the fund totaled approximately $30 billion.

The Reclamation Fund did not finance all Reclamation investments in the western United States. As a result of limited funding availability, a number of large dams and other Reclamation investments were financed by the General

* This is an edited, reformatted and augmented version of the Congressional Research Service Publication, CRS Report for Congress R41844, dated July 24, 2012.

Fund of the U.S. Treasury. Notwithstanding advances to the Reclamation Fund by Congress in 1910 and 1931, deposits into and appropriations out of the fund have been roughly equal over time. From the 1940s until the 1990s, the fund maintained a small, relatively stable balance. Beginning in the mid-1990s, balances in the fund began to increase significantly as receipts from mineral leasing and power sales increased, while appropriations from the fund largely remained static. By the end of FY2011, the fund had a balance of more than $9.6 billion, and it is expected to continue to grow.

Receipts deposited into the Reclamation Fund are made available to Reclamation by Congress through annual discretionary appropriations bills, which are subject to congressional budgetary allocations. Some have proposed that Congress appropriate some portion of the surplus balance in the Reclamation Fund to reclamation activities in western states, including new water storage projects or the rehabilitation of existing projects. These interests argue that the Reclamation Fund was set up to benefit western states and should now be used to increase investments in these areas.

As the balance of the Reclamation Fund continues to increase, Congress may reevaluate the Reclamation Fund's status, including its financing of new or ongoing activities. The Omnibus Lands Act of 2009 (P.L. 111-11) included provisions that will transfer $120 million per year from the fund from FY2020 through FY2034, without further appropriation, to a separate fund that provides for Indian Water Settlement construction projects. In the 112th Congress, a bill before the Senate (S. 3385) proposes to transfer another $80 million per year that would otherwise go to the Reclamation Fund from FY2013 through FY2029 for the construction of rural water projects. Major changes to the fund's mechanics may have scoring implications in the annual budgetary context and under congressional pay-as-you-go rules.

INTRODUCTION

The Reclamation Fund was established in 1902 as a special fund within the United States Treasury to aid the development of irrigation on the arid lands of western states.[1] It originated as a revolving fund supported by the proceeds of the sale of land and water in the western United States. Over time it, has been amended to receive proceeds from a number of disparate sources, including power generation and mineral leasing.

Since the mid-1990s, balances in the Reclamation Fund have increased significantly as appropriations made from the fund have not kept pace with receipts coming in to the fund. As of the end of FY2011, the fund had a balance in excess of $9.6 billion. Barring major changes by Congress in the form of increased appropriations from the fund or a redirection of its receipts, the fund's balance is expected to continue to increase.

This report provides general background information on the Reclamation Fund, including a short history of the fund and trends in its deposits and appropriations. It includes a brief analysis of the issues associated with using the current surplus balance for other means.

BACKGROUND

Early History

The Reclamation Act of 1902[2] authorized the Secretary of the Interior to construct irrigation works in western states and established the Reclamation Fund to pay for these projects. The Reclamation Fund was established as a special fund within the U.S. Treasury and was designated to receive receipts from the sale of federal land in the western United States.[3]

> All moneys received from the sale and disposal of public lands in ... [the western United States.] ... shall be, and the same are hereby, reserved set aside, and appropriated as a special fund in the Treasury to be known as the "reclamation fund, " to be used in the examination and survey for and the construction and maintenance of irrigation works for the storage, diversion, and development of waters for the reclamation of arid and semiarid lands in the said States and Territories, and for the payment of all other expenditures provided for in this Act.

The 1902 act made funding from the Reclamation Fund available for the purposes outlined in the legislation without further appropriation by Congress. This requirement was later revised in the Reclamation Extension Act (1914) to limit Reclamation's expenditures for carrying out the 1902 act to only those items for which funds are made available annually by Congress.[4]

Between 1902 and 1910, the Reclamation Service (later changed to the Bureau of Reclamation) authorized 24 projects across the West, and the balance in the fund reached as much as $68 million.[5] However, by 1910, estimates indicated that anticipated income and repayments would not be adequate to carry on the authorized construction program, and funds were borrowed from the U.S. Treasury on multiple occasions. In the act of June 25,

1910,[6] Congress authorized an advance of $20 million to the Reclamation Fund from the General Fund of the U.S. Treasury. Congress authorized an additional advance of $5 million from the General Fund in the act of March 3, 1931.[7] These funds were eventually reimbursed in 1938 under the Hayden-O'Mahoney Amendment, which among other things directed the Secretary of the Treasury to transfer funding accruing to the western states from lands within naval petroleum reserves.[8]

The Reclamation Fund was not adequate to fund many of Reclamation's large investments in water infrastructure. Dating to the late 1920s, Congress directed that the General Fund (in lieu of the Reclamation Fund) finance part or all of some of Reclamation's largest construction projects. By the end of the 1930s, most major Reclamation projects under construction were financed by the General Fund of the Treasury.[9] For instance, the Boulder Canyon Project Act of 1928 provided that construction of Hoover Dam would be financed from the General Fund of the Treasury rather than the Reclamation Fund.[10] In the 1950s and 1960s, other large, multiple- purpose Reclamation projects were built with support from the General Fund. Among these projects were those authorized in the Colorado River Storage Project Act (P.L. 485, which authorized Glen Canyon Dam, built in 1956) and the Colorado River Basin Project Act (P.L. 90-537, which authorized the Central Arizona Project in 1968).[11]

Revenue Sources

The Reclamation Fund was originally established to serve as a "revolving" fund,[12] but this concept proved impractical over time. When the fund was created, it was expected that project repayment and receipts from the sale of public lands (under the original statute, the fund receives 95% of these proceeds) would finance expenditures on new or ongoing projects. As previously noted, around 1910 Congress recognized that the existing Reclamation Fund revenue stream was inadequate to finance ongoing expenditures. Congress made the fund subject to annual appropriations in 1914, and directed additional receipts toward the Reclamation Fund over time, including those from revenues associated water and power uses and from sales, leases, and rentals of federal lands and resources (e.g., oil, gas, and minerals) in the 17 western states. Of these, natural resource royalties and power revenues (discussed below) have proven to be the most significant sources of revenue for the Reclamation Fund.

Receipts from natural resource royalties were initiated in the Mineral Leasing Act of 1920.[13] These receipts, which include 40% of the royalty payments received by the federal government for the production of oil, gas, coal, potassium, and other minerals on federal lands, currently generate the most revenue for the Reclamation Fund (see **Figure 1**). In recent years, these receipts have increased significantly (see the section, "Recent Trends").

Hydropower receipts were authorized to be received by the Reclamation Fund through the aforementioned Hayden-O'Mahoney Amendment, enacted on May 9, 1938.[14] The amendment provided that revenues associated with irrigation projects' power features be deposited into the Reclamation Fund.[15] The practical function of the change was to secure for the fund power revenues from large projects then under construction, such as Coulee Dam, Shasta Dam, and Parker Dam.[16] An additional significant source of revenues into the Reclamation Fund is sales of water contracts, which was authorized by Congress in 1920.[17] The primary sources of revenue for the Reclamation Fund are summarized below in **Table 1**.

Appropriations from the Reclamation Fund

Congress makes appropriations from the Reclamation Fund in annual appropriations acts. Appropriations from the Reclamation Fund are typically made for three separate accounts: the Bureau of Reclamation's Water and Related Resource account, the Bureau of Reclamation's Policy and Administration account, and the Western Area Power Administration's (WAPA's) Construction, Rehabilitation, and Operation and Maintenance account. Funds are made available from the Reclamation Fund only for projects authorized under the fund. Funds have been provided to WAPA since 1978, when the power marketing functions of Reclamation were transferred to the Department of Energy.[18] Appropriations are typically provided in annual Energy & Water Development Appropriation bills.

Recent Trends: Increasing Balances

After the early financial issues between the Reclamation Fund's establishment in 1902 and the supplemental funding from the General Fund in the 1930s, the fund maintained a relatively stable balance until the early 1990s. Beginning in the mid-1990s, the fund's balance began to increase significantly as revenues from power sales and natural resource royalties significantly exceeded appropriations from the fund. For every year since FY1994, receipts going into the Reclamation Fund have exceeded appropriations made from it by more than $100 million, and in some years receipts have exceeded appropriations by more than $1 billion.[19] The exception to this trend was FY2009, when the American Recovery and Reinvestment Act (ARRA, P.L. 111-5) appropriated funding for Reclamation from the Reclamation Fund. As of the end of FY2011, the fund had a balance in excess of $9.6 billion. Trends in the Reclamation Fund from 1990 to 2010 are summarized below in **Figure 1**.

Receipts deposited into the Reclamation Fund are derived from five general categories: natural resource royalties, sales of federal land, hydropower receipts, timber sales receipts, and other proprietary receipts.[20] Of these, natural resource royalties and hydropower revenues make up the majority of incoming receipts. From FY1990 to FY2011, an average of 87% of the Reclamation Fund's receipts came from these two sources.[21] In recent years, even more receipts have come from these sources. Over the last five years, an average of 91% came from the two sources (79% from natural resource royalties and 11% from hydropower receipts). A breakdown of the fund's receipts in FY2011 is provided in **Figure 2**.

Table 1. Reclamation Fund: Selected Major Sources of Revenue

Revenue Source	Description/Percentage	Year First Authorized	Code Reference
Public Land Sales	95% of proceeds from public land sales in western states	1902	43 U.S.C. §391
Reclamation Project Repayments	100% of receipts	1902	43 U.S.C. §391
Reclamation Project Water Contracts/Sales	100% of proceeds	1902	43 U.S.C. §392a
Reclamation Project Power Revenues	100% of proceeds	1938	43 U.S.C. §392a
Natural Resource/ Mineral Royalties	40% of bonuses, royalties, and rentals from onshore public lands[0]	1920	30 U.S.C. §191

Notes: Several smaller sources of revenue are not included in this table.

a. Pursuant to statutory requirements, receipts from mineral leasing in Alaska are collected and distributed to that state separately.

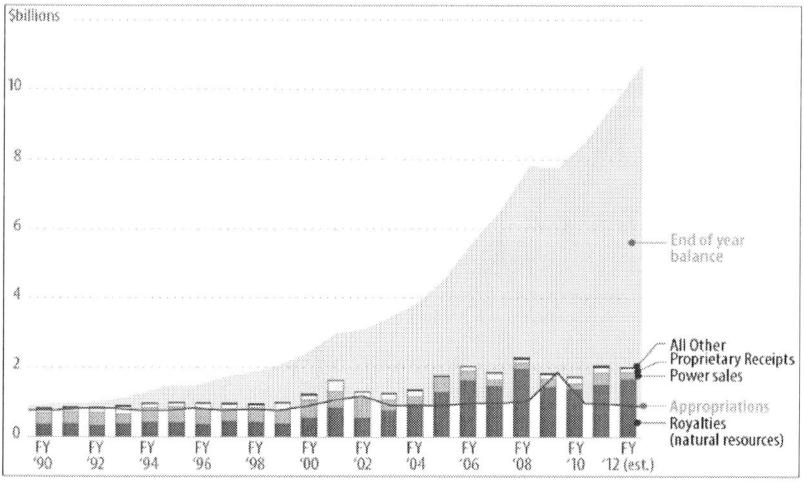

Source: CRS, with Bureau of Reclamation data. FY2012 data are estimates derived from the FY2013 budget request.

Notes: Increased appropriations in FY2009 reflect ARRA funding appropriated from the Reclamation Fund pursuant to statute. "All Other" includes multiple revenue streams, including timber sales (no more than $29 million annually since FY1990), land sales (no more than $20 million), and interest on the fund balance (no more than $55 million). "Power Sales" includes receipts from the sale of power by WAPA and Bonneville Power Administration (BPA). "Proprietary Receipts" includes several categories of Reclamation receipts, including those for repayment of operation and maintenance, construction, and loans, as well as those from rental of land and sale of project water and power (i.e., power not marketed by WAPA or BPA).

Figure 1. Reclamation Fund, FY1990-FY2012.

Limited data is available on the source (by state) of the receipts going into the Reclamation Fund for various purposes. For the largest portion of revenues, mineral royalties (which accounted for approximately 79% of all receipts in the last five years), CRS estimates that over the last five years, an average of 93% of the receipts from onshore public mineral leasing came from five western states: Wyoming, New Mexico, Colorado, California, and Utah.[22] Two states, Wyoming and New Mexico, account for about 64% of these receipts. For power revenues, Reclamation reports that the majority come from power generated on the Columbia River, the Central Valley Project, the Parker-Davis Project, and the Pick-Sloan Missouri Basin Program.[23] On average, this power has generated about 16% of Reclamation Fund revenues over the last 10 years.

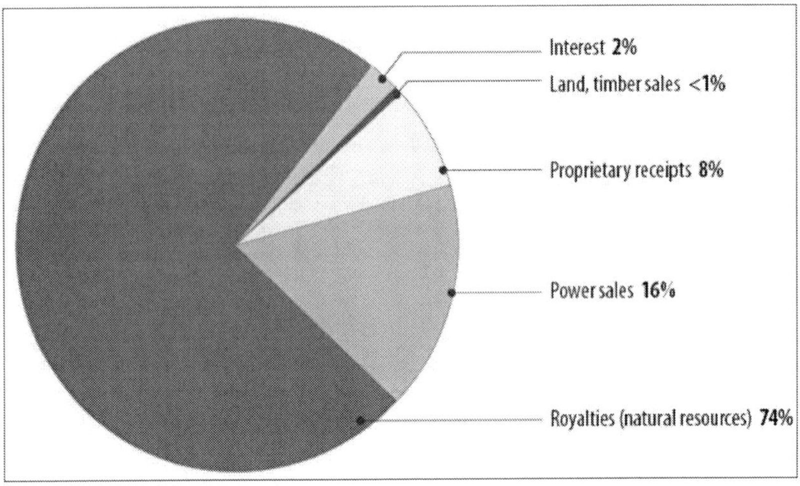

Source: CRS, with Bureau of Reclamation data.
Notes: Total receipts deposited into the fund in FY2010 were approximately $2 billion.

Figure 2. Reclamation Fund Receipts, FY2011.

PROPOSALS TO USE THE RECLAMATION FUND'S SURPLUS BALANCE

The increasing balance of the Reclamation Fund has caused some to call for directing these funds for new purposes or to supplement ongoing authorized expenditures. Such a change could take one or more forms, each of which may have an associated budget scoring impact. For instance, Congress could increase appropriations from the Reclamation Fund in annual discretionary appropriations, but such an increase would have to compete with other appropriations (including General Fund appropriations) subject to congressional 302 (b) allocations.[24] Separately, Congress could dedicate a stream of revenue from the Reclamation Fund for a subset of projects and make it available, with or without further appropriations (i.e., discretionary funding or mandatory funding) required. Congressional PAYGO requirements may necessitate offsets in spending corresponding to some of these changes.[25]

Some, including water users and others benefitting from Reclamation projects, note that the Reclamation Fund was intended to benefit water resource projects in western states, and spending its balance on the fund's intended purposes is a logical use of the fund. However, others may view other potential uses of the fund's surplus as being more pressing in the current fiscal climate.

These same interests argue that the large increases to mineral receipts were not foreseen when those disbursements were originally authorized, and may advocate for redirecting surplus balances to debt reduction or the states.

Congressional Interest

A change to the Reclamation Fund enacted by Congress in 2009 provides an example of the challenges associated with dedicating Reclamation Fund balances toward a particular purpose. In Title X of the Omnibus Lands Act of 2009 (P.L. 111-11), Congress redirected a portion of Reclamation Fund receipts for Indian water rights settlement projects. The bill established a separate fund (known as the Reclamation Water Settlements Fund) in the Treasury and directed the Secretary of the Treasury to transfer into the new fund up to $120 million annually between FY2020 and FY2034 that would otherwise go to the Reclamation Fund.[26] Significantly, the law directed that this funding be made available without further appropriation. However, in this case, the appropriation was made outside of the congressional scoring window for PAYGO costs, and thus did not require an offset.[27]

More recently, a bill in the Senate, the Authorized Rural Water Projects Completion Act (S. 3385), proposes to establish a new fund for rural water projects (similar to the Water Settlements Fund referenced above) that would receive, without further appropriation, as much as $80 million per year in funding that would otherwise revert to the Reclamation Fund. In contrast to the aforementioned water settlements fund, some portion of this funding, which is proposed for FY2013-FY2029, would fall within the 10-year scoring window. However, the legislation also contains a provision that would prevent the transfer from taking place if the redirection of funds would increase the deficit.[28]

End Notes

[1] In the early part of the 20th century, such efforts were commonly referred to as "reclamation" projects because they were "reclaiming" the lands for human use.

[2] 32 Stat 388; 43 U.S.C. §391. This act is also often referred to as the "Newland Act" or the "National Reclamation Act of 1902."

[3] Special funds are fund accounts for receipts and spending with specific taxes or revenues earmarked for a specific purpose. They are maintained separately from the General Fund of the U.S. Treasury (which funds most government operations). If a special fund takes in more receipts than it spends in a year, its surplus is added to the unified budget surplus.

[4] 43 U.S.C. §414.

[5] Correspondence with the Bureau of Reclamation, April 26, 2011.

[6] 43 U.S.C. §397.

[7] 43 U.S.C. §391a.

[8] 43 U.S.C. §391a-1.

[9] Correspondence with the Bureau of Reclamation, April 26, 2011.

[10] 45 Stat 1057. This act authorized construction of Hoover Dam.

[11] A solicitor opinion later found that the Reclamation Fund was not a proper financing source for some projects, including projects constructed under the Small Reclamation Projects Act of 1956 (70 Stat 1044) and the Colorado River Basin Salinity Control Act (88 Stat 266).

[12] Generally speaking, in a "revolving fund" a set of receipts continually finances a related set of expenditures, usually without further appropriation from Congress.

[13] 30 U.S.C. §191. Under the original act, in 1921, the Reclamation Fund received 52.5% of these proceeds. The act was amended in 1976 to decrease this amount to 40%.

[14] 43 USC, §391a-1, 392a.

[15] The amendment provided that after net power revenues have repaid project construction costs allocable to power, they are to be transferred to the General Fund as "miscellaneous receipts."

[16] The Boulder Canyon Project was specifically exempted from the act. These power revenues are directed to a separate fund, the Lower Colorado River Basin Project Fund, per the Colorado River Project Storage Act.

[17] 43 U.S.C. §521. Moneys derived from these sales are credited to the project from which the water is supplied.

[18] These functions were transferred in the Department of Energy Organization Act (P.L. 95-91). 42 U.S.C. §7152.

[19] In FY2006, receipts exceeded appropriations by $1.06 billion. In FY2008, receipts exceeded appropriations by $1.24 billion.

[20] Reclamation reports that these receipts include repayment of certain expenditures for construction and operations and maintenance, as well as sale of water at some projects, including the Central Valley Project.

[21] CRS, using Reclamation data.

[22] CRS estimate based on data from MMS, Summary of Mineral Revenues Distributed to States, 1920-2000. http://www.onrr.gov/Stats/pdfdocs/DisbAll01.PDF.

[23] Correspondence with the Bureau of Reclamation, April 29, 2011.

[24] 302(b) scoring allocations establish the maximum spending levels for each of the 12 appropriations bills. For more information, see CRS Report R40472, *The Budget Resolution and Spending Legislation*, by Megan Suzanne Lynch.

[25] "PAYGO" refers to requirements that legislation projected to increase direct spending or reduce incoming revenues must include equivalent amounts of spending cuts or revenue increases (or both). For more information, see CRS Report RL32835, *PAYGO Rules for Budget Enforcement in the House and Senate*, by Robert Keith and Bill Heniff Jr.

[26] 43 U.S.C. §407.

[27] In its cost estimate for the Senate-passed bill, the Congressional Budget Office estimated that the change would result in $900 million in costs outside of the 10-year scoring window.

[28] See S. 3385, Section 3(b)(3).

In: Federal Funds: A Selection of Programs ISBN 978-1-62618-005-5
Editor: Kieran Saccoccio

Chapter 7

LAND AND WATER CONSERVATION FUND: OVERVIEW, FUNDING HISTORY, AND ISSUES*

Carol Hardy Vincent

SUMMARY

The Land and Water Conservation Fund (LWCF) Act of 1965 was enacted to help preserve, develop, and assure access to outdoor recreation facilities to strengthen the health of U.S. citizens. The law created the Land and Water Conservation Fund in the U.S. Treasury as a funding source to implement its outdoor recreation goals.

The LWCF has been the principal source of monies for land acquisition for outdoor recreation by the four federal agencies—the National Park Service, Bureau of Land Management, Fish and Wildlife Service, and Forest Service. In the past, Congress typically has identified which areas are to be acquired with the funds it provides. The LWCF also funds a matching grant program to assist states in recreational planning, acquiring recreational lands and waters, and developing outdoor recreational facilities. A portion of the appropriation is divided equally among the states, with the remainder apportioned based on need, as determined by the Secretary of the Interior. The states award their grant money through a competitive selection process based on statewide recreation plans and establish their own priorities and criteria. Finally,

* This is an edited, reformatted and augmented version of the Congressional Research Service Publication, CRS Report for Congress RL33531, dated August 9, 2011.

beginning in FY1998, LWCF has been used to fund other federal programs with related purposes.

The LWCF is authorized at $900 million annually. While the fund accrues revenues and collections from multiple sources, nearly all of the revenues are derived from oil and gas leasing in the Outer Continental Shelf. Congress determines the level of appropriations each year, and yearly appropriations have fluctuated widely since the origin of the program. Of the total revenues that have accrued throughout the history of the program ($33.5 billion), less than half have been appropriated ($15.8 billion). FY2001 marked the highest funding ever, with appropriations exceeding the authorized level by reaching nearly $1 billion. For FY2011, the most recent fiscal year, the appropriation was $300.5 million.

The $15.8 billion appropriated throughout the history of the program has been unevenly allocated among federal land acquisition (62%), the state grant program (26%), and other programs (12%). Similarly, federal land acquisition funds have been allocated unevenly among the four federal agencies. More recent legislation (P.L. 109-432) provided that a portion of revenues from certain OCS leasing are provided without further appropriation to the state grant program. These funds are to supplement any funds appropriated by Congress.

There is a difference of opinion as to the appropriate level of funds for LWCF and how those funds should be used. Current congressional issues include deciding the amount to appropriate for land acquisition and identifying which lands should be acquired; deciding the level of funding for the state grant program and how funds should be allocated among the states; and determining which, if any, other programs to fund from the LWCF. The primary context for debating these issues is Interior appropriations legislation. Other issues of current debate include whether the LWCF should be permanently appropriated at the authorized level of $900 million, and whether revenues from additional activities should be directed to the LWCF.

INTRODUCTION

The Land and Water Conservation Fund (LWCF) Act of 1965[1] was enacted to help preserve, develop, and assure access to outdoor recreation resources. A main goal of the law was to facilitate participation in recreation and strengthen the "health and vitality" of U.S. citizens. The law sought to accomplish these goals by "providing funds" for federal acquisition and development of lands and other areas and by "providing funds for and authorizing" federal assistance to states in recreation planning, acquiring lands and waters, and development of recreation facilities.

The law created the Land and Water Conservation Fund in the Treasury as a funding source to implement the outdoor recreation goals it set out. The fund is currently authorized at $900 million annually through September 30, 2015. The LWCF is a "trust fund" that accumulates revenues from the federal motorboat fuel tax and surplus property sales. To supplement these sources to reach the annual authorized level of $900 million, the fund accumulates revenues from oil and gas leases on the Outer Continental Shelf (OCS). For many years, the OCS revenues have accounted for almost all of the deposits.

Monies in the fund are available for outdoor recreation purposes only if appropriated by Congress, and the level of annual appropriations has varied widely since the origin of the fund in 1965. One current issue is whether to provide permanent appropriations for LWCF, rather than continue the current procedure of providing appropriations each year. Also of current debate is whether to direct additional monies to LWCF, to be used for purposes provided for in the LWCF Act or for other purposes. Perennial congressional issues include (1) deciding the amount to appropriate for federal land acquisition, determining the level of acquisition funds for each of the four agencies, and identifying which lands should be acquired; (2) deciding the level of funding for the state grant program; and (3) determining what, if any, other programs should be funded through LWCF and at what level. The primary context for debating these issues traditionally has been the annual Interior appropriations legislation. For the most recent action on LWCF, see the "Land and Water Conservation Fund" section of the most recent CRS report on appropriations for Interior, Environment, and Related Agencies.[2]

How the Fund Works

The LWCF is not a true trust fund in the way "trust fund" is generally understood in the private sector. The fund is credited with revenues totaling $900 million annually, but these credited monies cannot be spent unless appropriated by Congress. Unappropriated funds remain in the U.S. Treasury and can be spent for other federal activities. From FY1965 through FY2011, about $33.5 billion has been credited to the LWCF. Roughly half that amount—$15.8 billion—has been appropriated.[3] Further, interest is not accrued on the accumulated unappropriated balance that has been credited to the LWCF. While some supporters assert that the LWCF was originally intended to be a revolving fund, whereby the money would be maintained in a separate account that could accrue interest, this has not been the case. The fund's basic purpose has not been altered even though the authorizing legislation has been amended, most notably to raise the funding ceiling and to mandate that offshore oil and gas leasing revenues should make up any shortfall from other specified financing sources.

Purposes of LWCF Appropriations

Appropriations from LWCF have been made for three general purposes: (1) federal acquisition of land and waters and interests therein; (2) grants to states for recreational planning; acquiring recreational lands, waters, or related interests; and developing outdoor recreational facilities; and (3) related purposes.[4] Each year, Congress determines the total appropriations from the Fund, and the amount for each of these three general purposes.

The LWCF Act states that not less than 40% of the appropriations from the fund are to be available for federal purposes. This language resulted from a 1976 amendment, at a time when funds were being appropriated for federal land acquisition and for the stateside program. Funding for other federal purposes did not occur until FY1998. This provision replaced language in the LWCF Act that had provided that, "in the absence of a provision to the contrary in the Act making an appropriation from the fund," the appropriation from the fund was to be 60% for state purposes and 40% for federal purposes. That language had specified that during the first five years in which appropriations were made from the fund, the President could vary these percentages by not more than 15 points to meet the needs of states and the federal government.

Federal Land Acquisition

The LWCF remains the principal source of funds for federal acquisition of lands for outdoor recreation. Most federal lands are acquired (and managed) by four agencies—the Forest Service (FS) in the Department of Agriculture, and the National Park Service (NPS), Fish and Wildlife Service (FWS), and Bureau of Land Management (BLM) in the Department of the Interior.[5] These four agencies manage about 95% of all federally owned lands. Of these agencies, only the FWS has another significant source of acquisition funding.

Specifically, under the Migratory Bird Conservation Fund the FWS has a permanently appropriated source of funding for land acquisition.[6]

The LWCF Act provides that "unless otherwise allotted in the appropriation Act making them available," appropriations from the fund for federal purposes are to be allotted by the President for certain purposes.[7] These purposes include water development projects with recreational benefits; land acquisition in areas administered by the Secretary of the Interior for recreational purposes; land acquisition in national park, national forest, and national wildlife system units. In practice, the appropriations acts typically identify the purposes for which the federal funds are to be used.

The process for appropriating funds for federal land acquisition is similar from year to year. The annual budget submission from each of the four federal agencies typically has included proposals for lands the agencies seek to acquire with requested LWCF funds. The number of specific acquisitions sought by the agencies varies from year to year. For instance, for FY2012 the three DOI agencies are seeking 116 acquisitions while the FS is seeking 38 acquisitions. By contrast, the FY2009 requests sought to fund relatively few acquisitions—10 for the three DOI agencies and none for the FS. The large backlog of potential acquisitions provides each agency with options in its annual request. Congress reviews agency requests, then determines which areas will be acquired and the funding level it will provide for each acquisition. In general, most of the funds have been earmarked to specific sites. For instance, in FY2010 Congress specified funds for 136 acquisitions by the four federal agencies.

The LWCF Act restricts appropriations to those acquisitions that have been previously authorized by law. However, it allows LWCF appropriations to be used for pre-acquisition work where "authorization is imminent and where substantial monetary savings could be realized."[8]

In recent years, Congress typically has provided the agencies with a portion of the acquisition funding for one or more related purposes. For instance, funds have been provided for acquisition management to cover the costs of land purchases, such as appraisals and title research. Acquisition funds also have been provided to cover the costs of land exchanges, as well as the acquisition of lands within the boundaries of federal land units ("inholdings") that may become available throughout the year. Further, in some cases funds have been appropriated for "emergencies" or "hardships," for acquisition of lands from an owner who must sell quickly and where the agency determines there is a need to purchase the lands quickly.

Appropriations laws typically provide that LWCF funds for land acquisition remain available until expended, meaning the funds can be carried over from fiscal year to fiscal year. Often an appropriation is not used in the fiscal year provided, because the process for completing a land acquisition has many components and often takes more than one year.[9]

Stateside Program

Another portion of the LWCF, administered by the NPS, provides matching grants to states (including the District of Columbia and U.S. territories) for recreation planning, acquisition of lands and waters, and facility development. Grants are provided for outdoor recreation purposes only, rather than for indoor facilities such as community centers. As of July 26, 2011, 41,641 grants have been provided to state and local governments for outdoor recreation projects. This figure includes 7,547 grants for acquisition; 27,106 grants for developing recreation facilities; 3,065 grants for redeveloping older recreational facilities; 682 state planning grants for studies of recreation potential, need, opportunity, and policy; and 3,241 grants for a combination of these activities.

Acquisitions funded through LWCF state grants must remain in recreation use in perpetuity, unless the Secretary of the Interior approves of the conversion of the land to another use and replacement lands are substituted. Conversions occur due to changing state needs, such as to use park lands to build schools, widen roads, and develop civic facilities. The NPS approves about 50-75 conversions yearly nationwide, according to the agency.

Appropriations to the state grant program typically do not include earmarks or other directions to the NPS to guide how these funds should be distributed or spent. The Secretary of the Interior apportions the appropriation for state grants in accordance with a formula set out in the LWCF Act.[10] The formula calls for a portion of the appropriation to be divided equally among the states.[11] The remaining appropriation is to be apportioned based on need, as determined by the Secretary.[12] Under law, the determination of need is to include the population of the state relative to the population of the United States, the use of outdoor recreation resources within a state by people outside the state, and the federal resources and programs within states. In current practice, population is the biggest factor in determining state need. No state can receive more than 10% of the total appropriation.

States have up to three years to use the money—the federal fiscal year in which the apportionment is made and the next two fiscal years. It is rare for a state not to use the money during this time, according to the NPS. Under law, the Secretary is to reapportion any amount that is not paid or obligated during the three-year period.

To be eligible for a grant, a state must prepare and update a statewide recreation plan. This plan usually addresses the needs and opportunities for recreation and includes a program for reaching recreational goals. It generally does not include specific projects. Under law, the plan is required to be approved by the Secretary, and in practice it is sent to the NPS for approval. The states award their grant money through a competitive process based on their recreation plans and their own priorities and selection criteria. They can use the money for state projects or for pass-through to localities. States send their top-ranked projects to the NPS for formal approval and obligation of grant money. Under law, payments to states are not to cover more than 50% of a project's costs, and in practice states typically receive a 50% federal payment. The remaining cost is to be borne by the state.[13]

Additional monies are provided for state grants under provisions of the Gulf of Mexico Energy Security Act of 2006.[14] Specifically, 12.5% of the revenues from certain OCS leasing in the Gulf of Mexico is directed to the stateside program in accordance with the terms of the LWCF Act. The funds are to be in addition to any amounts appropriated by Congress for LWCF. The money is available without further appropriation, and is available until expended. An estimated $8.2 million in proceeds from pertinent OCS leasing was collected in FY2008 and disbursed to the stateside program in FY2009. Since then, the disbursements to the stateside program under this authority have decreased. An estimated $0.2 million in revenue from such OCS leasing was dispersed to the stateside program in FY2011, and $0.1 million is projected to be dispersed in FY2012.[15] The funds are available to the states until expended, unlike the three-year duration of the funds appropriated annually for the stateside program.

Other Purposes

As noted above, the LWCF Act lists the federal purposes to which the President is to allot LWCF funds "unless otherwise allotted in the appropriation Act making them available."[16] A portion of the LWCF appropriation has been provided for other federal purposes (i.e., other than land acquisition) in FY1998 and each year since FY2000. Because there is no set of "other programs" specified to be funded from LWCF, Presidents have sought funds for a variety of programs and Congress has chosen which, if any, other programs to fund from LWCF. For instance, for FY2008, President George W. Bush sought LWCF funds for 11 programs within the FWS, FS, and other agencies, and Congress provided funding for two of these programs. Since FY1998, the LWCF has been used for a broad array of other programs, including the maintenance needs of the four land management agencies, FS highway rehabilitation and maintenance, the Historic Preservation Fund, the Payments in Lieu of Taxes program, FS State and Private Forestry programs, FWS State and Tribal Wildlife Grants, and FWS Cooperative Endangered Species Grants.

Funding History

Overview of FY1965-FY2011

Total annual appropriations from the LWCF have fluctuated widely since the origin of the program over four decades ago (see the bar graph in **Figure 1** and **Table 1** below). Until FY1998, LWCF funding rarely exceeded $400 million; from FY1977-FY1980, funding ranged from $509 million (FY1980) to $805 million (FY1978), and averaged $647 million annually. LWCF appropriations spiked dramatically in FY1998—to $969 million—from the FY1997 level of $159 million. FY1998 was the first year that LWCF appropriations exceeded the authorized level of $900 million.[17] They included $270 million in the usual funding titles for land acquisition by the four federal land management agencies; an additional $627 million in a separate title, funding both the acquisition of the Headwaters Forest in California and New World Mine outside Yellowstone National Park; and $72 million for other programs.

Another spike occurred in FY2001, when appropriations again exceeded the authorized level and totaled nearly $1 billion. This record level of funding was provided partly in response to President Clinton's Lands Legacy Initiative, which sought $1.4 billion for 21 resource protection programs including the LWCF. It also was provided in response to some congressional interest in securing increased and more certain funding for the LWCF. The 106th Congress considered legislation to fully fund the LWCF and to make it operate like a private sector trust fund. Such proposals sought to divert offshore oil and gas revenues to a Conservation and Reinvestment Act (CARA) Fund and to permanently appropriate receipts credited to the LWCF, among other related purposes.

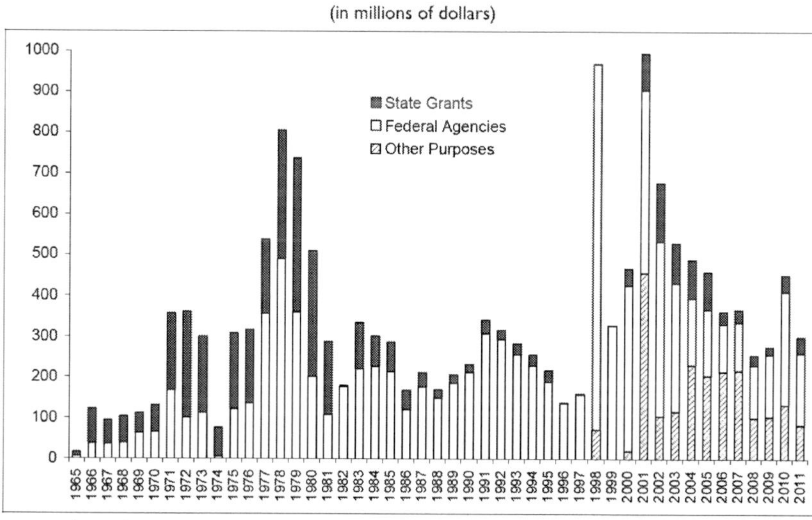

Source: The primary source for these data is the DOI Budget Office; data updated May 29, 2009. See the Land and Water Conservation Fund, MSExcel spreadsheet, on the Budget Office's website at http://www.doi.gov/budget/budget_general/bgindex.html (visited on August 1, 2011).

Notes: The graph does not reflect $76 million provided for the transition quarter from July 1, 1976, to September 30, 1976.

Figure 1. LWCF Appropriations, FY1965-FY2011.

Table 1. LWCF Appropriations, FY1965-FY2011
(in millions of dollars)

Fiscal Year	Land Acquisition	State Grants	Other Programs	Total
1965	$6	$10	$0	$16
1966	$38	$84	$0	$122
1967	$36	$59	$0	$95
1968	$40	$64	$0	$104
1969	$64	$48	$0	$112
1970	$66	$65	$0	$131
1971	$168	$189	$0	$357
1972	$102	$259	$0	$361
1973	$113	$187	$0	$300
1974	$5	$71	$0	$76

Table 1. (Continued)

Fiscal Year	Land Acquisition	State Grants	Other Programs	Total
1975	$122	$186	$0	$308
1976	$136	$181	$0	$317
1977	$356	$182	$0	$538
1978	$491	$314	$0	$805
1979	$361	$376	$0	$737
1980	$202	$307	$0	$509
1981	$108	$180	$0	$288
1982	$176	$4	$0	$180
1983	$220	$115	$0	$335
1984	$227	$75	$0	$302
1985	$213	$74	$0	$287
1986	$121	$47	$0	$168
1987	$176	$35	$0	$211
1988	$150	$20	$0	$170
1989	$186	$20	$0	$206
1990	$212	$20	$0	$232
1991	$309	$33	$0	$342
1992	$294	$23	$0	$317
1993	$256	$28	$0	$284
1994	$228	$28	$0	$256
1995	$189	$28	$0	$217
1996	$137	$1	$0	$138
1997	$158	$1	$0	$159
1998	$896	$1	$72	$969
1999	$328	$0	$0	$328
2000	$406	$41	$20	$467
2001	$449	$90	$456	$995
2002	$429	$144	$105	$677
2003	$316	$97	$116	$529
2004	$165	$94	$230	$488
2005	$164	$91	$204	$459
2006	$119	$30	$213	$362
2007	$120	$30	$216	$366
2008	$129	$25	$101	$255
2009	$152	$19	$104	$275

Fiscal Year	Land Acquisition	State Grants	Other Programs	Total
2010	$278	$40	$133	$450
2011	$177	$40	$84	$301

Source: The primary source for this data is the DOI Budget Office; data updated May 29, 2009. See the Land and Water Conservation Fund, MSExcel spreadsheet, on the Budget Office's website at http://www.doi.gov/ budget/budget_general/ bgindex.html (visited on August 1, 2011).

Notes: The graph does not reflect $76 million provided for the transition quarter from July 1, 1976, to September 30, 1976.

When it became clear that CARA legislation would not be enacted, Congress included aspects of the legislation in the FY2001 Interior and Related Agencies Appropriations law (P.L. 106-291). These provisions established the Conservation Spending Category (CSC), with the LWCF as a major component in the CSC. The CSC provisions set a target for total funding for all the component programs in FY2001 at $1.6 billion, including $1.2 billion through Interior appropriations and $400 million through Commerce appropriations. Under law, the target was to increase each year until it reached $2.4 billion in FY2006. However, Congress generally did not use the CSC structure in appropriating funds to the LWCF and related programs. The CSC was authorized in Interior Appropriations law through FY2006, while the Commerce Appropriations law authorized it for only FY2001.

Total LWCF appropriations, and the funding levels for each federal agency, the stateside program, and other programs, have declined over the past decade (from FY2002 to FY2011). During this decade, appropriations declined by 62% from the FY2002 high ($677.2 million) to the FY2008 low ($255.1 million), while ending the decade in FY2011 with a 56% decrease (to $300.5 million). **Table 2** lists appropriations from FY2002-FY2011.

Allocation among Land Acquisition, Stateside, and Other Purposes

The $15.8 billion appropriated from the fund through FY2011 has been unevenly allocated among federal land acquisition, the stateside program, and other purposes, as shown on the bar graph above. The largest portion of the total—$9.9 billion (62%)—has been appropriated for federal land acquisition. The four federal land management agencies have received differing portions of this $9.7 billion. Specifically, the NPS has received $4.2 billion (43%); the FS, $2.7 billion (27%); the FWS, $2.1 billion (21%), and the BLM, $0.8 billion (8%).[18]

Table 2. Total LWCF Appropriations, FY2002-FY2011
(in millions of dollars)

Purpose	FY2002	FY2003	FY2004	FY2005	FY2006	FY2007	FY2008	FY2009	FY2010	FY2011
Land Acquisition										
Bureau of Land Management	$49.9	$33.2	$18.4	$11.2	$8.6	$8.6	$8.9	$14.8	$29.7	$22.0
Fish and Wildlife Service	$99.1	$72.9	$38.1	$37.0	$28.0	$28.0	$34.6	$42.5	$86.3	$54.9
National Park Service	$130.0	$74.0	$41.7	$55.1	$34.4[a]	$34.4	$44.4	$45.2	$86.3	$54.9
Forest Service	$149.7	$132.9	$66.4	$61.0	$40.9	$41.9	$41.2	$49.8	$63.5	$32.9
Total Land Acquisition[b]	*$428.8*	*$316.0*[c]	*$164.6*	*$164.3*	*$119.2*	*$120.4*	*$129.1*	*$152.2*	*$277.9*	*$164.7*
State Grants	$143.9	$97.4	$93.8	$91.2	$29.6	$29.6	$24.6	$19.0[d]	$40.0	$39.9
Other Programs	$104.6[e]	$115.5[f]	$229.7[g]	$203.5	$213.1	$216.1	$101.3	$104.1[h]	$132.5	$83.8
Total	**$677.2**[e]	**$528.9**[fc]	**$488.1**[g]	**$459.0**	**$361.9**[a]	**$366.1**	**$255.1**	**$275.3**	**$450.4**	**$300.5**

Source: The primary source for this data is the DOI Budget Office; data updated May 29, 2009. See the Land and Water Conservation Fund, MSExcel spreadsheet, on the Budget Office's website at http://www.doi.gov/ budget/budget_general/ bgindex.html (visited on August 1, 2011).

a. The NPS land acquisition and total appropriation figures are reduced by $9.8 million due to the use of prior year funds for NPS federal land acquisition.

b. Figures for FY2006, FY2007, FY2010, and FY2011 include appropriations for DOI Departmental Management for land acquisition appraisal services that are not shown in the figures above. The respective amounts are $7.3 million, $7.4 million, $12.1 million, and $12.1 million.

c. This figure includes $3 million for the Bureau of Indian Affairs for Indian Land and Water Claim Settlements that is not shown in the figures above.

d. This figure has been reduced by $1.0 million due to the use of prior-year funds.

e. This figure reflects a $25 million rescission of FY2001 funds for State Wildlife Grants.

f. This figure reflects a $40 million rescission of FY2002 funds for the Landowner Incentive Program and a $10 million rescission of FY2002 funds for the Private Stewardship Grants Program.

g. This figure includes $5 million for Bureau of Indian Affairs settlements and $5 million for FWS resource management.

h. This figure has been reduced by $8.0 million due to the use of prior-year funds.

The stateside program has received the second largest portion of LWCF appropriations—$4.1 billion (26% of the total, which includes funds for grant administration and funds under GOMESA). In the early years, more funds generally went to the stateside program than to the four federal agencies combined. For instance, stateside appropriations exceeded federal land acquisition appropriations during 12 of the 16 years from FY1965 to FY1980. The stateside program has declined as a portion of total LWCF appropriations since the early 1980s, and received no appropriations (except for program administration) from FY1996 through FY1999. Over the past decade (FY2002-FY2011), funding for the stateside program has ranged from a low of $19 million (FY2009) to a high of $144 million (FY2002). Stateside funding has averaged 15% of total LWCF appropriations over the decade, and 9% of LWCF funding over the past five years.

Other purposes have received the remaining portion of total LWCF appropriations—$1.8 billion (12%). No funds were provided for other purposes until FY1998. By contrast, 30% of LWCF appropriations from FY1998 through FY2011 have been for other programs. While the funds have been provided for various purposes to different agencies, the FWS and FS have received the largest shares: about $1.1 billion and $489 million respectively of the $1.8 billion appropriated for other purposes since FY1998.

Both the dollar amount and percentage of LWCF appropriations provided to other purposes have varied widely throughout this period, as shown in **Table 3** below. The current dollar value of the appropriations for other purposes was much higher in FY2001 than any other year, when these appropriations were used to fund programs in the Clinton Administration's Lands Legacy Initiative. The highest percentage of funds provided for other purposes occurred in FY2006 and FY2007, in response to President Bush's request for funding for an array of other programs. In some years, Congress has appropriated significantly less for other purposes than the Administration has requested. For instance, for FY2008 the Bush Administration sought $313.1 million for other programs of a total request of $378.7 million. Congress appropriated $101.3 million for other programs of a total of $255.1 million.

Legislation[19]

A variety of bills pertaining to the LWCF are pending in the 112th Congress. One bill (S. 1265) would provide permanent appropriations for

LWCF at the authorized level of $900 million, rather than continue the current procedure of providing appropriations each year. The bill does not address how the appropriations would be allocated among LWCF purposes or agencies. Similar bills were introduced in the 111th Congress. One such 111th Congress bill (S. 3663) would have provided for permanent appropriations of $900 million for FY2011-FY2015. In other fiscal years, either a lesser amount or none of the appropriations would have been permanently appropriated.

The 111th Congress bills contained differing provisions as to how the appropriations would be allocated.[20]

Other 112th Congress bills would direct additional sources of funds to the LWCF, with the sources varying among the bills. For instance, H.R. 1372 and S. 205 would direct payments for oil and gas leasing in particular areas of the Outer Continental Shelf to the LWCF. By contrast, revenues under other legislation—H.R. 1628—would be derived from a tax on single-use carryout bags (e.g., disposable plastic bags). The bills vary as to whether they would constitute additional funds for the LWCF beyond the $900 million currently authorized. They differ too in terms of how the funds can be used, for instance, for any purpose currently authorized by the LWCF Act or for only a particular purpose, such as the stateside program.

Table 3. LWCF Appropriations for Other Purposes, FY1998-FY2011
(in millions of dollars)

Fiscal Year	Total LWCF Appropriation	Appropriation for Other Programs	Other Programs as % of Total Appropriation
FY1998	$969.1	$72.0	7%
FY1999	$328.2	$0	0%
FY2000	$466.9	$20.0	4%
FY2001	$995.4	$455.9	46%
FY2002	$677.2	$104.6	15%
FY2003	$528.9	$115.5	22%
FY2004	$488.1	$229.7	47%
FY2005	$459.0	$203.5	44%
FY2006	$361.9	$213.1	59%
FY2007	$366.1	$216.1	59%
FY2008	$255.1	$101.3	40%
FY2009	$275.3	$104.1[a]	38%
FY2010	$450.4	$132.5	29%
FY2011	$300.5	$83.8	28%

Source: The primary source for this data is the DOI Budget Office, data updated May 29, 2009.

a. This figure has been reduced by $8.0 million due to the use of prior-year funds.

Some measures would amend the LWCF Act to "secure recreational public access" to federal land. For instance, S. 1265 includes a provision to provide not less than 1.5% of the annual authorized funding for projects that would secure recreational public access to federal land for hunting, fishing, and other recreational purposes. H.R. 1997 and S. 901 seek to secure recreational access to federal land where such land has "significantly restricted access for hunting, fishing, and other recreational purposes." Such access can be secured through federal acquisition of land, rights of way, or other interests from willing sellers. These companion bills direct the Secretary of the Interior and the Secretary of Agriculture to ensure that of the amounts requested for LWCF each year, not less than 1.5% or $10.0 million, whichever is greater, is used for recreational access projects identified on priority lists developed by the Secretaries.

Still other bills provide for the management of lands acquired with LWCF funds, setting out prohibitions on uses of these lands. For example, S. 138, which would amend the California Desert Protection Act, would generally prohibit the disposal of certain lands that were acquired with LWCF funds. It also would generally prohibit activities that would create impacts contrary to the conservation purposes for which the land was acquired, such as rights-of-way, leases, livestock grazing, infrastructure development, mineral entry, and use of off-highway vehicles. The Secretary may authorize exceptions.

Current Issues

There are differing opinions as to the appropriate level of LWCF appropriations and for what these funds should be used. The LWCF has broad support from resource protection advocates, many of whom seek stable and predictable funding through consistent levels of appropriations or permanent appropriations. Most of these advocates seek higher appropriations in general. The Obama Administration, for instance, proposed increased LWCF funding for FY2010 and FY2011, and appropriations at the authorized level of $900 million for FY2012. Some advocates have specific priorities, such as higher acquisition funding for one of the four federal agencies, the state grant program, or a particular site or area. Advocates of higher federal land acquisition funding promote a strong federal role in acquiring and managing sensitive areas and natural resources. Some advocates of higher LWCF funding seek permanent appropriations, as discussed in the "Legislation" section.

Others seek reduced levels of funds for LWCF based on varied concerns. They include concerns about further acquisition of privately owned land by the federal government either generally or at specific sites, especially in the West, where federal ownership is already concentrated. The concerns involve preferences for private ownership, limits that federal agencies may place on uses of private lands, and reduced local tax revenues that result from public ownership. Some opponents believe that maintaining (and rehabilitating) the land and facilities that federal agencies already own should take priority over further acquisitions. Since federal agencies cannot use LWCF funds for maintenance, supporters of this priority favor more funding to other accounts that can be used for maintenance and less for LWCF. Others seek LWCF reductions as part of a broader focus on reducing the large federal deficit, or on the grounds that there is inadequate cooperation among LWCF programs and between LWCF and other programs.[21]

If funding for land acquisition is relatively low, choices may be more difficult and there may be more competition for limited funds. Since the early 1990s, the appropriations debate has grown more complicated as perspectives on resource protection have changed. Alternatives to acquisition which may provide potentially lower levels of protection but at less cost (such as easements) have become more widely used by federal agencies. Also, resource protection is discussed increasingly for either larger areas with multiple landowners—such as ecosystems, landscapes, or watersheds—or for managing systems where only a portion of the land is in public ownership. In these complex situations success depends on cooperation and partnerships, and the LWCF may be viewed as less critical or looked to as one component in cooperative protection efforts.

One area of congressional focus has been the stateside program, with debate over the level of funds for grants. The Bush Administration did not request funds for new stateside grants for several years on the grounds that state and local governments have alternative sources of funding for parkland acquisition and development, the current program could not adequately measure performance or demonstrate results, and large federal deficits require a focus on core federal responsibilities. At least one 111th Congress bill (H.R. 2916)[22] had sought to prohibit stateside funds from being used to acquire land or make improvements in state or local parks. Stateside supporters assert that the program contributes significantly to statewide recreation planning; state leadership in protection and development of recreation resources; and long-term outdoor recreation overall, and particularly through locally sponsored projects that are readily accessible to communities. They see the program as a way to help fiscally constrained local governments and leverage state and local funds for recreation. Further, advocates assert that investments in recreation save money in other areas; for instance, they say that these investments promote healthier lifestyles and thus save health care expenditures.

Whether to change the way that funds are apportioned to the states is under consideration. The Obama Administration proposed that at least 40% of the appropriations for state grants be distributed equally to all states, and that the balance be provided through a new competitive grants program. Under current law, a portion of the appropriation is to be distributed equally among the states, with the percentage varying depending on the total amount of appropriations.[23] Further, the Secretary of the Interior has discretion to apportion the balance based on need, and population has been the biggest factor in determining need. In determining need under the proposed competitive grant program, the Secretary would consider the extent to which projects provide access to natural areas in large urban areas; reconnect young people and their families to the outdoors, especially in disadvantaged communities; provide access to blueways/waterways; and protect, restore, and connect open space and natural landscapes, among other factors.[24]

Another focus has been on which, if any, programs other than land acquisition and stateside grants should be funded through the LWCF. Some seek to channel LWCF funding to a broader array of programs to protect federal lands. For instance, the Bush Administration sought LWCF funds for cooperative conservation programs through which federal land managers partner with other landowners to protect natural resources and improve recreation on lands under diverse ownership. The Obama Administration also has supported the use of LWCF funds for other programs, although generally fewer than the Bush Administration. Traditional fund beneficiaries have expressed concern about expanding the uses of appropriations if that expansion is accompanied by reductions in the amount available for federal land acquisition or state grants.

End Notes

[1] Act of Sept. 3, 1964; P.L. 88-578, 78 Stat. 897. 16 U.S.C. §§4601-4, et seq.

[2] The most recent report is CRS Report R41896, *Interior, Environment, and Related Agencies: FY2012 Appropriations*, coordinated by Carol Hardy Vincent.

[3] These figures are derived primarily from the Office of Budget, Department of the Interior, at http://www.doi.gov/ budget/budget_general/bgindex.html. Under the entry for the Land and Water Conservation Fund, MSExcel Spreadsheet, see the table entitled *Land and Water*

Conservation Fund Receipts, Appropriations and Unappropriated Balances Reported by Treasury.

[4] Hereinafter, these purposes are referred to respectively as (1) federal land acquisition, (2) the stateside program, and (3) other purposes.

[5] For an introduction to these agencies and their responsibilities, see CRS Report R40225, *Federal Land Management Agencies: Background on Land and Resources Management*, coordinated by Ross W. Gorte.

[6] For more information on the Migratory Bird Conservation Fund, see the FWS land acquisition section of CRS Report RL34273, *Federal Land Ownership: Current Acquisition and Disposal Authorities*.

[7] 16 U.S.C. §460l-9(a).

[8] 16 U.S.C. §460l-9(b).

[9] In the past, LWCF funds were among the first to be borrowed for wildland fire fighting when funds appropriated for fire fighting are insufficient. Borrowed funds typically were repaid in a subsequent appropriations bill.

[10] 16 U.S.C. §460l-8.

[11] Specifically, the law provides that 40% of the first $225.0 million, 30% of the next $275.0 million, and 20% of all additional appropriations are to be apportioned equally among the states.

[12] The apportionment among states (including the District of Columbia and U.S. territories) for each of the last nine fiscal years—FY2002-FY2010—is on the NPS website at http://www.nps.gov/ncrc/programs/lwcf/funding

[13] For more information on the stateside program, see the *Land and Water Conservation Fund State Assistance Program: Federal Financial Assistance Manual* on the NPS website at http://www.nps.gov/lwcf/manual/lwcf.pdf.

[14] §105, Division C, P.L. 109-432.

[15] U.S. Dept. of the Interior, National Park Service, *Budget Justifications and Performance Information*, Fiscal Year 2012, p. OCS-1.

[16] 16 U.S.C. §460l-9(a).

[17] The LWCF had accumulated receipts sufficient to cover an appropriation exceeding the annual authorization. Specifically, in 1997 the LWCF had a balance of $11.9 billion in unappropriated receipts, which represented the difference between the receipts into the Fund and the appropriations from the Fund since its creation.

[18] Another $41.9 million (0.4%) of the total appropriations for federal land acquisition was provided to other agencies or offices (e.g., to the Office of the DOI Secretary for land appraisal services).

[19] For information on legislation to provide appropriations from the LWCF for FY2012, see the "Land and Water Conservation Fund (LWCF)" section of CRS Report R41896, *Interior, Environment, and Related Agencies: FY2012 Appropriations*, coordinated by Carol Hardy Vincent.

[20] For instance, like S. 1265 in the 112th Congress, S. 2747 of the 111th Congress did not address how the appropriations would be allocated. H.R. 3534 (111th Congress) stated that the House and Senate Appropriations Committees may provide by law for the allocation of monies in the fund to activities eligible under the LWCF Act. S. 3663 (111th Congress) would have required the President to submit with his annual budget a priority list for federal land acquisition. Appropriations were to be made for those acquisitions unless Congress enacted legislation containing an alternate list. If the congressional list provided for less funding than was available, projects on the President's list also would have been funded.

[21] See, for example, the report of the House Appropriations Committee on H.R. 2584, providing FY2012 appropriations for Interior, Environment, and Related Agencies: H.Rept. 112-151, pp. 14-15.

[22] Similar legislation has not been introduced in the 112th Congress as of July 29, 2011.

[23] The LWCF Act provides that 40% of the first $225.0 million, 30% of the next $275.0 million, and $20% of all additional appropriations are to be apportioned equally among the states.

[24] U.S. Dept. of the Interior, National Park Service, *Budget Justifications and Performance Information, Fiscal Year 2012*, pp. LASA-53-56.

In: Federal Funds: A Selection of Programs
Editor: Kieran Saccoccio

ISBN 978-1-62618-005-5

Chapter 8

DRINKING WATER STATE REVOLVING FUND (DWSRF): PROGRAM OVERVIEW AND ISSUES*

Mary Tiemann

SUMMARY

The Safe Drinking Water Act (SDWA) Amendments of 1996 authorized a drinking water state revolving loan fund (DWSRF) program to help public water systems finance infrastructure projects needed to comply with federal drinking water regulations and to meet the act's health objectives. Under the program, states receive capitalization grants to make loans to public water systems (privately and publicly owned) for drinking water projects and certain other SDWA activities. Since FY1997, Congress has provided more than $16 billion for this program, including $2 billion in the supplemental funding the American Recovery and Reinvestment Act of 2009 (ARRA; P.L. 111-5). Through June 2010, the DWSRF program had provided a total of $14.6 billion in assistance and supported 8,519 projects; with the 20% state match, bond proceeds, and other funds, the program had provided a total of $20.027 billion in assistance.

* This is an edited, reformatted and augmented version of the Congressional Research Service Publication, CRS Report for Congress RS22037, dated February 24, 2012.

The Environmental Protection Agency's (EPA's) latest (2007) survey of capital improvement needs for public water systems indicated that water systems need to invest $334.8 billion on infrastructure improvements over 20 years to ensure the provision of safe water. EPA reports that this amount is similar to the 2003 needs estimate of $276.8 billion ($331.4 billion when adjusted to 2007 dollars). The latest survey reflects continued improvement in the reporting of needs for infrastructure rehabilitation and replacement, and also reporting funding needs related to compliance with SDWA regulations and security-related needs.

Key program issues include the gap between estimated needs and funding; the growing cost of complying with SDWA standards, particularly for small communities; the ability of small or economically disadvantaged communities to afford DWSRF financing; and the broader need for cities to maintain, upgrade, and expand infrastructure unrelated to SDWA compliance.

ARRA provided $2 billion for the DWSRF program for drinking water infrastructure projects, and $4 billion for a similar Clean Water SRF to fund municipal wastewater infrastructure projects in the form of capitalization grant loans. Under the DWSRF program, the supplemental funding was also allocated as capitalization grants to the states, which states use to provide financial assistance (subsidized loans and grants) to public water systems for infrastructure projects. The ARRA supplemental funding, and subsequent appropriations, have come with new requirements (such as a 20% reserve for "green" projects and the application of Davis-Bacon prevailing wage requirements to projects receiving any DWSRF funding). States have expressed concern that the added requirements have reduced their ability to determine project priorities, increased project costs, and placed new strains on the state/federal partnership.

In the 112th Congress, congressional action has focused on appropriations. For FY2012, the President requested $999.0 million for the DWSRF program, and Congress provided $919.4 million in P.L. 112-74 (before applying an across-the-board rescission of 0.16%). In this act, Congress made the green infrastructure reserve discretionary, and expanded the application of Davis-Bacon requirements to the DWSRF program to include FY2012 and all future years. The Administration has requested $850 million for the program for FY2013. Other approaches to financing water infrastructure also have been proposed. For example, H.R. 402 would establish a National Infrastructure Development Bank, and H.R. 1802 and S. 939 would remove the volume cap on private activity bonds for drinking water and wastewater facilities; the Senate Finance Committee's Surface Transportation Reauthorization bill includes similar provisions.

INTRODUCTION

The quality of water delivered by public water systems has been regulated at the federal level since enactment of the 1974 Safe Drinking Water Act (SDWA). Since then, EPA has issued regulations for more than 90 contaminants, and all states (except Wyoming) have assumed primary responsibility for administering and enforcing the federal drinking water program. The 104th Congress substantially revised the SDWA in 1996 (P.L. 104-182). The amendments were the culmination of a multi-year effort to amend a statute that was widely criticized as having too little flexibility, too many unfunded mandates, and an arduous but unfocused regulatory schedule.

Among the key provisions, the 1996 amendments authorized a drinking water state revolving loan fund (DWSRF) program to help public water systems finance projects needed to comply with SDWA regulations. A key provision, Section 1452, authorized a drinking water state revolving loan fund (DWSRF) program to help public water systems finance improvements needed to comply with federal drinking water regulations and to address the most serious risks to human health. The law authorized the Environmental Protection Agency (EPA) to make grants to states. A state uses its annual capitalization grant from EPA to "capitalize" the state's revolving loan fund to provide an ongoing source of water infrastructure funding for communities generally through repayment of loans to the state fund. States must match 20% of their annual grant and develop intended use plans each year indicating how the allotted funds will be used. States may use the DWSRF to provide loans and other assistance to eligible public water systems for expenditures that EPA has determined will facilitate SDWA compliance or significantly further the act's health protection objectives. Eligible projects include installation and replacement of failing treatment facilities, distribution systems, and certain storage facilities. Projects to replace aging infrastructure are eligible if they are needed to maintain compliance or to further public health protection goals. Projects to consolidate water supplies also may be eligible. This program is patterned after the Clean Water Act SRF (CWSRF) program for financing municipal wastewater treatment projects that was authorized under the Water Quality Act of 1987.

Public water systems that are eligible to receive DWSRF assistance include community water systems (whether publicly or privately owned) and not-for-profit noncommunity water systems.[1] States generally may not provide DWSRF assistance to systems that lack the capacity to ensure compliance with the act or that are in significant noncompliance with SDWA requirements, unless these systems meet certain conditions to return to compliance. Systems owned by federal agencies are not eligible. Although the law authorizes assistance to privately owned community water systems, some states have laws or policies that preclude privately owned utilities from receiving DWSRF assistance.[2] Because many of the nation's 52,000 community water systems (especially small systems) are privately owned, this limitation has raised issues in such states.

The SDWA as amended authorized appropriations for DWSRF capitalization grants at a level of $599 million for FY1994 and $1 billion annually for each of FY1995 through FY2003, for a total appropriations authority of $9.6 billion. Although the authorization of appropriations expired in 2003, the program has continued to receive funding.

For each of FY2008 and FY2009, Congress provided $829.0 million through regular appropriations acts. The American Recovery and Reinvestment Act of 2009 (ARRA; P.L. 111-5) provided another $2 billion for water infrastructure projects via the DWSRF program, for a combined total of roughly $2.83 billion for FY2009. (See ARRA discussion in the "Legislative Activity" section below.)

For FY2010, in P.L. 111-88, Congress approved $1.39 billion for the DWSRF. For FY2011, the President requested $1.29 billion, and under several continuing resolutions, the program was generally being funded at FY2010 levels (through March 4, 2011, under P.L. 111-322). The full- year continuing resolution (P.L. 112-10) reduced the level to $965.0 million for FY2011 ($963.1 million after applying an across-the-board rescission of 0.2%).

For FY2012, the President requested $999.0 million, and Congress provided (P.L. 112-74) $919.4 million, before applying an across-the-board rescission of 0.16%. This amount brings cumulative DWSRF program appropriations to some $16.4 billion for FY1997 through FY2012. For FY2013, the President has requested $850 million. **Table 1** provides annual funding levels for the program since its inception in 1997.

Table 1. Drinking Water State Revolving Fund Program Funding, FY1997-FY2012
(in millions of dollars, nominal dollars not adjusted for inflation)

Fiscal Year	Authorizations	Appropriations
1997	$1,000.0	$1,275.0
1998	$1,000.0	$725.0
1999	$1,000.0	$775.0
2000	$1,000.0	$816.9
2001	$1,000.0	$823.2
2002	$1,000.0	$850.0
2003	$1,000.0	$844.5
2004	—	$845.0
2005	—	$843.2
2006	—	$837.5
2007	—	$837.5
2008	—	$829.0
2009	—	$829.0
2009 ARRA Supplemental		$2,000.0
2010	—	$1,387.0
2011	—	$963.1
2012	—	$919.4
2013 (request)	—	($850.0)
Total		$16,399.0[a]

Sources: Prepared by CRS using the most recent information available from House, Senate, or conference committee reports accompanying the annual appropriations bills that fund EPA and Administration budget documents, including the President's annual budget requests as presented by OMB, and EPA's accompanying annual congressional budget justifications. "ARRA" refers to the American Recovery and Reinvestment Act of 2009 (P.L. 111-5). FY2012 enacted amounts are as presented in P.L. 112-74 and the conference report (H.Rept. 112-331), which do not reflect a 0.16% across-the-board rescission required in Section 436 of P.L. 112-74. EPA is directed to apply this rescission to the amounts specified in the law.

a. Funds available to states are reduced by amounts EPA sets aside from the annual appropriation. For example, EPA reserved $2 million to reimburse small systems for monitoring for unregulated contaminants, and 1.5% for grants to Indian tribes (roughly $19.26 million for FY2011).

Program Results

In contrast to direct grants for construction projects, which would not create an ongoing funding source, the revolving fund program was designed to provide seed money to states in the form of capitalization grants to help generate a sustainable source of funding in each of the states over time. Through June 2010, cumulative funding for federal capitalization grants provided in annual appropriations reached $12.3 billion. When combined with the 20% state match, bond proceeds, loan principal repayments, and other funds, a total of $19.8 billion in DWSRF funds was available for loans and other assistance during this time frame. Also through June 2010, 8,519 projects had assistance agreements, and 5,248 of these projects had been completed; total assistance provided by the program reached $20.027 billion.[3]

DWSRF Allotments and Set-Asides

Under SDWA Section 1452(a)(1), EPA is required to allot DWSRF funds among the states based on the results of the most recent quadrennial needs survey (discussed below). Each state and the District of Columbia must receive at least 1% of available funds, and as much as 0.33% of the total appropriation must be made available for grants to the Virgin Islands, the Commonwealth of the Northern Mariana Islands, American Samoa, and Guam.[4] Before distributing funds among the states, EPA sets aside from the annual DWSRF appropriation $2 million to pay for monitoring of unregulated contaminants in small and medium systems, and 1.5% for grants to Indian tribes and Alaska Native Villages ($12.26 million for FY2011). EPA is also authorized to reserve annually up to $30 million to reimburse states for operator training and certification costs if separate funding is not provided under Section 1419 of the SDWA; EPA reserved the full amount for several years, but reserved none after FY2003, as state training programs had matured. To provide technical assistance to small systems, EPA may reserve up to 2%, with a $15 million cap; however, funding for this activity is provided under Section 1442, and EPA has not set aside funds for this purpose.[5]

The SDWA also includes several set-asides and directives that apply to states. These provisions offer states flexibility in tailoring their individual DWSRF programs to address state priorities. They also demonstrate the emphasis that the 1996 amendments placed on enhancing compliance, especially among smaller systems. The act requires states to make available at least 15% of their annual allotment for loan assistance to systems that serve 10,000 or fewer persons, to the extent that the funds can be obligated to eligible projects. The act also allows states to use up to 30% of their DWSRF grant to provide additional assistance, such as forgiveness of loan principal or negative interest rate loans, to help economically disadvantaged communities (as determined by the state).

Among other optional set-aside provisions, states may reserve as much as 4% of their DWSRF allotment to cover the costs of administering the DWSRF program and an additional portion to help pay the costs of other mandates added by the 1996 amendments. Specifically, states may set aside as much as 10% for a combination of the following: public water system supervision programs, technical assistance through source water protection programs, state capacity development strategies, and operator certification programs. To use DWSRF funds for these purposes, states must match these expenditures with an equal amount of state funds. States may use an additional 2% of funds to provide technical assistance to systems that serve 10,000 or fewer persons. States also have the option of using as much as 15% for a combination of the following: loans for the acquisition of land or conservation easements; loans to implement voluntary source water protection measures; technical and financial assistance to systems as part of a capacity development strategy; and development and implementation of ground water protection programs. Expenditures may not exceed 10% for any one of these activities. (Other SDWA provisions include funding authority for several of these programs and activities.)

To further enhance public water system compliance, the 1996 amendments added new capacity development and operator certification requirements. The law required EPA to withhold part of the DWSRF grant from any state that did not meet these mandates. Section 1420 required states to establish capacity development programs that include (1) legal authority or other means to ensure that new systems have the technical, financial, and managerial capacity to meet SDWA requirements and (2) a strategy to assist existing systems that are experiencing difficulties in coming into compliance.[6] States also were required to adopt programs for training and certifying operators of community and non-transient non-community water systems.

Congress designed the DWSRF program to give states implementation flexibility. Congress provided states flexibility in setting priorities between the SDWA and Clean Water Act SRF programs to accommodate the divergent drinking water and wastewater needs and priorities among the states. The SDWA authorized states to transfer as much as 33% of the annual DWSRF allotment to the CWSRF or an equivalent amount from the CWSRF to the DWSRF. The act authorized these transfers through FY2001. In 2000, EPA recommended that Congress continue to authorize transfers between the SRF programs to give states flexibility to address their most pressing water infrastructure needs. Subsequent conference reports to accompany EPA fiscal year appropriations have authorized states to continue transferring funds between these programs.

DRINKING WATER INFRASTRUCTURE NEEDS

SDWA Section 1452(h) requires EPA to assess the capital improvement needs of eligible public water systems and to report to Congress every four years.[7] Concurrently, and in consultation with the Indian Health Service and Indian tribes, EPA must assess needs for drinking water treatment facilities to serve Indian tribes (§1452(i)).[8] EPA is required to distribute the DWSRF funds to the states based on the results of the latest needs survey. Eligible systems include nearly 53,000 community water systems (publicly or privately owned) and 21,400 not-for-profit nontransient noncommunity water systems.

EPA conducted its third survey of capital improvement needs for public water systems in 2003.[9] Based on this survey, EPA estimated that systems needed to invest $276.8 billion on drinking water infrastructure improvements over 20 years to comply with drinking water regulations and/or to ensure the provision of safe water. EPA reported that the amount exceeded the 2001 needs survey estimate of $165.5 billion (in 2003 dollars) by more than 60%. EPA attributed the large increase to several factors. The 2003 survey included funds needed for compliance with several regulations (including the revised arsenic and radium rules) and pending rules for radon and other contaminants. It also identified $1 billion in security-related needs. Most significantly, water systems made efforts to improve their reporting of needs for infrastructure rehabilitation and replacement, which EPA determined had been under-reported in the previous surveys.

Issued in 2009, the latest (2007) needs survey estimated that public water systems need to invest $334.8 billion on infrastructure improvements over 20 years (2007 through 2026) to achieve regulatory compliance and ensure the provision of safe water. EPA reported that this amount is similar to the 2003 needs estimate of $331.4 billion, when adjusted to 2007 dollars. The agency noted that the survey reflects the use of more consistent methodologies for needs estimation among the states, and continued improvements in reporting of needs related to infrastructure rehabilitation and replacement.[10]

Although all of the infrastructure projects in the needs assessment would promote the health objectives of the act, EPA reported that just 16% ($52.0 billion) of the funding needed was attributable to SDWA regulations, while $282.8 billion (84%) represented nonregulatory costs. Most nonregulatory funding needs typically involve installing, upgrading, or replacing transmission and distribution infrastructure to allow a system to continue to deliver safe drinking water. These system problems often do not cause a violation of a drinking water standard, but projects to correct infrastructure problems may be eligible for DWSRF funding if needed to address public health risks. Projects attributable to SDWA regulations (including proposed regulations) typically involve the upgrade, replacement, or installation of treatment technologies.

The survey presented the 20-year needs estimates by category: transmission and distribution, treatment, source, storage, and other. The largest needs category, installation and rehabilitation of transmission and distribution systems, accounted for $200.8 billion (60%) of total 20-year needs. Water treatment needs constituted the next largest category, accounting for $75.1 billion (22%) of total needs, while water storage accounts for $36.9 billion (11%), and source (projects needed to obtain safe water supplies, including rehabilitation and installation of wells) accounts for $19.8 billion (6%) of total 20-year needs.

The 2007 Needs Survey also included $422.0 million for projects to address security needs. However, EPA concluded that security-related needs were underestimated, as many water systems incorporate these costs into the costs of broader construction projects rather than report them separately.

For further perspective, the needs survey breaks down the 20-year needs estimates according to system size and ownership. Large community water systems (serving more than 100,000 people) accounted for $116.3 billion (36%) of total 20-year need; medium systems (serving from 3,301 to 100,000 people) accounted for $145.1 billion (45%); and small systems (serving 3,300 or fewer people) accounted for $59.4 billion (19%). Not-for-profit noncommunity water systems have estimated needs of $4.1 billion. American Indian and Alaska Native Village water systems have combined estimated 20-year needs of $2.9 billion. The estimated needs reported by American Samoa, Guam, the Commonwealth of the Northern Mariana Islands, and the U.S. Virgin Islands totaled $889.4 million.

EPA noted that the total needs estimate may be conservative for several reasons: (1) systems are required to meet stringent documentation criteria when identifying needs; (2) many systems did not fully understand their security needs at the time of the assessment; (3) capital improvement plans often cover fewer than 10 years, while the survey tries to capture 20-year estimates; and (4) the survey is limited to eligible needs, thus excluding projects related to dams, raw water reservoirs, fire protection, operation and maintenance, and future growth.

Other needs assessments have also been prepared, including EPA's 2002 Gap Analysis. This study identified potential funding gaps between projected needs and spending from 2000 through 2019. EPA estimated a potential 20-year funding gap for drinking water capital and operations and maintenance ranging from $45 billion to $263 billion, depending on different scenarios.[11]

PROGRAM ISSUES

With the authorization of the DWSRF program, Congress acted to help public water systems finance infrastructure projects needed to achieve or maintain compliance with SDWA requirements and protect public health. While this federal/state program provides an important means for addressing drinking water needs, a substantial gap remains between financing needs and available funds. The 2007 needs survey identified $334.8 billion in drinking water infrastructure needs over 20 years, while the DWSRF program was authorized at $9.6 billion over seven years (FY1997-FY2003). The appropriated amounts, augmented by the state match, leveraging, repayments, and interest earnings, have created significant financing capacity among the state DWSRFs. However, many expect a funding gap to persist, and new SDWA requirements are expected to drive up future estimates of needs.

Other SDWA mandates are eligible for DWSRF funding, thus increasing competition for these resources. The DWSRF program embraces competing objectives, and thus, this competition is perhaps unavoidable. On the one hand, the fundamental purpose of the program is to capitalize revolving funds in the states in order to generate a perpetual source of funding for drinking water projects. On the other hand, Congress authorized multiple set-asides to fund other drinking water program priorities and requirements, such as system compliance capacity assurance, operator certification, and small system technical assistance. Overall, states may use as much as 31% of their grant for the set-asides and another 30% to provide loan subsidies to economically disadvantaged communities. While these options offer states flexibility to tailor their programs to meet individual needs, using funds for these activities could significantly erode the corpus of state funds and slow the rate at which they become capitalized. A concern for states is that, to the degree that Congress relies on the DWSRF to fund other SDWA requirements instead of providing separate appropriations, the potential of the DWSRF program is diminished.

Perhaps a larger issue is the need for communities to address drinking water infrastructure needs that are outside the scope of the DWSRF program. Communities typically must address several categories of infrastructure requirements unrelated to SDWA compliance and, thus, ineligible for DWSRF assistance. These categories include future growth, ongoing rehabilitation, and operation and maintenance of systems. EPA has reported that outdated and deteriorated drinking water infrastructure poses a fundamental long-term threat to drinking water safety, and that in many communities, basic infrastructure costs can far exceed SDWA compliance costs. As reported in EPA's most recent (2007) drinking water needs assessment, just 16% of the 20-year estimated need is attributable to SDWA regulations. Although the DWSRF program does not address certain categories of needs and excludes many noncommunity water systems from coverage, with this program Congress has added a major tool to the mix of federal, state, and local initiatives intended to help communities ensure the safety of water supplies.

LEGISLATIVE ACTIVITY AND ISSUES

In recent years, House and Senate committees have held hearings on the clean water and drinking water SRF programs, infrastructure needs, and funding issues and options. Funding bills have been introduced repeatedly. A fundamental and persistent question has concerned the long-term federal role in water infrastructure financing. A newer subset of questions concerns how the latest recession, economic recovery efforts, and deficit reduction efforts might affect the type and level of federal involvement. For example, how might deficit reduction objectives impact recent congressional efforts to develop a small system grant program or sustainable funding source, such as a water infrastructure trust fund? Other persistent water infrastructure issues include the gap between funding and estimated needs; the growing cost of complying with SDWA standards, particularly for small communities; the ability of small or economically disadvantaged communities to afford DWSRF financing; and the broader need for cities to maintain, upgrade, and expand infrastructure unrelated to SDWA compliance. Another issue for the states concerns the new requirements, not present in the SDWA, that Congress has imposed on state capitalization grants through ARRA and subsequent appropriations acts. These include a 20% Green Project Reserve and Davis-Bacon prevailing wage conditions. (See discussion below.)

Despite ongoing legislative interest, budgetary constraints and other concerns have posed challenges to efforts to enact new water infrastructure funding legislation. In the face of large needs, scarce federal resources, and debate over the federal role in funding water infrastructure, EPA, states, and utilities have increasingly focused on alternative management and financing strategies to address costs and promote greater financial self-reliance among water systems. Strategies include establishing public-private partnerships, improving asset management, and adopting full-cost pricing for water services. Such approaches are meant to improve the financial and managerial sustainability of water systems; however, they may be limited in their ability to fully meet needs, particularly among poorer communities and small water systems. Consequently, interest in exploring new infrastructure financing options—such as an infrastructure bank—and expanding federal assistance has persisted.

111th Congress

In the 111th Congress, water infrastructure funding issues received early attention in the context of economic stimulus proposals. Consideration of such proposals raised a number of issues. For example, how might project readiness be balanced against traditional program priorities? Given multiple considerations—including speed and efficiency in creating jobs, public health need, economic need, or ensuring urban/rural equity or equity among the states—how would priorities be set? And how many projects were shoveled ready? The American Water Works Association estimated that at least $10 billion in drinking water infrastructure projects were "ready to go" and could move forward rapidly given funding.[12] The U.S. Conference of Mayors estimated that $15.36 billion in identified "ready to go" water and wastewater projects could generate 133,000 jobs.[13] Although much uncertainty surrounded estimates associated with the potential benefits of a stimulus package, the backlog of water infrastructure projects was much larger than any proposed level of funding. Water sector advocates asserted that stimulus funding was especially needed to address a nationwide backlog of projects pending that had been hampered by the credit crisis.

American Recovery and Reinvestment Act of 2009

The stimulus debate resulted in the supplemental appropriations package, the American Recovery and Reinvestment Act of 2009 (ARRA; P.L. 111-5). ARRA included $2 billion for drinking water infrastructure projects to be administered through the DWSRF program, and $4 billion for wastewater infrastructure projects through the Clean Water SRF program. Congress waived the 20% state match requirement for these grants. ARRA required states to use at least 50% of the funds to further subsidize loans (including forgiveness of principal, negative interest loans, and grants) to eligible recipients. States also were required to reserve at least 20% of the funds for green infrastructure, water efficiency improvements, or other environmentally innovative projects. A key program change was that ARRA applied Davis-Bacon prevailing wage requirements to construction projects that received assistance of any kind from these funds. (This requirement had not been applied previously to the DWSRF program.)[14] The act also required American steel, iron, and manufactured goods to be used in construction and repair of water infrastructure projects that received ARRA funding.

ARRA provided that, notwithstanding the existing state project rankings, priority for the supplemental funding would go to projects on state priority lists that were ready to proceed to construction within 12 months of enactment (by February 17, 2010). The EPA administrator was directed to reallocate funds that were not under contract or construction by that date. All states met this deadline, and no funds were redistributed.[15]

Water Infrastructure Authorizing Bills

Beyond the stimulus debate, drinking water and other water infrastructure issues received attention. In 2009, the Senate Environment and Public Works Committee reported, amended, S. 1005, the Water Infrastructure Financing Act (S.Rept. 111-47). The bill was similar to this committee's measure in the previous Congress, proposing to authorize $20 billion over five years for clean water SRF capitalization grants and $14.7 billion over five years for DWSRF capitalization grants. As discussed, the states use their annual capitalization grants from EPA to "capitalize" the state revolving loan fund to provide an ongoing source of water infrastructure funding for communities generally through repayment of loans to the state. S. 1005 also would have authorized new grant programs for critical water quality and drinking water infrastructure projects. During markup, the committee adopted several amendments, including one to specify that the Davis-Bacon Act prevailing wage requirement would apply to all projects financed in whole or in part through a clean water or drinking water SRF. Davis-Bacon language was not included in the bill as introduced. The full Senate did not take up the reported bill.

The Senate Environment and Public Works Committee had reported a water infrastructure financing bill in each of the four preceding Congresses. The application of Davis-Bacon requirements to the DWSRF program has been one of the policy issues that have hampered further action on these bills. Additionally, a jurisdictional issue has been that, while the Senate committee has jurisdiction over both the Clean Water Act (CWA) and Safe Drinking Water Act, this jurisdiction is split in the House between the Energy and Commerce Committee (SDWA) and the Transportation and Infrastructure Committee (CWA).[16] The House Transportation and Infrastructure Committee reported and the House passed clean water SRF legislation (H.R. 1262) in the 111th Congress, which proposed to make the clean water SRF more similar to the DWSRF. The DWSRF is a newer, more flexible program, and in the past several years no companion reauthorization bill for the DWSRF had been offered in the House. In July 2010, the House passed one such bill, the Assistance, Quality, and Affordability Act of 2010 (H.R. 5320, H.Rept. 111-524). As passed, H.R. 5320 would have reauthorized the DWSRF for three years (for a total of $ 4.8 billion), applied Davis-Bacon prevailing wage provisions to projects financed in any way by a DWSRF, specified certain eligible uses of the fund (such as rehabilitation of aging infrastructure and projects that improve energy or water efficiency), and made other changes to this program and the act more broadly. The bill proposed to expand DWSRF program priorities to include projects designed to improve the economic and environmental sustainability and long- term viability of water systems. H.R. 5320 was referred to the Senate Environment and Public Works Committee, where no further action occurred.

The Water Protection and Reinvestment Act, H.R. 3202, as proposed in the 111th Congress would have established a dedicated water infrastructure trust fund supported by specified product and corporate taxes rather than general revenues. The trust fund was to be supported by taxes on a range of products that can affect water quality or treatment costs, such as pharmaceuticals and personal care products (PPCPs). The bill also would have imposed taxes on water-based beverages and some corporate profits.

Related legislation in the 111th Congress included companion bills H.R. 537 and S. 3262, the Sustainable Water Infrastructure Investment Act of 2009.

These bills would have amended the Internal Revenue Code of 1986 to provide that the volume cap for private activity bonds (PABs) would not apply to bonds for water supply or wastewater facilities. A key purpose of this legislation was to provide alternative financing for water infrastructure investments. The House Ways and Means Committee reported the Small Business and Infrastructure Jobs Tax Act of 2010 (H.R. 4849, H.Rept. 111-447), which incorporated the text of H.R. 537 to lift the state volume cap on tax-exempt PABs for water or wastewater treatment facilities. The House passed the bill, but no further action occurred during the 111th Congress.

112th Congress

Congressional attention thus far in the 112th Congress has focused largely on appropriations bills. For FY2011, the full-year continuing resolution (P.L. 112-10, Division B, Title VII, §1738) provided $965 million for the DWSRF program ($963.1 million after applying the required across-the-board rescission of 0.2%).[17] For FY2012, the President requested $999.0 million, and, in P.L. 112-74, Congress provided $919.4 million (before applying the 0.16% across-the-board rescission). In the FY2012 appropriations, Congress further expanded the application of Davis-Bacon to the DWSRF program:[18] "For fiscal year 2012 and each fiscal year thereafter, the requirements of section 1450(e) of the Safe Drinking Water Act (42 U.S.C. 300j-9(e)) shall apply to any construction project carried out in whole or in part with assistance made available by a drinking water treatment revolving loan fund as authorized by section 1452 of that Act (42 U.S.C. 300j-12)."

As discussed, the application of Davis-Bacon prevailing wage requirements to construction projects funded in any part by DWSRF funds is one of the recently added appropriations conditions criticized by state financing and regulatory authorities and others for limiting state program flexibility. This requirement had not been applied historically to this program, although many states have similar requirements. The FY2012 appropriations also modified the green infrastructure reserve requirement first added in 2009 ARRA. The green project reserve was reduced from 20% to 10% for the Clean Water SRF and was made discretionary for states under the DWSRF. The act also applies Buy American requirements to SRF construction projects.

In addition to appropriations, other legislation concerning infrastructure funding has also been offered. As in the previous Congress, legislation has been introduced to remove the volume cap on private activity bonds (PABs) for drinking water and wastewater facilities. These tax-exempt bonds provide a financing tool to stimulate private sector investment in public projects. Federal law imposes state bond caps limiting the ability of state and local governments to use PABs to finance drinking water and wastewater infrastructure projects.[19] The Sustainable Water Infrastructure Investment Act of 2011 (H.R. 1802 and S. 939) would remove the cap to:

> accelerate and increase overall investment in the Nation's critical water infrastructure; facilitate increased use of innovative infrastructure delivery methods supporting sustainable water systems through public-private partnerships that optimize design, financing, construction, and long-term management, maintenance and viability; and provide for more effective risk management of complex water infrastructure projects by municipal utility and private sector partners.

Supporters note that the proposed legislation would expand opportunities for private investment in the water infrastructure market and generate significant private capital at a very low cost to the government.[20] Others argue against subsidies, generally, and the loss of revenue that would result from such an approach. Congress generally has limited the use of tax-exempt bonds for private activities because of concern about their overuse.

Other legislation that would impact water infrastructure projects includes H.R. 1684, the Keep American Jobs from Going Down the Drain Act. This bill would amend the SDWA and the Clean Water Act to largely prohibit the use of SRF funds for water project construction, alteration, maintenance, or repair unless the steel, iron, and manufactured goods used in the project are produced in the United States. The provisions essentially codify the Buy American requirements contained in the ARRA supplemental appropriations and subsequent appropriations.

H.R. 395, the Healthy Communities Water Supply Act of 2011, would amend the Clean Water Act to extend the authorization of appropriations for the pilot program for alternative water source projects. This bill also would require the EPA administrator, when making grants under the program, to consider whether a project is located in an area which is served by a public water system serving 10,000 individuals or fewer. Similar to bills in the past four Congresses, the Small System Drinking Water Act (S. 999) proposes an alternate approach to address the chronic shortage of drinking water infrastructure funding relative to needs, particularly among small, rural communities: S. 999 would amend the SDWA to prevent the enforcement of certain drinking water regulations unless adequate funding was available.

Taking a different funding approach from the SRF programs, H.R. 402 and H.R. 3259/S. 1550 would establish a national infrastructure development bank that would be used to fund water, transportation, and other infrastructure.

The debate over debt reduction will likely be a key factor influencing the outcome of any infrastructure financing proposals in this Congress.

End Notes

[1] A community water system is one that serves at least 15 service connections used by year-round residents or that regularly serves at least 25 year-round residents. Noncommunity water systems regularly provide water to people, but not year-round (e.g., schools and workplaces with their own wells).

[2] Some states have legislative or regulatory restrictions on providing DWSRF assistance to private systems. According to EPA, some states have made a policy decision to restrict assistance to private systems because of concerns about endangering the tax-exempt status of bonds issued to provide the state match. In 2003, EPA reported that 21 states had provided DWSRF assistance to private systems, 12 states had restricted assistance to private systems, and 17 states did not have restrictions, but had not yet provided assistance to private systems. States restricting assistance to private systems include Alabama, Arkansas, Colorado, Georgia, Kansas, Louisiana, Mississippi, Nebraska, North Carolina, Oklahoma, Tennessee, and Wyoming. Source: U.S. Environmental Protection Agency, *The Drinking Water State Revolving Fund Program: Financing America's Drinking Water from the Source to the Tap, Report to Congress,* EPA-918-R-03-009, May 2003, pp. 36-37, http://www.epa.gov/ogwdw/dwsrf/pdfs/dwsrf_congressreport-main.pdf.

[3] Program statistics are available at http://www.epa.gov/safewater/dwsrf/dwnims.html. For further discussion of the DWSRF program, see EPA Report to Congress, *Drinking Water State Revolving Fund: Investing in a Sustainable Future*, EPA 816-R-08-002, March 2008, http://www.epa.gov/safewater/dwsrf.html.

[4] For FY2010, Congress authorized EPA to reserve up to 1.5% of the appropriated DWSRF funds for territories (P.L.111-88).

[5] DWSRF state-by-state allotments and set-asides are available at EPA's website, http://www.epa.gov/safewater/dwsrf/allotments/index.html.

[6] 42 U.S.C. §300g-9.

[7] 42 U.S.C. §300j-12(h).

[8] 42 U.S.C. §300j-12(i).

[9] Environmental Protection Agency, Drinking Water Infrastructure Needs Survey and Assessment: Third Report to Congress, June 2005. EPA 816-R-05-001. This and earlier needs surveys are available online at http://www.epa.gov/safewater/needssurvey/index.html.

[10] Environmental Protection Agency, 2007 *Drinking Water Infrastructure Needs Survey and Assessment: Fourth Report to Congress*, EPA 816-R-09-001, March 2009, http://www.epa.gov/safewater/needs.html.

[11] U.S. Environmental Protection Agency, *Clean Water and Drinking Water Infrastructure Gap Analysis Report*, EPA 816-R-02-020, September 2002.

[12] American Water Works Association, *Massive Stimulus Program Being Readied; Congress Needs to Hear from Drinking Water Sector*, Washington, DC, Report, December 11, 2008.

[13] U.S. Conference of Mayors, *Mainstreet Economic Recovery, "Ready to Go" Jobs and Infrastructure Projects,* p. 1.

[14] The Department of the Interior, Environment, and Related Agencies Appropriations Act, 2010 (P.L. 111-88), included \$1.387 billion for the DWSRF program, and applied Davis-Bacon

prevailing wage requirements to these FY2010 funds. Specifically, the act contains the following language in Title 11 under the heading, "Administrative Provisions, Environmental Protection Agency": "For fiscal year 2010 the requirements of section 1450(e) of the Safe Drinking Water Act (42 U.S.C. 300j-9(e)) shall apply to any construction project carried out in whole or in part with assistance made available by a drinking water treatment revolving loan fund as authorized by section 1452 of that Act (42 U.S.C. 300j-12)."

EPA guidance on this Davis-Bacon provision extended coverage to include all assistance agreements concluded during FY2010, regardless of the source of funding. For more information, see CRS Report R41469, *Davis-Bacon Prevailing Wages and State Revolving Loan Programs Under the Clean Water Act and the Safe Drinking Water Act*, by Gerald Mayer and Jon O. Shimabukuro.

[15] For additional information and discussion, see CRS Report R40216, *Water Infrastructure Funding in the American Recovery and Reinvestment Act of 2009*, by Claudia Copeland, Megan Stubbs, and Charles V. Stern.

[16] For a discussion of Clean Water Act legislation, see CRS Report R40098, *Water Quality Issues in the 111th Congress: Oversight and Implementation,* by Claudia Copeland.

[17] The rescission is required per Division B, Title I, §1119 of P.L. 112-10.

[18] U.S. Congress, House, Conference Report, *Military Construction and Veterans Affairs and Related Agencies Appropriations Act*, 2012, 112th Cong., 1st sess., December 15, 2011, H.Rept. 112-331, p. 236.

[19] The federal tax code allows state and local governments to use tax-exempt bonds to finance certain projects that would be considered private activities. Congress uses an annual state volume cap to limit the amount of tax-exempt bond financing and restricts the types of "qualified private activities" that would qualify for tax-exempt financing to types of projects specified in the tax code. For a review of private activity bonds, caps, qualified programs, and congressional action, see CRS Report RL31457, *Private Activity Bonds: An Introduction*, by Steven Maguire.

[20] See, for example, National Utility Contractors Association, *Clean Water Council and Sustainable Water Infrastructure Investment Coalition Talk Strategy*, 2011, http://www.nuca.com/i4a/pages/index.cfm?pageid=2615.

In: Federal Funds: A Selection of Programs ISBN 978-1-62618-005-5
Editor: Kieran Saccoccio

Chapter 9

INTERNATIONAL SPECIES CONSERVATION FUNDS*

Pervaze A. Sheikh and M. Lynne Corn

SUMMARY

International species conservation is addressed by several funds, including those under the Multinational Species Conservation Fund (MSCF) and the Neotropical Migratory Bird Conservation Fund (NMBCF). This report provides a brief overview of MSCF and NMBCF and their funding and legislative status.

MULTINATIONAL SPECIES CONSERVATION FUND

The Multinational Species Conservation Fund, which currently benefits tigers, the six species of rhinoceroses, Asian and African elephants, marine turtles, and great apes (gorillas, chimpanzees, bonobos, orangutans, and the various species of gibbons), has generated a tremendous amount of constituent interest. The fund supports conservation efforts benefitting these species, often

---

* This is an edited, reformatted and augmented version of the Congressional Research Service Publication, CRS Report for Congress RS21157, dated April 16, 2012.

in conjunction with efforts under the Convention on International Trade in Endangered Species (CITES), to which the United States is a party.[1]

MSCF provides funding in the form of technical and cost-sharing grants to range countries for the conservation of African and Asian elephants, rhinoceroses, tigers, great apes, and marine turtles and their habitats. The grants target species and address habitat conservation, law enforcement, and technical assistance for conserving species under the MSCF. Efforts to conserve species under the MSCF benefit from funding and in-kind support provided by partners and collaborators. According to the U.S. Fish and Wildlife Service (FWS), which runs the program, almost $87.0 million was provided by partners and collaborators for efforts under the MSCF from FY2007 to FY2011. This is nearly double the amount appropriated ($56.0 million) for these efforts during the same period. Funds might also come from purchases of the Multinational Species Conservation Funds Semipostal Stamp (authorized under P.L. 111-241).[2] On September 22, 2011, the U.S. Postal Service introduced the "Save Vanishing Species" semipostal stamp. It will be available for no less than two years.

For FY2013, the Administration requested $10.0 million for species programs under MSCF, which is $0.5 million above the FY2012 enacted level of $9.5 million. Funding for these species programs comes to FWS within the Interior, Environment, and Related Agencies Appropriations Act. **Table 1** shows funding levels for the MSCF and the NMBCF for FY2008-FY2012 and the FY2013 request. The MSCF is authorized under five acts, described below:

- The African Elephant Conservation Act (16 U.S.C. §4201) authorizes matching grants for conservation, research, management, and protection of this species. Projects are carried out in cooperation with African nations and non- governmental organizations (NGOs). Appropriations are authorized for $5.0 million annually from FY2007 to FY2012.
- The Rhinoceros and Tiger Conservation Fund (16 U.S.C. §5301) assists in conserving tigers and the six species of rhinos. Matching grants support governments and NGOs in projects to conserve habitat, survey populations, improve law enforcement, and educate the public. Appropriations are authorized for $10.0 million annually from FY2007 to FY2012.
- The Asian Elephant Fund (16 U.S.C. §4261) is similar to the above programs in purposes and scope. An additional emphasis, where the

elephants are draft animals, is to promote their humane treatment and encourage captive breeding. Appropriations are authorized for $5.0 million annually from FY2007 to FY2012.

- The Great Ape Conservation Fund (16 U.S.C. §6303) is similar to the above programs in purposes and scope. Species of interest are lowland and mountain gorillas, chimpanzees, bonobos (a species closely related to chimpanzees), orangutans, and the species of gibbons (Genus Hylobates—about 8-10 species, according to anthropologists). Appropriations are authorized for $5.0 million annually from FY2006 to FY2010.
- The Marine Turtle Conservation Act (16 U.S.C. §6601) was passed on July 2, 2004. This law provides grants for the conservation of marine turtle populations and their nesting habitats in the wild. This law authorizes $5 million in annual appropriations from FY2005 to FY2009 for conservation efforts and establishes a marine turtle conservation fund within the MSCF.

NEOTROPICAL MIGRATORY BIRD CONSERVATION FUND

The Neotropical Migratory Bird Conservation Act (16 U.S.C. §§6101-6109) provides grants for the conservation of hundreds of bird species that migrate among North and South America and the Caribbean. The act requires spending 75% of the funds on projects outside of the United States. The act was reauthorized in 2006. The legislation expands the program to include Canada, authorizes appropriations until 2009, and creates a separate fund for the NMBCF. Authorization for appropriations expired in FY2010. The FY2013 request for this program is $3.8 million, equivalent to the FY2012 enacted level. (See **Table 1**.)

LEGISLATIVE ACTIVITY

The 112th Congress is considering reauthorizing funding for several conservation funds organized under the MSCF. A summary of these efforts is listed below:

- H.R. 50 proposes to extend the authorization for funding the African Elephant Conservation Fund, the Rhinoceros and Tiger Conservation Fund, and the Asian Elephant Conservation Fund at their current level to FY2016.
- H.R. 1760 would reauthorize the Great Ape Conservation Act for an additional five years (FY2012 to FY2017), allow for multi-year grants to facilitate the continuation of conservation projects, and authorize a panel of experts to meet every five years to make recommendations on conservation plans and strategies, among other things.
- H.R. 1761 would reauthorize funding for the Marine Turtle Conservation Act at $5 million annually from FY2012 to FY2017. The bill would amend language that limits conservation activities authorized under the bill to marine turtles in foreign countries. The proposed language would allow conservation activities to address marine turtles in both foreign countries and U.S. states, territories, and possessions.
- H.R. 3510 would reauthorize the Multinational Species Conservation Funds Semipostal Stamp Act by extending the availability of stamps to the public to six years instead of two years.

Table 1. Appropriations for Multinational Species Conservation Fund and Neotropical Migratory Bird Conservation Fund, FY2008-FY2013 Request
(in U.S. $ thousands)

Multinational Species Conservation Fund	FY2008 Enacted	FY2009 Enacted	FY2010 Enacted	FY2011 Enacted	FY2012 Enacted	FY2013 Request
African Elephant	$1,477	$2,000	$2,000	$1,697	$1,645	$1,697
Tiger and Rhinos	1,969	2,500	3,000	2,695	2,471	2,695
Asian Elephant	1,477	2,000	2,000	1,697	1,645	1,697
Great Apes	1,969	2,000	2,500	2,194	2,059	2,194
Marine Turtle	984	1,500	2,000	1,697	1,646	1,697
Total MSCF	**7,876**	**10,000**	**11,500**	**9,980**	**9,466**	**9,980**
Neotropical Migratory Bird Conservation Fund	4,430	4,750	5,000	3,992	3,786	3,786

Source: U.S. Fish and Wildlife Service, *U.S. Fish and Wildlife Service Fiscal Year 2013 Budget Justifications*, Department of the Interior, Budget Justification, 2012, pp. MS-1, http://www.fws.gov/budget/2013/FY%202013%20FWS%20Greenbook%20Final.pdf.

End Notes

[1] For more information, see CRS Report RL31654, *The Endangered Species Act: A Primer*, by M. Lynne Corn, Kristina Alexander, and Eugene H. Buck, and CRS Report RL32751, *The Convention on International Trade in Endangered Species of Wild Fauna and Flora (CITES): Background and Issues*, by Pervaze A. Sheikh and M. Lynne Corn.

[2] Proceeds from the sale of certain postage stamps would be used to help implement the MSCF. According to P.L. 111-245, funds from the stamps should not offset annual appropriations to the MSCF, nor should they be taken into account in any decision related to funding MSCF or FWS. The stamps would be available to the public for at least two years.

INDEX

D

E

F

I

J

K

L

M

N

O

P

Q

R

S

T